Praise for *The Full Spirit Workout*

"I met Kate Eckman a decade or so ago, while she was modeling in one of my style seminars, and I remember thinking, 'Wow, she's beautiful, but — more interestingly — she just radiates happiness.' Now, having read her book, I know it's a quality she worked hard to acquire. I'm thrilled she's sharing her techniques with the world, because we all deserve to shine as brightly as Kate."

— **Clinton Kelly**, Emmy Award–winning television host, stylist, and author of *Freakin' Fabulous*

"This is the workout that the whole world needs right now. It's a workout you will actually feel like doing, and it works wonders!"

— **Susie Moore**, author of *Stop Checking Your Likes*

"Kate Eckman is the real deal. One of my favorite things about Kate is that she not only has achieved a great deal in her life but is someone who puts in the work. Minute by minute and day by day, she is fearless in the practice of becoming a better person. This book, and the full spirit practices it contains, is sourced from real experience and is a gift to whoever has the privilege and pleasure of reading it."

— **Eduardo Placer**, story doula and founder and CEO of Fearless Communicators

"Kate Eckman's *The Full Spirit Workout* is a practical guide to finding the fulfillment and freedom that come with meeting everything in your life on its own terms — with an edge! That edge is a spiritual practice and understanding that tips the scales from fear and denial to self-love and joy, strength, and flexibility. Kate has lived what she teaches, and her journaling exercises and meditations alone will take you home to yourself, where your new story waits."

— **Gail Larsen**, teacher and author of *Transformational Speaking*

"*The Full Spirit Workout* shares strategies you can use immediately. It will help athletes, executives, and entrepreneurs alike reach new levels of success and perform at the highest level."
— **Plaxico Burress**, Super Bowl champion, New York Giants

"*The Full Spirit Workout* is a fun way to reconnect with yourself and recharge your life. With Kate Eckman as your personal trainer, this book gives you all the practices you need to create a fitness regimen for your inner well-being — and build a healthy, empowered, and intuitive life!"
— **Kim Chestney**, author of *Radical Intuition*

"Kate's book will help you think curiously, feel energized, and live confidently."
— **Jason Wachob**, founder and co-CEO of mindbodygreen

"Kate Eckman is a force of nature, and her smart, sassy book, *The Full Spirit Workout*, will motivate and inspire you to embrace who you are and shine brightly."
— **Beth Kempton**, bestselling author of *Wabi Sabi: Japanese Wisdom for a Perfectly Imperfect Life*

"*The Full Spirit Workout* is not just a good book to read — it's a great book that is a must-read! Coach Eckman provides an honest, heartfelt, real-world approach to improving your emotional and spiritual fitness. This resource is innovative, playful, and most importantly, practical. I thoroughly enjoyed it."
— **Alan Stein Jr.**, keynote speaker and author of *Raise Your Game*

"You have so much love and light inside you, and Kate Eckman wants to unleash it onto the world. In *The Full Spirit Workout*, she teaches you how to build confidence, live authentically, and find a blissful sense of self-acceptance."
— **Christine Hassler**, bestselling author of *Expectation Hangover*

the
FULL SPIRIT
WORKOUT

the FULL SPIRIT WORKOUT

A Ten-Step System to Shed Your Self-Doubt,
Strengthen Your Spiritual Core,
and Create a Fun and Fulfilling Life

KATE ECKMAN

Foreword by Courtney Carver

New World Library
Novato, California

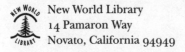

New World Library
14 Pamaron Way
Novato, California 94949

Text design by Tona Pearce Myers

Library of Congress Cataloging-in-Publication Data

Names: Eckman, Kate, author.
Title: The full spirit workout : a ten-step system to shed your self-doubt, strengthen your spiritual core, and create a fun and fulfilling life / Kate Eckman.
Description: Novato, California : New World Library, 2021. | Includes bibliographical references. | Summary: "Drawing an analogy between physical health and spiritual health, the author provides a spiritual exercise regimen to promote resilience, cultivate a positive mindset, and develop greater emotional intelligence"— Provided by publisher.
Identifiers: LCCN 2020057926 (print) | LCCN 2020057927 (ebook) | ISBN 9781608687213 | ISBN 9781608687220 (ebook)
Subjects: LCSH: Spiritual life. | Spiritual formation.
Classification: LCC BL624.2 .E25 2021 (print) | LCC BL624.2 (ebook) | DDC 204—dc23
LC record available at https://lccn.loc.gov/2020057926
LC ebook record available at https://lccn.loc.gov/2020057927

First printing, April 2021
ISBN 978-1-60868-721-3
Ebook ISBN 978-1-60868-722-0
Printed in Canada on 100% postconsumer-waste recycled paper

 New World Library is proud to be a Gold Certified Environmentally Responsible Publisher. Publisher certification awarded by Green Press Initiative.

10   9   8   7   6   5   4   3   2   1

For Sam and Raf,
thank you for holding my hand every day

Contents

Foreword

Honesty and integrity are values I hold dear, maybe the dearest, which is why writing this foreword is easy (even though I've never done this before). Kate Eckman is the living, breathing, human version of this book. She embodies every word. When we first met, Kate was a little sweaty and a lot smiley. She had just finished a meditation session and was sipping a CBD tonic, beaming, and all I could think was, "I'll have what she's having."

We always think about working out as physical exercise. We picture working out in gyms and yoga studios, on tennis courts, and while out for a run — just as we used to think about taking care of our health only as physical, though it's so much more than that. *The Full Spirit Workout* is a practice in creating strength and resilience in our minds and hearts. It's for our spiritual health, our mental health, our emotional health, and of course our physical health, too — because there is no more denying that it's all connected, and we are all connected.

I met Kate in a meditation center / bookstore / crystals-and-facemasks (the moisturizing kind) emporium in New York City. I'd planned to walk out with a new book and maybe a candle, and instead I left with a new friend, which isn't always an easy feat as an adult.

Kate meets you where you are, in real life and in this book. The reason she knows where you are is that she's been there. Her vulnerability in sharing what she's learned, from a place of "Yep, I was there, too" instead of "I'm reporting my research," is welcome and needed. Kate's woo-woo is rooted in what she has learned is best for her based on her real-life experiences, and that's a level of woo I can embrace and incorporate into my own life.

I've tapped into Kate's thoughtful words outside of this book, too. Her post on Instagram "being ok if it happens and being ok if it doesn't, is a very powerful place to be" has helped me navigate some really hard moments and has become a personal mantra. I'm so grateful that practices like repeating mantras, taking deep breaths, meditating, and working on what's within me change what is around me. And likewise, just because things are chaotic around me doesn't mean things have to be chaotic within me.

From sharing personal stories and wise advice to inviting you to journal and meditate, coaching you along the way, and then giving you permission to choose stillness, stop pretending, and stay in your pajamas all day, this book is all about knowing, forgiving, loving, and trusting yourself. It's not always easy to work on ourselves and to let our hearts lead the way, but I promise that if you navigate this book with curiosity, you'll find clarity. If you put Kate's words into action, you'll discover how strong you are, how much you deserve out of life, and how working on yourself is a gift not only to you but to everyone around you.

— **Courtney Carver**, author of *Soulful Simplicity* and *Project 333* (www.bemorewithless.com)

Introduction

If you looked at my life from the outside, you might be surprised to learn that I spent most of my years getting in my own way. Despite achieving many goals and building a successful career, I was often in turmoil, filled with anxiety and insecurity. My life was all about impressing other people or attaining some image of success that I'd borrowed from society. But who was I on the inside? Who was the *real me*? And what did that real me *really want*? For a long time, I had no idea.

If you're anything like I was, you're tired of living a life based on comparison, competition, fear, and lack. You're looking for a system that helps you live your life based on love, support, faith, abundance, and authenticity. Maybe you're doing all the so-called right things to be happy and successful, but something's still missing. Maybe you're afraid you aren't good enough. (Join the club!) Maybe you feel like you're going nonstop...but for what purpose? Maybe you're asking yourself, *Is this as good as it gets?*

You might even have asked yourself, *Isn't there a way to shed my excess emotional pounds? Isn't there a way to get spiritually fit so that I finally feel confident, fulfilled, peaceful, abundant, loving, and joyful?*

1

Just as strong physical muscles help you live more effectively, strong spiritual muscles can give you the power to navigate your internal world, as well as the external world. Just as physical fitness involves a strong core, spiritual fitness will help you develop a strong *inner* core. And just as consistent reps of exercise get the body fit, the reps and exercises in *The Full Spirit Workout* will help you shed the self-doubt that holds you back from achieving the fun, fulfilling life you desire and deserve!

But this workout conditions you on the inside — no sweating required. Instead, I will help you cultivate small, meaningful moments of mindfulness and stillness throughout the day, making it fun and easy to come back home to yourself with enthusiasm and joy.

How do I know the Full Spirit Workout can work? Because I'm the proof! It's how I turned my life around, and I know in my heart of hearts that this program can help you do the same.

Today, my life is eons away from where it was when I was filled with anxiety and self-doubt. Now, I own my greatness. I live a fulfilling, joyous life, and I've helped many others do the same. I still have to work at it, but because I have consistently followed the principles in this book, the work I've done on my spirit has translated into more blessings on the outside. Every day, I'm filled with such gratitude.

So how did I come to develop the Full Spirit Workout? Well, let's just say the journey was more grueling (but also more strengthening) than a thousand burpees.

My Wake-Up Call

It took a hefty wake-up call for me to change the way I looked at myself and my life. It happened on a mid-December day as I was speed-walking through Midtown Manhattan near Times Square. (Speed-walking is my usual pace.) I was surrounded by noisy sirens, rush-hour crowds, and chaos, but the mayhem and turmoil inside me were even more overwhelming. As stressed New Yorkers hustled past in all directions, I began to feel like I was out of my body…and out of my mind. My breath quickened, and I started to hyperventilate. I couldn't breathe. I began to panic.

It had been just six weeks since a man I considered to be one of the great loves of my life jumped to his death, nearly a year to the day after another dear friend also took his life. Like many suicides, they came as a complete shock to all of us who loved them. There were no warning signs, no drugs, no indications of mental illness or even unhappiness, let alone depression.

Frightened and anxious, I grabbed my phone and called my brother, John, a physician. It was nothing short of a miracle that he picked up. My brother rarely answers his phone, especially during business hours.

"Babe [as I call him], I'm freaking out. I can't…breathe. I think…I'm having a…panic attack or something. Can you… please call in a prescription…for Lexapro? I've taken it for anxiety before. I'm just…a few blocks…from a pharmacy."

I managed to drag myself through the masses down Seventh Avenue to the pharmacy, breathing fast and sobbing the whole way. The good thing about New York City is that people leave you alone when you walk down the street sobbing. *That's also the sad thing about New York City — people leave you alone when you walk down the street sobbing.*

When I approached the counter, the pharmacist greeted me with such friendliness that I burst into even heavier sobs. I texted my friend Lily while my prescription was being filled: "I'm crying my eyes out at a pharmacy while I wait for antianxiety medication. Yes, I've become *that* girl."

"What? Are you serious? Are you okay? Kate, that's not you! You're one of the happiest people I know," she responded.

I had never seen myself as "that girl" either, but in that moment, there was no denying that's who I had become.

After I took the first dose of Lexapro, I texted my brother: "I just want to take the whole bottle and go to sleep."

He texted back: "I'm calling the cops."

"*No!* I'm kidding."

"You don't joke about things like that, Kate!"

The truth is that I wasn't really kidding. The pain I was experiencing felt like too much to bear, and I desperately wanted it to go away, whatever that took. I had never been suicidal, but suddenly, I had fallen asleep to the truth of who I was and caught a glimpse of what my friends Sam and Raf must have been feeling when they decided to take their own lives.

As close as I was to both of them, neither one took me or anyone else into his confidence about his darkest feelings. My own saving grace was that I was willing to sob in front of that pharmacist, and I was willing to reach out to my brother for help. Other angels showed up that day and after — people I like to call "God in drag" (i.e., God in human form). As I disclosed my pain to each of them, starting with my brother, they helped me resist the urge to empty that bottle down my throat.

If I'd been like Sam or Raf, though, who were taught to keep their pain hidden and buried, I don't know what would have happened to me that day.

During the six weeks between Sam's death and that morning when I contemplated swallowing the pills, I had been going, going, going on the same frantic hamster wheel that Sam had always traveled on. I booked my schedule solid without giving myself the proper self-care or space I needed to let the depth of my pain out.

I realized I couldn't run on that wheel any longer. I was exhausted. It wasn't just the pain of losing two friends to suicide; it was the constant hustle of trying to prove my worth to myself and the world through an endless list of accomplishments, achievements, accolades, and awards (what I call the "four As").

I had to face not only the loss of my dear friends but also the fears that their deaths were bringing up in me. Sam, in particular, had been like my male counterpart — like a mirror image of me. We were both known for being the life of every party and everyone's best friend. But like so many, we placed our worth in the material world. We thought success was measured by what we looked like, how many jobs we booked, how much money we had in the bank, and so on.

Like me, both Sam and Raf appeared to the outside world as though they had all those things and more. In the minds of most people who met them, they were the cream of the crop — successful and good-looking with enviable lives. Since Raf's death, I've learned that he was harboring a deep secret and was worried his family and friends wouldn't accept him if they knew. In other words, he was scared and ashamed to live his truth. Sam was living on a teeter-totter. A single rejection from a casting agent was enough to send him plummeting down.

Their deaths forced me to face a difficult truth: when

we allow our self-worth to be defined by people and sources outside ourselves, we can never have enough or be enough. When we depend on the approval of others, we stand on the edge of a cliff, ready to tumble from even the smallest setback.

Was I on a similar path? A part of me was scared I was going to end up like them. After all, there I was nursing a bottle of pills as though it could be my savior. Who had I become?

Striving to Become "Enough"

My childhood set the stage for that woman I became, who put so much stock in what others thought. Like most of us, I grew up with the belief that other people's opinions about me were paramount. When we think that we aren't enough, we don't feel safe and secure in the permanence of our loved ones' feelings for us. If I could just be enough (beautiful, smart, educated), do enough (achieve, accomplish, perform), and have enough (money, notoriety, "success"), my life would be "perfect" and complete. I would win the eternal love of my parents and everyone around me. I would be safe because I wouldn't be alone.

I felt safer when I got good grades, for example, and people reflected back to me that I was a good girl. I felt safer when I could make myself pretty enough to get attention from boys and when I could be funny enough to gain popularity with girls. I felt safer when I became a star athlete, making my parents proud as I broke records as a competitive swimmer and earned an athletic scholarship to Penn State. And when I got into the best journalism school and became a writer and television anchor.

Then, when I moved to New York for a job opportunity that fell through, I discovered that I had the right physicality to become a "plus-size" model (which, according to the modeling industry, is size 6 and up). So I reinvented myself, signing with one of the biggest modeling agencies in the world, and soon became an international TV personality as well. It's interesting that I chose a career that's all about outward appearances — a field that's supposedly the final confirmation that you're beautiful. At least that's what most women imagine. If you become a model, it means you're pretty *enough*, right?

The irony, though, is that when you get paid for how you look, everyone constantly zeroes in on your perceived "flaws" or "imperfections" — always telling you what's "wrong" with you. You lose jobs based on hair color, hip size, natural female weight fluctuations, and age. Your photo or video appears in an ad, and people online feel they have license to rip every inch of you apart from the comfort of their home computers — as if you aren't a real person sitting behind a computer at home yourself. I was told, for example, that I needed a gym membership and was called derogatory names while working as a size 12 swimsuit model.

Modeling brought out every insecurity I'd ever harbored about myself and some I didn't even know I had. As a result, I started working even harder to try to be better, more, "perfect," so that I wouldn't have to face the constant rejections that my profession brought with it. But it isn't like there's some *perfect* destination that will stop the casting rejections or the negative online comments. There's simply no such thing.

If I didn't want to end up so caught up in what others

thought of me that I couldn't go on living, I had to stop looking outside myself for my value. I had to stop trying so desperately to *achieve* and *accomplish* in order to show the world that I was worth knowing and loving. I had to stop striving for some elusive image of perfection and give myself permission to be imperfect, authentic me. *That*, I discovered, is true perfection. So I started my quest to accept all that I am — confident, vulnerable, intelligent, flawed, sassy, silly Kate. I started on a quest to connect with my spirit and become *spiritually fit*.

Answering the Wake-Up Call

The suicides of my beloved Raf and Sam, coupled with that day in the pharmacy, shook me to my core. To call these events a wake-up call is an understatement, and I knew my life depended on answering it. So I dove headfirst into studying, meditating, writing, praying, and working hard to find the keys to a better way of life that would allow me to generate self-esteem and contentment from within. As a devout student of *A Course in Miracles*, a metaphysical self-study book and curriculum, I learned how to retrain my mind to think differently. I unsubscribed from the thought system of the world that's based on fear and instead plugged into core beliefs based on love. I learned how to surrender my ego. And I learned how to shed emotional flab and connect with my spirit within. Slowly, I began to develop a process that felt very much like a physical workout, only for my inside! And over time, it worked. Then, I tried it with my coaching clients, and it worked for them, too.

I'm now able to live in faith rather than fear. (And I no longer feel the need to take Lexapro or other pharmaceuticals. While I advocate for anyone with a serious mental illness who needs these medications, I believe that most of us are capable of getting off that hamster wheel, too.)

I now operate from this core belief: *I am complete.* I'm still a work in progress, of course, but my life is no longer about what I do or about striving to prove my worth. Instead, it's about who I am. And I owe all of that to working on my *spiritual fitness.*

Imagine a life that isn't about how to "get this" or "do that," but instead about *being* the person who naturally attracts all that your heart desires. You just have to believe how powerful you are! Increased performance and resilience, more meaningful relationships, newfound confidence and well-being, true fulfillment, and fun are available to you when you get your spirit in shape.

Here's the Plan

To get your spirit in tip-top condition so that you can have the life you've always wanted, here's what we're going to do:

Step 1: Stretch Your Comfort Zone. Just like we need to stretch before we work out physically, we need to stretch before we start our spiritual fitness regimen. The truth is that everything you've ever wanted is just on the other side of "comfy," so in this step, you'll learn how to stretch your comfort zone and "unsubscribe" from struggling.

Step 2: Lift Yourself Up. Step 2 will show you how to redefine beauty so that you can lift yourself up on a daily basis, feeling beautiful (or handsome) from the inside out — even if you don't feel confident or comfortable in your body right now.

Step 3: Feel the Burn. This step might burn just a little as you go deeper and discover the false, limiting beliefs that are holding you back from achieving what you desire. We'll also redefine relationships as "soul assignments" and tools for growth so that you can move on from breakups more easily.

Step 4: Strengthen Your Core Confidence. In this key step, you'll learn how to strengthen your spiritual core, much like we strengthen our physical core in exercise programs. To do that, you'll firm your spiritual flab by creating new beliefs to replace the old, outworn ones. You'll also practice self-forgiveness and explore your core values.

Step 5: Build Your Emotional Muscles. We all know that if we want to be physically fit, we have to train our physical muscles. The same is true of our emotional muscles. In this step, you'll learn to flex your feelings and shed your emotional skin in order to become more emotionally resilient and maintain your equilibrium.

Step 6: Boost Your Mental Metabolism. Every athlete knows that the mind is an important component of physical fitness. It's important for spiritual fitness, too. Just like physical metabolism affects our energy, your mental metabolism — through your positive or negative self-talk — will affect your energy every day. In this step, you'll learn new self-talk habits to boost your mental metabolism for a maximum experience of joy.

Step 7: Step Up Your Spiritual Stamina. The Full Spirit Workout isn't a fad or a boot camp. It's a regimen for life that requires spiritual stamina. But that isn't like other kinds of stamina that are about self-determination, will, or gritting our teeth. It's about constantly returning to vulnerability. It's about choosing to be open and tender. In this step, you'll learn to choose trust so that you can make yourself available for transformation and renewal over and over.

Step 8: Embrace Your Endorphins. Through our glands and brain, we produce endorphins that reduce our pain and increase our feelings of well-being. Through spiritual fitness, we can create the equivalent of a runner's high on a regular basis. The exercises in this step will help you learn how to regularly release spiritual endorphins through a connection with the divine.

Step 9: Rock the Freedom Freestyle. The freedom freestyle is when you'll really start to make spiritual fitness work for you and become a way of life. You'll explore what you truly want and how to *allow* abundance rather than try to will it into being. This will include letting go of resistance to what's good for you and discovering how to be of service by putting your unique gifts to use, rather than requesting "things."

Step 10: Cool Down with Inner Calm. This step shows you how to get off the treadmill and cool down with newfound inner calm, or, as I like to say, "calm-fidence." We'll practice radical self-acceptance and create "to-be" lists rather than to-do lists. Through it all, you'll reinforce your ability to maintain your spiritual fitness through daily practices that keep you steady and strong while you create the fun and fulfilling life of your dreams.

The magic happens when we approach our spiritual fitness with creativity, playfulness, and delight. This is your invitation to get radically honest about what is happening inside you at your core. Just like physical exercise, spiritual exercise can be challenging but also extremely rewarding, and we always feel so much better after a great workout, even if we resist it at first. You won't need weights or a jump rope for these exercises, but you will need a journal and something to write with. Feel free to grab your meditation pillow if you have one, light some candles, and cozy up with your favorite blanket.

Can you feel the excitement of possibility? Are you fired up? Let's work out!

CONTRACT

On this day, _____, I, _____, agree to embark on the Full Spirit Workout and officially unsubscribe from the struggle.

_____

Signature

STEP 1

Stretch Your Comfort Zone

A man grows most tired while standing still.

— CHINESE PROVERB

We all know our muscles crave stretching, and they become tight and contracted when we don't stretch them. What most of us don't realize is that our spirit craves stretching, too, and it can become equally tight and contracted if we don't take the time to bend and expand. We crave stretching so much, in fact, that employees have said in surveys that their favorite bosses are the ones who push them to learn and achieve more.

Spiritual stretching is about allowing for the fresh opportunities that come when we expand our comfort zone. But what exactly is our "comfort zone," anyway? Well, I like to think of it as an arbitrary boundary that we create in our minds based on fear. When we are unfamiliar with an idea or something else, we push it away, as it's easier and more comfortable to stay in what we know and have tested. It helps us feel secure, but at what cost? If we stay in that zone, we never discover how juicy life can really be.

Unfortunately, many of us stay stuck in our comfort zones, afraid to venture out of them and stretch our spirits, because discomfort is so...well, uncomfortable. But only when we move outside that zone can we grow and truly transform our lives to live up to our full potential. When was the last time you wanted to try something new but hesitated, then stuck with what felt comfortable? (Key here: being stuck.)

Consider this insight from author T. Harv Eker: "Nobody ever died of discomfort, yet living in the name of comfort has killed more ideas, more opportunities, more actions, and more growth than everything else combined."

Oftentimes we don't even realize we are sabotaging our chances at true fulfillment — abundance, joy, lasting success. We self-sabotage by not believing we are worthy or deserving of having what we truly desire. We make excuses. We waste countless hours and brain cells scrolling through social media, exhausting ourselves with comparison and judgment. We think, *If only I had her looks, money, husband, cute dog, beautiful home, and opportunities, I could be happy, too.* We allow our worn-out, limiting beliefs (some of which are subconscious) to take the wheel and make decisions for us that aren't in our best interest. We think these beliefs are keeping us "safe," but ultimately they are keeping us from our true potential and the life we crave. Our undisciplined, inflexible minds block our blessings. But if we can allow ourselves to take that first step into the unknown, we will find we are more courageous, bold, capable, and resilient than we ever imagined. And through personal experience, I've discovered that when we take risks and rise to the challenge, we stretch and grow in ways that catapult us to new levels of excitement. We feel lit up from the inside out, and our life reflects that back to us with improved relationships, career opportunities, financial success, and freedom.

In my twenties, I gave up a cushy entertainment reporting gig in Hollywood to move to Chicago and give my relationship with my then-boyfriend a real shot. I thought he was the man I would eventually marry. I struggled with leaving LA, especially the sunshine and year-round warm weather. Southern California always felt like home to me. I put my condo on the market, and it ended up selling at the peak of the US real estate bubble. My home had tripled in value in just three years. In fact, the week after my home sold, my real estate agent called to tell me that prices were already coming down. I felt as though I had won the lottery. Just six months prior, I had no intention of ever leaving LA.

This isn't the part of the story where I tell you I absolutely loved living in Chicago and married the love of my life. The truth is, I missed California terribly, nearly froze to death, even in April and May, and ultimately broke things off with the kindest, most decent man who was willing and able to love me in a way I still haven't fully experienced since. I wholeheartedly wanted to feel the same way about him, but I simply wasn't in love with him. The original reason I moved to Chicago was for romantic love, which sadly ended, but I was able to leave with another kind of love — a love of writing and storytelling — and my master's degree from

Northwestern University's Medill School of Journalism. This was the beginning of my TV news career, which was anything but glamorous, unlike the celebrity-filled red carpets of Hollywood reporting. I would soon experience just how underpaid most journalists are, but it was okay. I had the money from my winning lottery ticket, aka the sale of my California home, to help me along the way. This is often the case when we take risks: the universe steps in to assist us.

But first we have to be *willing* to stretch our spirits and become more flexible. It's a vital first step in this spiritual fitness process: when we neglect it, we can "pull" an emotional muscle — we can hurt ourselves. Oftentimes, we are too "comfortable" in our pain and in what's not working. That's why stretching is so important and can prevent future injuries. One of my favorite spiritual principles from *A Course in Miracles* teaches that our good intentions are not enough; our willingness is everything.

We understand how important stretching is to our bodies before and after we exercise. It increases blood flow and circulation for a healthier body and sends oxygen to the brain for a clearer mind. Stretching allows us to perform more efficiently on every level. Ultimately, we can achieve more when we devote even a few minutes a day to this simple practice. So why would we ever skip this much-needed, beneficial step?

Yet, honestly, I've never been great about stretching my body before or after working out. I'm always eager to get right into running, swimming, lifting. I know I'm not alone in this, either: in my exercise classes, many people leave after the main workout, skipping stretching altogether. I rarely go to yoga classes because I always feel like I'm the least flexible in the class, and I'm much more comfortable participating in activities where I can excel and feel accomplished. I think sometimes I feel resistant to stretching because I don't want to be up close and personal with the reality that flexibility isn't my strong suit. I may also be inclined to think, *I don't have time, I don't enjoy it, it feels uncomfortable. My muscles are so tight, what's the point?* The truth is, that's just me trying to stay in my comfort zone.

The idea of a "comfort zone" goes back to a classic experiment in psychology. In 1908, psychologists Robert M. Yerkes and John D. Dodson explained that a state of relative comfort creates a steady level of performance. To *maximize* performance, we need to be in a state of relative anxiety — a space where our stress levels are slightly higher than normal. They refer to this space as "optimal anxiety," and, as you might have guessed, it's just outside our comfort zones.

Their theory is that we gain drive and ambition, and become more productive, when we push the boundaries of our comfort areas. We can do this by giving ourselves deadlines and expectations. Or we can do it by giving up our need to distract ourselves with "busyness" as a way of *avoiding* having to try new experiences.

I believe any change, even positive change, can feel uncomfortable. It requires courage. It forces us to break free from the box inside our minds that says it's safer and easier to just keep doing what we're doing. Stretching ourselves and trying new things means we have no choice but to show up as an improved and enhanced version of ourselves, even if just to survive the new circumstances we've willingly put ourselves into.

It's Not Easy

In 2009, I left my career as a TV news reporter in South Florida to spend several weeks living and working in Zimbabwe with my then-boyfriend, Raf. He was a wildlife biologist studying African wild dogs, and I was going to work as a freelance journalist for *Travel Africa* magazine.

When the opportunity arose, I knew I had to go on that trip. So many of my colleagues couldn't believe it when I left the business and packed myself off to backcountry Africa. But it was a once-in-a-lifetime chance, and I knew I owed it to myself to give it a try. (Don't you just love it when our truth, our highest and most ideal self, speaks to us, if we allow it to flow through us?)

I was thrilled to be traveling to Africa for the first time and to get the opportunity to see all the incredible wild animals face-to-face, but it was far from easy. This was by no means a rich American's African safari. We stayed in the bush with no air-conditioning and less-than-desirable living conditions. As a self-proclaimed high-maintenance woman who loves room service, bubble baths, fluffy robes and slippers, and luxury skin-care products, I was pushed way beyond my comfort zone.

I desperately want to tell you that I loved every second of my experience there, but the truth is that I recall crying at times because I was so uncomfortable, hot, sweaty, and dirty. Sometimes, I just craved US Wi-Fi, clean showers, and even fast-food restaurants.

The eye-opening and life-changing experiences I had in Africa made it all worthwhile, though. I got to meet and interview incredible women who had given up their cushy lives to dedicate everything they had — time, money, energy — to help save the elephants, hippos, rhinos, and other threatened species from deplorable conditions and frequent poaching. They were shining examples of people truly sacrificing life's comforts for a purpose greater than themselves. Meeting them was awe-inspiring and helped me get over myself and want to devote more time to serving others.

I also couldn't ignore the reality of how spoiled so many of us are around the world, especially in the States. I watched children walking miles to school with bare feet in 100-degree heat. Women carrying large buckets of water on their heads, again in bare feet. I gave my five-dollar Walmart flip-flops and some hand sanitizer to Nicky, my host in the bush, and she was so elated you'd have thought I bought her a Mercedes.

When I returned home, I wept, thinking about how fortunate I am, how much I have taken for granted at times, and how blessed I was to take this trip. Yes, being with my boyfriend and seeing the wildlife were incredible experiences. But even more so was seeing myself in this environment, so far out of my comfort zone, yet *growing* with the flow, doing the best I could, and learning to truly appreciate all the comforts I took for granted as an American. This stretched my spirit by allowing me to see how insignificant many of our "problems" really are. While I don't want to belittle our feelings or experiences, this trip to Africa was a reminder to put them into perspective. It stretched me into the art of taking a step back and noticing, actually noticing, what's going on around me and within me. This gave me the capacity to change how I interpret not just the outer world, but my inner world. My spirit, rather than my mind, now had permission to lead the way. This opened me up to an entire new world, showing me there is always something deeper, more magnetic and mysterious, and even grander to discover and explore. The best part? We don't have to hop on a plane or travel to Africa; we just have to be willing to go within.

That trip was one of the defining moments of my life. Raf and I got to experience Victoria Falls together, and so much more, and all those memories occupy a precious place in my heart and soul. Raf and I ultimately broke up, and he later took his own life, but I am grateful for what we shared there and how much he helped me grow.

My Zimbabwe trip was one of the deepest spiritual stretches I've ever completed, and I feel like a deeper, richer person because of it. I encourage you, too, to buy the ticket, take the ride — even if it's just a metaphorical one.

Some stretches are very deep, and we stay in them a while, strengthening, lengthening, becoming more powerful. Other times, we just need a quick stretch. For example, take the first time I drove in New York City. I realized it was not an option to be anything but aggressive — not to be a jerk, but simply to survive and not get plowed over. I found you must be simultaneously aggressive and hyperfocused, so as to not hit pedestrians or bicyclists while also not getting run over by cabs or buses. New York City driving truly teaches a person to live outside her comfort zone (or any driving safety laws she thought could and would protect her).

You're Going to Be Great

I vividly remember the first live shot I did as a TV news reporter. It was in Panama City Beach, Florida, where I had recently arrived, fresh from journalism school.

But first, let me back up and say that the simple fact of living in Panama City Beach represented some serious stretching. As I mentioned, I'd given up a red-carpet reporting job in Hollywood and headed to journalism school in Chicago, where I'd spent hours reporting from Cook County Juvenile Court. This move sounded insane to so many around me. Yet I remember thinking how much more rewarding it was to talk to judges about improving conditions for troubled inner-city youths than it was to talk to Angelina Jolie about her new movie.

But back to that first live shot. I remember feeling so nervous, a little shaky, thinking, *What if I mess up? What happens if I forget what I'm going to say? Will viewers and coworkers laugh at me for not being amazing?*

If I could speak to my younger self that day, I would share the same message I'd give any of you who try something for the first time and feel a little unsure of yourself, worried about judgment from yourself and others: "You are going to be great! Even if you don't perform 'perfectly' (as if there were any such thing), you still will have showed up and done it! And you will continue to get better and better, until it becomes almost effortless. Just keep going!"

And more, I would add, "I'm so proud of you. You have dared to put yourself out there, and share your truth openly and vulnerably. You are a success, not because of anything you have achieved or accomplished but because you are *you*. Have fun with it. Dare to suck or not be great…at first. Smile. Laugh. Go ahead. Stop thinking you have to have it all figured out and do everything 'flawlessly.' Your messy is sexy. Own it."

People don't care about what you're saying and doing as much as you think they do. They're more concerned with what they themselves are saying and doing.

You are learning. You are growing. You are becoming more of who you are every day. And whether you recognize it or not, everything in your life has prepared you for this moment. Think of experiences you have been through that can show you why you are more prepared and perfect for the present moment than you realize.

In my case, a seventeen-year competitive swimming career — where we got up on the blocks, and then it was, "Take your mark," *Beep!* and off we went, whether we were "ready" or not — prepared me for a live TV career so perfectly. For both, I had to be truly present in the moment and let all my practice and inner knowing take over while consciously blocking out both inner and outer noise and distractions.

That presence is key. I invite you to lean into the present moment and allow yourself to be guided. In the years since that live shot, I've expanded from a TV reporter into a TV personality, model, public speaker, and more. Half the time I do a live presentation on TV or elsewhere, I walk off camera or offstage and think to myself, *I don't even know how I did that.* The words, the message, the presentation just flowed. I focus on having fun and doing my best, and forget the rest. That's true success to me.

And as for that first shot? I wasn't perfect. Far from it. But I did it, and in the end, taking that leap was what landed me where I am today.

Not Everyone Will Like You

News flash: not everyone is going to like you. I'm a recovering people pleaser, so this is a big one for me — especially considering that as a model, pleasing clients during auditions was the way I made money for years. I literally needed people to like me, and pick me, to pay my bills.

A huge turning point for me was when I was up for a national commercial featuring Sofía Vergara that paid a life-changing amount of money. The client told my agent I was exactly what they were looking for. I went on three call-backs. I was so excited about the opportunity and exposure, in addition to the paycheck.

I didn't get the job. I remember feeling completely devastated. It's hard for me to even admit this, but at the time, I truly thought it was because I wasn't good enough in some way I should have fixed. Not pretty enough, not the perfect shape or size, not young enough, or not up to snuff in my audition performance. The core message that ran through my entire body at this rejection was, *I'm not good enough.*

I couldn't help but laugh with relief when I eventually saw the commercial and discovered that a petite African American woman had gotten the part. It wasn't about me at all. The casting directors simply wanted someone who looked very different from me, which happens a lot. In hindsight, it was another reminder of that core lesson: so much that happens to us, and in our interactions with other people, isn't about *us* at all.

At the time, though, it hurt. It stung. I had been going on more huge auditions than ever before, but I wasn't booking any jobs. *There must be something wrong with me*, I thought. My self-esteem had plummeted without my even realizing it. I didn't wake up to this reality until I wrote an article for mindbodygreen.com and one of their editors titled it, "I'm a model + had low self-esteem. How I found calm in a competitive industry."

I remember getting an email from the editors that my story was live, and feeling horrified and embarrassed when I saw the title. Ouch! I really had to let it sink in for a minute:

I was a model with low self-esteem. What an oxymoron. Or actually…of course I was a model with low self-esteem — all we do is get picked apart and told what's "wrong" with us. How could we *not* have low self-esteem? Our entire livelihood is based on what we look like. And not just on what we look like, but on someone else's opinion of our looks, which really has nothing to do with *us* at all but rather with our mom, dad, grandma, and grandpa's genetics. And as a plus-size model, jeez, I wasn't even fitting into society's extra-small standard of beauty.

So, slowly, I realized the title of that article was a gift. It was like this little hall pass to own my insecurities, to talk openly about them and encourage others to own and embrace their perceived flaws and insecurities, too. We are all in this together, after all.

I had stretched out of my comfort zone of trying to *appear* to have it all together while striving for unattainable perfection. And it turns out my willingness to stretch this way would kick off a beautiful new journey for me — as an author, executive leadership coach, keynote speaker, and champion for living from the spirit (love) rather than ego (fear).

Which brings me back to the question of our willingness to stretch ourselves. I allowed myself to be *willing* to admit that my self-esteem needed a massive (inner) makeover. I was willing to speak openly and honestly about it. I was willing to discipline my emotional muscles daily because that inner critic can be mean, loud, and extra bitchy. I was willing to show up, be uncomfortable, cry, notice my depression when repressed thoughts and feelings surfaced, go to therapy, do the work, meditate, pray, ask for help — to not just give myself love but also to remember I *am* love and to connect deeply with a higher power.

For me, that higher power is God, and my God is un-conditional love. "God" can be a loaded word for many, I know. But by it, I mean unconditional love — a tremendous source of goodness, guidance, and powerful energy that is always with and within me. The willingness to connect to that source and plug into it daily has transformed my life, and I'm so happy it can do the same for you, if you are willing.

Choose Peace

A friend recently said to me, "I just want to feel at peace."

"I understand," I said. "That is the ultimate goal for all of us. Are you willing to choose peace?"

"Yes," she said. Then I saw her eyes light up, like, *Wow, that was easy!*

And it *is* that easy. If you want love, choose to be in love, starting with yourself. I believe if peace and love are what we truly want, we will choose peace and love. Oftentimes, we *think* we want them but are still stuck in past wounds that make us feel more at home and "safe" in chaos, lack, and trauma. But just like we can decide to be willing to stretch before a workout because we know it will make us perform better and avoid injury, we can be willing to choose thoughts that empower us to get out of our comfort zone. That leads us into the life that's waiting for us to claim it — a life where we get to live in our divine perfection.

I don't think you have to move to a different city, change careers, start a new relationship, adopt a new workout rou-tine, or go vegan to stretch your comfort zone, although I highly recommend all of that. It can be as simple (not easy, mind you, but simple) as choosing to look in the mirror and notice something you love about your body rather than thinking, *Gosh, I'm looking older* or *Ugh, I have stomach rolls.*

Say to yourself, *I am willing to feel love, peace, and joy, instead of this.* Make that a daily practice, and I promise you will start to think, look, feel, and be your most glorious self.

When we stretch our comfort zones, we automatically get to discover our greatness, our highest self. We find our true essence and desires, naturally attracting what lights us up and gives our lives meaning and purpose. Simply put, it is healing to stretch. And when we are willing to stretch, the universe responds to even our slightest invitation to assist us in our efforts. We are never alone. We are always cocreating.

If you've ever started a new business or family, I'm guessing it wasn't easy, and it wasn't painless. (If you are a parent, you are my own personal hero!) But I'll bet that allowing yourself to expand your personal boundaries and devote your most precious resource — time — to your cherished new venture opened up the space you needed to take on this exciting challenge.

When I recently took on a new project outside my comfort zone, I was able to keep taking steps forward because I first allowed myself to experience my heavy feelings and cry to a supportive friend. My tears washed the space clear for me to express myself. I'm learning that one of the worst things we can do is to pretend uncomfortable feelings like worry, stress, sadness, fear, and discomfort don't exist — or that we're somehow too precious, too positive, or too evolved to feel something other than pleasant feelings. When we are in that place of loneliness, fear, sadness, and discomfort, it's important not to try to jump right to gratitude or "positivity." Sometimes crying and acknowledging how much things suck, or how heavy our feelings weigh on us, put us on the fast train to returning home to ourselves, where appreciation and gratitude occur naturally. This certainty offers me peace, just as it did during that uncertain time.

The period of forced isolation we all experienced during the pandemic was a deep stretch for all of us, and while seclusion could feel uncomfortable, I also noticed benefits. For example, many of us learned, or relearned, how little we really need. It helped me remember to be more simple and minimal in my day-to-day living. We also had more time to reflect on and challenge old ways of thinking — giving us spiritual fitness workouts. I brainstormed new ways to help clients and, in turn, myself. I saw old problems in a new light and was able to devote energy to discovering new ways of being because, quite simply, why not?

And just like physical exercise has cumulative effects over time, so does spiritual fitness. Once we start stepping out of our comfort zone, it gets easier. We become more and more comfortable with our own discomfort. Awesome, right?

JOURNALING EXERCISE
Stretching for Tight, Stuck, Dissatisfied Mental Muscles

Sit quietly with your pen and journal. Gently close your eyes and begin to scan your mind and body. What feels tight? Where do you feel soreness? What is bringing you dissatisfaction right now? Take your time. Really check in with yourself. There are no right or wrong answers. Simply notice what's popping up for you. Try to identify where your mental and emotional "muscles" feel out of alignment. Write these observations in your journal.

For example, maybe your emotional responses feel tight. In other words, you keep telling yourself to just be grateful for what you have — which is great — but are you bypassing your feelings of disappointment, sadness, or loneliness? Maybe your heart feels sore from trying to keep it together all day in front of your children. You could use a good cry, relaxing walk, comforting book, or heartfelt conversation with a loved one. Maybe you need to speak openly to a trusted coach or therapist about what you're experiencing, so the emotions no longer feel stuck in your body.

Maybe you need your partner, parent, or boss to acknowledge your hard work around the home or office. Perhaps you need to acknowledge yourself or let yourself off the hook. You are doing your best. When was the last time you told yourself, *Great job!*? Or maybe you're not doing your best and need to explore why. Maybe you are dissatisfied that you've been searching for so much of your sense of self-worth from external sources and it's making you feel horrible. Or maybe your relationships — both romantic and platonic — could use some TLC.

Now let's explore some of your fears. What are you scared of? Resist the urge to shrink back into what's comfortable, and allow your mind to keep expanding. Understand that growth and a deeper knowledge of yourself lives in the uneasiness. Take a moment to let yourself dwell in any uneasiness so you can move forward freely.

If it feels good, write down whatever thoughts and emotions surfaced for you in your journal. Next, move on to the following questions:

1. How is sticking to what is familiar and safe keeping you stuck?
2. List three small steps you can take to stretch your comfort zone in order to maximize your full potential.
3. Psychologists say our comfort zone is a reflection of our self-image, how we think and expect things to be. How are your thoughts and expectations holding you back?
4. If or when you stretched your comfort zone in the past, how did that instill confidence in you?
5. How can stretching your comfort zone enhance the level of meaning and purpose you find in your work?
6. What are you learning about yourself while stretching?
7. If you knew you were capable of achieving your true potential, what would you try?

Daily Mantras to Stretch Slowly and Take Bite-Size Risks

1. I accept exactly where I am on my journey right now.
2. I break the illusion of perfection and stop trying to appear to have it all together.
3. I ditch self-imposed standards.
4. I release my fear of what others will think.
5. I am okay with letting people down in order to establish a healthy boundary.
6. I surrender expectations from myself, others, situations, and experiences.
7. I gamble for fun, by having the courage to try again and again.
8. I give up conforming to social standards and pressures.

9. I embrace awkwardness.
10. I'm open to making a new friend who is outside my world (work, school, play).
11. I see myself as a success already.
12. I do life on my own terms. I make my own rules.
13. I say Yes! to new experiences that allow me to blossom (whether it's living in Africa, speaking publicly, starting my own business, leaving the job or relationship that no longer feels good, falling in love, getting sober).
14. I celebrate every small stretch as a big success toward the freedom of spiritual fitness.

Ultimately, if you ever want to achieve anything noteworthy or out of the ordinary, expanding your comfort zone is a must! Know that while you may feel intimidated now, you will become comfortable with time. After all, if we want to become a more elevated version of ourselves — the version who can accomplish our cherished goals — we cannot stand still and unstretched.

 REACH FOR THE SKY MEDITATION

I know of nothing that will lift your spirit higher than meditation, because it changes more than just your mind and thoughts. Scientific studies have proved that meditation actually changes your brain waves. It also soothes your emotions and expands your spirit. It's true spiritual fitness in progress!

All the meditations in this book are listed on my website (www.kateeckman.tv) with audio versions that you can use. If you prefer, however, you can read and record them yourself. Just don't keep your eyes open and read as you meditate. You won't be able to stay in a meditative state that way.

If you've never meditated before, don't worry! There's nothing you have to do but breathe and relax as best you can. There's no wrong way to do it.

Take a moment to get comfortable in your meditation space. Close your eyes gently. Feel the heaviness of your eyelids as you take a deep breath in through your nose and out through your mouth. Good. Continue this simple, relaxed style of breathing throughout your meditation.

When you're ready, invite the following words into your mind and heart while allowing them to be absorbed into your subconscious mind, shifting the way you experience yourself and your life.

The comfort and security I seek lie within.

I am fully present, clear, confident, and joyful. I have let go of the need to be guarded, distracted, distant, or stressed.

When I allow myself to stretch my comfort zone, it enhances the way I enjoy and experience life.

My brain feels stimulated, and my mental health is boosted.

I am more flexible and resilient.

I am no longer stuck in a rut.

My self-improvement and personal development game is strong. I am strong.

I achieve more in less time.

When I stretch, I can relax. When I relax, joy flows through my mind, body, spirit, relationships, career, and life.

On the other side of my comfort zone is my most au-thentic, fierce, fun, gorgeous, successful, joyful, true, high-est self — my divine perfection.

I experience a deeper faith and connection to Source. I understand that my comfort zone is just an illusion of safety and control. It's barely keeping me afloat. Stretching out of my comfort zone, breaking free from the limitations in my mind, is about trust. I trust the voice within that tells me to go on the adventure, try something different, be someone happier, fall in love.

I trust that the universe wants me to succeed. I trust I am being guided. I am protected. I am safe. I am loved. I am love. I have faith in everything working out for the highest good for all more than I have faith in everything working against me. I am willing to stretch. I am willing to live a life way better than anything I ever could have imag-ined. I am willing to do the exercises in The Full Spirit Workout *consistently, and I welcome my transformation.*

Take a moment to soak all this wisdom into every cell of your body, relaxing and releasing with every breath. When you are ready, gently open your eyes, and return to the room.

 ## A WALKING MEDITATION FOR FLEXIBILITY

We all have a brilliant source of wisdom deep within us that has all the answers. We just have to become more practiced at listening to it. One of my favorite ways to do this is by go-ing on a walking meditation.

I used to live on the Hudson River, across from Man-hattan, and there is a beautiful track right there where I would go for guidance. I didn't meet with a sage, teacher, or coach — instead, I took myself on a walk.

It doesn't matter where you go for your walk, though many find it inspiring to be surrounded by beauty and nature. You can listen to music or go earphone-free, listening only to that inner guide.

While moving your body at a comfortable pace, ask yourself this: *If I take away money, what other people think, geography, and all other external circumstances — what do I really want to do?*

Let your heart, not your mind, answer. You should hear a response almost immediately. Don't edit, judge, or try to resist what comes up.

When I asked myself this question, the answer blew me away. It revealed that I want everything I'd been telling myself and others I didn't want. I pride myself on being a fiercely independent career woman with my own money, and — up until very recently — a huge part of my identity was wrapped up in being a single woman who is open to a life partner but doesn't want to get married or have children.

So when I asked myself this question and my heart answered, *I want to be a wife and mother,* I began to weep. My experience illustrates how often we do things in the name of what we think we want or think we should do, what society deems as worthy, what others will think or are impressed by, and so on.

This walking meditation exercise has opened me up to myself in such a profound way, and I know it can do the same for others. I love this exercise because it's fun, easy, and free, and it can be done at any time. Once we get clear on our heart's true desires, we can go back and do a sitting meditation, asking what inspired action steps to take.

When we get quiet, go within, clear ourselves from distractions, and ask for divine guidance, it is always available to us. It's like a computer file that cannot be deleted. We just have to choose to download it, and continue to redownload it regularly.

 COACH KATE CHECK-IN

Imagine that you and I are running on a track, training together. I get a little bit ahead, but then I turn back to check in and see how you're doing. Are you out of breath? Feeling overwhelmed? I'm here to help you, but you should know that *you* can stretch your comfort zone whenever you need to expand, grow, and truly transform, just by opening yourself to fresh opportunities and possibilities.

Putting yourself out there in a real and vulnerable way can feel uncomfortable at first, but try to embrace it. I'm here to share with you firsthand that stretching your comfort zone works! But I do believe any stretch or change, even positive change, can make us feel uneasy. It requires courage. It forces us to break free from the boxed-in voice inside our minds that says it's safer and easier to just keep doing what we've been doing. It forces us to show up as a better version of ourselves.

Confused about how to keep going? Don't worry — I've got you! And I won't let you give up. I'm your ultimate personal trainer and coach. So let's say this step's affirmation together. Live it, breathe it, own it.

STEP 1: STRETCH YOUR COMFORT ZONE *AFFIRMATION*

I am courageous and bold as I step out of what is familiar and into endless new possibilities. I know I am never alone and will always be supported and guided by the same force that holds galaxies together. I am transforming because I am choosing to be transformed. And so it is!

STEP 2
Lift Yourself Up

*There is no diet or doctor that can prevail
against a strongly held belief.*

— MARIANNE WILLIAMSON

Would you put on a bathing suit, walk into a corporate office, stand under horrific fluorescent lighting, be filmed on a camera phone, and then appear on a major news organization's Facebook Live feed — in front of more than one hundred thousand viewers?

That's exactly what I did when a swimsuit client hired me to model the latest swimwear trends for summer alongside a size 2 model. The point was to show different styles on different body types.

Of course, Facebook Live allows viewers to ask questions and make comments. Most people were extremely kind and body-positive, but some were mean-spirited. One person said

I needed a gym membership. One man typed, "No fat chicks." Another questioned how I was even a swimsuit model.

I wish I could say these comments didn't affect me at all, but for a few hours, I found myself questioning how I truly felt about my body. I had to acknowledge the times when I've dished out some pretty harsh and unjust criticism of this vessel of flesh and bone that serves me so well. The Facebook Live experience harkened back to the times I used to think my appearance defined my self-worth. The times I compared myself to the size o models standing next to me and felt uncomfortable being the "big girl" on set, questioning why I couldn't also have their "perfect" body type. The times I chose to overindulge with food and alcohol and then felt mad at my body for not looking or performing in a certain way.

But comparing our bodies to others keeps us small — we shrink to make others comfortable — and lowers our energy. Quite simply, it makes us feel like crap, yet we all do it. I meet many naturally thin women who tell me they wish they had my curves, while I have sometimes wished I had a slimmer stomach. When we compare like this, we waste precious time and energy that could be spent nurturing the body we've been given. And while this is a particular problem for women, it's more and more a problem for men, too. Ageism especially plagues men today, which is why plastic surgeons have seen more of them in their offices, trying to make sure they're still competitive both socially and professionally. Trust me, this step — lifting ourselves up — is for all of us, regardless of gender.

The good news is that we have a choice. That's what I quickly realized that day on set after reading those Facebook

Live comments. I could choose to internalize those few hateful judgments and feel horrible about my looks, or I could choose to be the victor by stopping with the comparisons and lifting myself up.

Now, I know lifting yourself up in this way can feel as hard as pull-ups. But you owe it to yourself to build this skill because the better you become at lifting yourself up, the better you'll feel every day of your life. You'll be able to quickly recover from the moments when you fall back into your old patterns, and you'll be able to brush off the negative opinions of others, knowing that what they say is a reflection on *them*, not on you.

That's why Lift Yourself Up is the critical step 2 of this Full Spirit Workout process. When you have this one in your spiritual workout arsenal, so much of your life will improve naturally.

The Nature of Judgment

I read a story recently about a guy who called comedienne Sarah Silverman the c-word online. She responded in an amazing way because she recognized this man was in pain. After engaging with him online, she found out that he suffered from back pain and hadn't been able to get the care he needed. So she figured out how to pay for him to get better care, and his attitude toward her immediately softened. What a revelation to discover that he was just using her as an easy target for feelings he didn't know how to process in a healthier way.

This is a lesson not only in compassion and making a difference in someone else's life, but also in the nature of judgment. How many times have we all taken someone else's unkind words to heart, not realizing that they were probably just lashing out due to stress, indigestion, or grief?

Of course, as a model, I've made a choice to put myself out there, knowing that I might be judged harshly. But I'm a grown woman; I can handle it. I'm especially concerned about all the young people in the world who are my size or bigger, which is the majority of the population. How do they feel when they see and hear larger bodies criticized in this way? The message it sends is "You're not attractive, worthy, or good enough unless you're thin." Heck, even size o supermodels like Chrissy Teigen have spoken publicly about being body-shamed and called "fat." Then, there are the models who are criticized for being *too* thin or the men who are judged for being too "scrawny." Few, if any, people seem to get a pass.

It has been a long journey for me, but the shame of not fitting into society's itsy-bitsy standard of beauty has now been replaced by the grace of self-acceptance and the knowledge that I'm so much more than what I look like in a swimsuit (especially in poor lighting).

Here's what I know for sure: healthy looks and feels different on everyone. One size doesn't fit all when it comes to body types and health. I would have been dead a long time before I ever reached a size 2. I take after my dad's side of the family and was never built to be that small. Each of us has to own and honor our own body type and make healthy decisions that are best for us rather than strive for some false ideal. Besides, society's so-called ideals change from decade to decade. The era of Marilyn Monroe as the "perfect woman" wasn't that long ago.

What I've learned is that when you're confident in your

own skin, just as you are, others are naturally drawn to you. But the irony is that it's a challenge to feel comfortable in your own skin if you *identify* with that skin. Instead, we need to see ourselves as souls first and foremost. This is one of the reasons spiritual fitness is *so important!* Our bodies are simply the vehicles that our souls use to experience joy, creativity, and love. They're wonderful vehicles, but vehicles just the same. As Beyoncé sings in her hit single "Pretty Hurts," "It's the soul that needs the surgery."

When I went to work the day I was on Facebook Live, I focused on making the swimsuits look lovely and comfortable. When I watch the video now, all I see is a woman glowing from the inside out, smiling and having fun. That's my new definition of beauty — self-confidence and owning who I am. That's drop-dead gorgeous to me, and it comes from within, not from the size of my body or the color of my hair.

Let's Redefine Beauty

Considering that I'm a plus-size model, you would think I'd be happy to see ad campaigns that use women of different shapes, sizes, ages, and ethnicities. And to some degree, I am.

As a curvy model, I've benefited professionally from this trend, and it's refreshing and uplifting after so many years of thin models shilling products.

But even these new, diverse-bodied ads are sending an incomplete message. Changing our perceptions about body image shouldn't be about "bigger is better." It should be about encouraging acceptance of *all* body types. Skinny-shaming isn't any less offensive than fat-shaming. This idea that "real women have curves" misses the mark. We're all real, whether we have curves or not!

Then there are the advertisers who tell us, "You're beautiful just the way you are." But doesn't that reinforce the belief that beauty is all about what we look like? We're taught that physical beauty determines our value and that physical beauty is power.

So if our physicality determines our worth, what happens if we become disfigured? What happens when we age? Do we have no value unless we measure up physically? That's the damaging message we get from society, and it couldn't be more false.

We don't need "real models" with our same skin tone or body type to reassure us of our self-worth. Placing all our energy on physical beauty just sets us up for failure.

What if we concentrated less on changing society's *standards* of beauty and instead changed our own *definition* of beauty? What if we were to make beauty about who we are and learn to see it without a mirror or a compliment? Wouldn't that be something?

Of course, I know this is easier said than done. I often hear people say that they value what's on the inside. Then they look in the mirror and think, *I want fuller lips, my nose is too big, I need to fix my teeth, I hate that my eyes look tired and puffy, if only I had thicker hair,* and on and on. Or they look at the person next to them in a restaurant and think, *Wow, I wish I could wear that, but my thighs are too big,* or worse, *Can you believe that comb-over? What was he thinking?* It's easy to pay lip service to the importance of inner beauty, but the challenge is to practice that belief on a daily basis and become more conscious and aware of our thoughts about appearance.

That's why I now make an effort to limit the messages I receive from the media by consciously choosing not to follow social media accounts, watch TV shows or movies, or read books, publications, or websites that reinforce negative feelings about my body. Instead, I spend more time going inward and being still, reminding myself of the innate beauty in all of us and our inherent worth as children of God. And whenever I compare myself to someone else, I quickly say, "Comparison is the thief of joy."

There's nothing wrong with keeping up our looks if it makes us feel good, but appearance alone shouldn't be what defines us. We have to begin to look at ourselves with more compassion, grace, and acceptance.

Let's start by getting a handle on the negative thoughts you have about your body. Then, later in this step, we'll replace them with new, positive thoughts so that you can truly lift yourself up! Be brutally honest with yourself because it's only when you bring these thoughts to light that you have the opportunity to change them.

When you notice your thoughts, you separate yourself from them. You become the observer of your negative thoughts, which allows you to create new, more positive thoughts. As Eckhart Tolle said,

> The beginning of freedom is the realization that you are not "the thinker." The more you start watching the thinker, a higher level of consciousness becomes activated. You then begin to realize that there is a vast realm of intelligence beyond thought, that thought is only a tiny aspect of that intelligence. You also realize that all the things that truly matter — beauty, love, creativity, joy, inner peace — arise from beyond the mind. You begin to awaken.

Isn't that exciting? We don't have to be a slave to our thoughts about our bodies or anything else. Let's start right now to experience that kind of freedom.

 JOURNALING EXERCISE
Sweat Out the Toxic Thoughts about Your Body

Write down the answers to the following five questions on a piece of paper. Please don't write them on an electronic device because I want you to be able to physically destroy the paper after your negative thoughts have been written.

1. When you hear the word "beauty" or "attractiveness," what words or images immediately pop into your mind? Don't edit your thoughts.

2. How far is your own body from this image of beauty or attractiveness? Do you have any of the attributes you wrote down, or do you have none of them? If your image of attractiveness is very different from how you look, can you see how this definition of beauty is damaging to you?

3. When you think of your body, what are the first three descriptive words that come to mind?

4. What's your core belief about your body? You might write, "It's too big." "It's ugly." "It's strong but not as fit as I'd like." "It's the vehicle through which all life experiences are possible." "It's the home to my heart, my soul." Write whatever comes to mind.

5. What harmful, unloving, destructive "attack thoughts" (thoughts of anger) have you had about your body

lately? You might have thought, *I hate my belly fat* or *I wish I looked good in shorts* or *These dark spots on my skin are so ugly.* If you can't recall any attack thoughts, pay attention during the next week, and notice if you put your body down or become angry with it. Write down the thoughts so that you can destroy the paper later.

Take this piece of paper on which you've written your judgments about your body, rip it into tiny pieces, and either throw them away or burn them. As you do so, make a commitment to yourself to stop putting your body down. Over time, you'll become more aware of your attack thoughts. When they come up, you can choose to release them, think a new thought, and construct an improved, more compassionate opinion about your body.

If you notice more negative thoughts about your body in the next few days, weeks, and months, feel free to write them down and destroy them as well. Each time, recommit to changing how you talk to yourself about your body. Remind yourself that you are a beautiful soul, not a physical body. Your body is just a suit of clothes. The real you is your spirit and the love within you.

My Biggest "Beauty Secret"

Think about the people you love most in the world. Is there anyone you love simply because they're physically attractive? You might appreciate their physical beauty just as you appreciate a lovely flower or a sunset, but I'll bet their physicality has nothing to do with your love for them. I'm sure the same is true of the people who love you. They don't love you for how you look — not even the people you've had a romantic relationship with. And let's get real: If someone loves you solely for how you look, don't you consider that person to be disturbingly superficial?

My friends say they love me because I'm compassionate, funny, genuine, honest, loyal, and fun to be around. I've never once had a friend tell me they love me and want to hang out with me because of how I look. Even men I've dated have said that what makes me beautiful to them is my personality and heart. That's what is sexy!

Furthermore, I've looked perfectly camera ready at times yet still felt incredibly insecure and lacking in self-confidence. Then there have been other times when I've met a friend for dinner wearing simple clothes and absolutely no makeup, yet I felt attractive because I was at peace within myself, not needing any outside validation or approval. I was just so happy to be with my friend, laughing and catching up. And I felt loved, which made me feel beautiful from the inside. I wasn't worried about impressing anyone.

In fact, when I look at my body through the lens of love, that love is reflected back to me from others. They either tell me I'm beautiful or they simply don't focus on my looks at all. They magically appreciate all of me! (Of course, it isn't magic at all. It's simply a reflection of my own self-love.)

We've all met someone who, though not the most physically beautiful person we've ever seen, exudes a generosity of spirit and becomes enormously attractive to us because of it. The reverse is also true. We've all met somebody who's beautiful by society's standards but is filled with negativity, anger, or jealousy. Suddenly, that person isn't so gorgeous anymore, right?

It just goes to show that it's never really about what we look like; it's about how we feel *on the inside*!

Now, I'm not going to pretend that it isn't a huge challenge to love ourselves in a world that's constantly telling us not to. But I think our time is far better spent cultivating our inner characteristics rather than working on "problem areas" to attract a partner, win approval from others, or try to conform to society's very narrow view of beauty. The physical workouts aren't going to help us love ourselves more. That's an inside job, which is what the Full Spirit Workout is all about. And the more we believe in ourselves regardless of how we look, the more we automatically attract people into our lives who see us that way, too.

So what's my biggest beauty secret? *Valuing myself for something other than my appearance, and focusing on what I can offer the world.*

When I focus my attention where it belongs, I find it easier to change my mind about my body. When I appreciate and value my body for getting up every day, even when I'm tired or ill, I treat it much kindlier than if I see it as an object that lets me down because it doesn't look like the images in the media.

Stop for just a moment and think about all that your body does for you every day. Even if you have a significant physical challenge, your body still serves you in amazing ways. Your heart beats without your conscious involvement. Your eyes express your feelings, your lips kiss, your mouth tastes. You might go to work, exercise, meet with friends, write an article, play the guitar, laugh out loud, eat wonderful food, talk to others, listen to music, look at a gorgeous sunset, feel the arms of someone you love around you, give birth to a beautiful baby (a true miracle!), and so much more.

Remember that you're a spirit going about life in a body that's here as your vessel for expressing love. Again, it's an instrument of purpose that allows you to experience and express joy. That's miraculous, isn't it? Rather than beating ourselves up for not fitting some arbitrary image, why don't we choose to instead appreciate all that our bodies give us? It's self-sabotage to pin all our self-worth on our appearance when our souls are so much more important and meaningful.

So right now, let's do a meditation to begin to disengage from this idea that our bodies have to look a certain way and that they're more important than what's beautiful about us on the inside.

 ## POSITIVITY PULL-UPS MEDITATION

A meditation is certainly more passive than pulling yourself up in a workout, but the positivity pull-ups we'll do in this meditation are just as powerful! So don't skip this part.

If you're new to meditation, don't fret. Remember to simply breathe and relax as best you can. There's no wrong way to do it.

To start the meditation, sit comfortably. Don't lie down, as you might fall asleep. Begin to inhale and exhale naturally, allowing your body to relax. Gently close your eyes as you continue this cycle of deep, cleansing breathing.

As you breathe, notice a ball of white light over your head. The light begins to grow, surrounding your entire body like a soft, warm, glowing blanket. You feel safe and comforted inside this nurturing cocoon.

Let the light penetrate your pores and enter your body so that it's no longer just surrounding you, but also filling you until every cell in your body is infused with this gorgeous, glowing light.

As you sit immersed in this light, imagine that you're inhaling love each time you breathe in. As you exhale, release anything within you that isn't love. You don't have to know what any of those things are. Just imagine that anything gray is leaving you through your breath. See and feel this energy leaving your body through your head or through your feet with every exhale. Let it go.

Recall as best you can the negative comments you wrote down and destroyed in the writing exercise. Imagine now that you're exhaling these thoughts away. They're no longer a part of your psyche. Say, "Goodbye, you're no longer welcome here," as they leave you on your breath and float away in the air. Watch them disappear for good.

Now, think about all the wonderful things your body does for you every day. Think about what you experience through all your senses — sight, hearing, smell, touch, and taste. Think of the last thing you saw that you loved, the last piece of music you heard that filled you with joy, the last item or person you touched with love, the last wonderful smell you experienced, and the best taste you've ever had. Think of how your body allows you to work and experience this life you've been given. Fill yourself with the gratitude your body deserves for all it's done for you.

In this moment, apologize to your body for not appreciating it fully and for perhaps expecting it to live up to some false ideal. Say you're sorry, and then say a heartfelt "Thank you!" to your body. Commit to appreciating your body every day and without the judgments you've placed on it in the past.

Finally, take a moment to connect with your soul. You don't have to know what that feels like. Just tell yourself that you're connecting with your soul, and trust that you are (because you are!). Say "Thank you!" to your soul as well, and tell your soul that you're sorry for having belittled its importance. Commit to appreciating your soul regularly and placing it front and center in your life, knowing that your true attractiveness as a person has to do with who you are within. Commit to lifting yourself up every day.

When you're ready, open your eyes, wiggle your toes, and shake your arms and legs to come back into full waking consciousness.

Take a few moments to simply sit and relax, gazing forward softly. Feel free to smile as you feel gratitude for this beautiful moment of stillness. Then, gently return to your day.

 **JOURNALING EXERCISE**
Confidence Crunches

Now that you've completed the meditation and altered your energy, making a commitment to both your body and soul to appreciate them more and stop treating them poorly, let's go a bit further with a little more writing. This time you can write either on a device or in a paper journal. I call these "confidence crunches" because like the crunches you do when you exercise physically, these journaling exercises will *tone* your ability to think lovingly about your body, yourself, and others.

1. You've thought about how much you appreciate what your body does for you every day. So to counteract the negative thoughts you've had about your body, write down five qualities that you love about it. These can relate to either function or appearance — whatever feels right to you. For example, you might write: "I love that my body is great at sleeping deeply and giving me terrific rest; I love the green flecks in my dark brown eyes; I love that my body can allow me to pick up and hold my daughter," and so on. Keep what you've written, and refer to it whenever you return to your old habit of negative self-talk about your body.

2. Next, think about someone you love dearly. This is a person you adore. Write down five qualities that you admire about this person.

3. Now, write down five positive qualities about yourself. Note that you wouldn't be able to recognize the traits you just wrote down about your loved one if you didn't have the capacity to express those traits yourself! If you struggle with this part of the exercise, ask a dear friend or family member to write down five traits about you that they admire. I wrote down that I'm compassionate, kind, joyful, intelligent, and have a great sense of humor.

4. Write down how you can use those characteristics toward your body. Here's what I wrote: "I have *compassion* for my body when I can only run for 20 minutes and not my normal 45 minutes. I'm *kind* to my body by fixing myself a healthy lunch. I'm *joyful* as I relax in a lavender salt bath and meditate for 30 minutes.

I'm *intelligent* as I allow for eight hours of sleep. I
have a *sense of humor* when I decide to walk seven
miles in brand-new shoes around Manhattan and
then care for my bloody ankles."

5. Make a plan to do three simple things to lift yourself
up this week by showing your body how much you
love, honor, and accept it exactly as it is right now.
Here's what I wrote: "I'm going for a run at the track
that overlooks the Hudson River and all of Manhattan at sunset. I'm going to take a bubble bath, meditate, pray, go to bed early, and get nine hours of
sleep to prepare for a business trip."

Dare to Shine!

I recently had a conversation with a girlfriend about how upset she felt about gaining weight (nearly fifty pounds). It felt
disingenuous to simply coddle her and say, "Oh, but you still
look great. You're *so* beautiful!" I could sense and feel her
pain because I'd been through my own thirty-pound weight
gain. I understood all too well the shame and discomfort she
was feeling.

I also felt strongly that her weight gain was about keeping people at bay, not fully showing up as her best self. But I
didn't want to be presumptuous and speak for her, so I simply created the space for her to speak her truth. It worked.
Pretty quickly, she blurted out, "I'm so scared that if I look
really good at my usual weight and feel amazing, I'll cheat
on my husband!"

There it was — the fear of being "too beautiful" and attracting the attention of men, which could lead to temptation. She was actually no longer in love with her husband and

still married to him primarily for the sake of their children. It was a huge aha moment for her. As Marianne Williamson so eloquently said in her book *A Woman's Worth*, "There is no diet or doctor that can prevail against a strongly held belief."

It's difficult to show up fully in the world and shine, proclaiming, "I love myself and my life!" We fear others will think we're arrogant, or they'll feel jealous. So we shrink ourselves in order to do what we perceive will make others comfortable. But how does it serve anyone to pretend? And aren't we more of an example to the world when we're filled with joy and love? That's when our self-love can overflow and allow us to love and serve others even more.

I believe our life purpose is to be happy, express joy, and spread love. So who are we to not shine as brightly as we're capable of shining?

Spiritual fitness helps us feel worthy of shining. It provides us with deep, meaningful connections with others and a life of purpose so that we're much less likely to believe that food, money, sex, drugs, a job, a relationship, or a plastic surgery procedure will fill us up. We know unequivocally that nothing in the outside world can offer us more than momentary pleasures, and what we look like isn't so important in the scheme of things.

Let's see ourselves through a new lens and lift ourselves up every day starting today. As hard as it may seem at times, it really doesn't require as much muscle as pull-ups, but pulling yourself up out of the doldrums of self-criticism is the kind of skill that will serve you for the rest of your life.

In the remaining steps of the Full Spirit Workout, we'll spend more time on self-love. (Spoiler alert: the "secret" to self-love is remembering or discovering that we actually *are* love.) But knowing how to lift yourself up is the best warm-up I know for the rest of our workout.

 ## COACH KATE CHECK-IN

- What actions can you take to shine as brightly as you're capable of?
- What inner beauty characteristics can you cultivate to help you feel this way?
- Who can support you in creating this new lens of love for yourself?
- How will you know when you're shining as brightly as you're capable of?

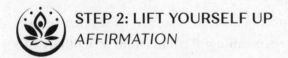 ## STEP 2: LIFT YOURSELF UP
AFFIRMATION

I am gorgeous because I was created by the same force that created the sun, the moon, the stars, and the ocean. I am stunning because I am a powerful force of love. Now, that is beautiful!

STEP 3
Feel the Burn

No problem can be solved from the
same level of consciousness that created it.

— ANONYMOUS

When I was four years old, my mom enrolled me in swim lessons at the Miami Hills Swim and Tennis Club in Cincinnati, Ohio. I didn't really like it. I didn't much care for my swim instructor, Mark, either. After lessons one day, I overheard him talking to my mom, and from what my four-year-old self could gather, Mark didn't think I was a very good swimmer.

I remember thinking to myself: *I love my mom and dad and want them to be proud of me. I don't want them to have a daughter who's a bad swimmer, especially since they're so athletic.*

As an adult, it breaks my heart that my four-year-old self took a comment from some guy at a swim club and translated it into a mentality that said: I need to perform at a high level so others, especially my mom and dad, will be proud of me and, in turn, I will feel worthy, safe, valuable, and loved.

As an eight-year-old, I stood in front of the record board at Miami Hills Swim and Tennis Club and saw my name under every event. At eighteen, while looking at that same board, I saw that I had all but two of the records, in every event, in every age group. I was a state and national champion and went off to Penn State University on a swimming scholarship. You would think I felt on top of the world, but my obsession with performance left me with the pain of anxiety.

I find it fascinating that even (or I guess *especially*) as young children, we can hear one comment, create a story, and make meaning out of it that isn't based on facts or on any truth whatsoever. Then we go about our lives, unconsciously collecting evidence for why *that* belief is true, and we make it our core belief system. All too often, we center this subconscious belief system on negative ideas.

A healthier thing to do would be to take notice of a genuine compliment or positive feedback and make *those* the pillars of our belief system.

Better yet, we could lean into our own inner wisdom that knows without a doubt that we are worthy, safe, valuable, and loved simply because we are children of God. We are good enough because we are. It's as simple as that. I think most of us will understand this intellectually if we really stop and articulate it, but we haven't consistently done the empowering inner exercises and outer practices to internalize this and let it work on our mentality.

That's why spiritual fitness is imperative — it helps us

combine our intellectual understanding (the head) with our instinctive wisdom (the body) and then implement them in our practice (the hand). I've come to learn that to simply know something is not enough. We create new healthy beliefs and habits by *doing* and practicing consistently.

When I think of how to express this concept, an image of Prince playing the electric guitar comes to mind. When I watched Prince, he looked like he wasn't trying or thinking. He wasn't in his head, trying to remember what note came next. He was one with the guitar, the notes, the music — he was in a completely unconscious flow state and therefore allowed us, the audience, to be in complete flow with him. Prince's knowledge of the songs went much deeper than just in his head; he knew them in his heart, in his body, and he could therefore organically implement the song flawlessly.

It's like driving a car. I don't get in and think, *Okay, now put your foot on the brake, start the car, and try to think about how to drive.* I hold the knowledge of how to drive within my body because I have done it so many times. Yes, I have to be conscious and pay attention to traffic laws, other drivers, the weather, and so forth, but I don't have to think or worry about the *how.*

As a swimmer, it was never enough to simply know how to swim, or to think about swimming the race and winning. I had to show up every day and train, working on my strength, power, endurance, stroke technique, breath control, starts, turns, finishes, you name it. There was never a time when I thought, *Okay, I'm fast enough now. I'm the state record holder. I got the college scholarship. I'm good. I can stop training so hard now.* In fact, it was the complete opposite. Once I reached a certain level, I had to train even harder to keep up my skills and be able to compete at a high level against other hard-working, dedicated, talented swimmers.

And just like physical exercise, spiritual workouts only work if we do. We can have the best coach in the world, but our coaches can't swim the laps, do the meditation, sleep, or build strong emotional muscles for us. That's our job. Are there days we won't feel like going to swim practice or sitting down to meditate? Absolutely. And of course, we all need to take time off to rest and just have carefree fun. I'm not suggesting you do any of these exercises out of fear or stress or obligation. I'm simply inviting you to be willing to show up to your consistent, empowered practice of choice. Similar to what happens with physical workouts, you'll begin to crave these practices because you will feel so much better (think: runner's high) and achieve so much more in less time when you do them.

When we allow negative thinking based on fear and lack to seep into our consciousness, we unknowingly let *it* call the shots and dictate how we feel about ourselves. Showing up consistently for yourself through spiritual practices allows you to unlearn all these lies and mistaken beliefs that have taken root in your subconscious — and come back home to yourself, and your truth.

Cleanse Your Misconceptions

On one hand, the belief that I needed to perform at a high level to make others proud made me a very driven, determined, hardworking young girl and woman. But at what cost? I certainly paid a price and gave away my well-being, freedom, and power over my own self-worth by adopting this thought system — a thought system not based on any truth.

The truth is that neither Coach Mark's opinion nor anyone else's opinion matters. Remember, our thoughts and feelings about ourselves are the only ones that truly matter. We discussed this in step 2, and I remind myself of this regularly. Then I go a little deeper and remind myself that the God of my own understanding has such a perfect image of me, and I do these Full Spirit Workout exercises to lean into and embody that inner knowing and truth on a consistent basis. In that way, my spirit has developed quite a strong six-pack!

The problem with attaining our sense of worth, well-being, happiness, peace, or anything else we value from sources other than ourselves is that it sets us up for failure When we do this, we can never have enough or be enough. We may achieve a goal, win the prize, get the job, find the dream partner, make the money, or acquire awesome stuff and be really, really happy — for about fifteen minutes. Then it's on to the next thing, the next goal, the next shiny object, and the more we achieve and the higher we climb, the more and more *stuff* it takes to fill us up and satisfy us. We are constantly on the hunt for more, better, different, and we often find ourselves in a state of dissatisfaction and even despair because of it.

I recently received my certification in the wildly popular Science of Well-being course at Yale University. It explores what psychological science says about the good life. This course uses science-based research to demonstrate that achieving the things we think will make us happy — career and financial success, "perfect" looks or partner, good grades, luxury goods, and so forth — does not actually lead to improved well-being. Let me say that again because it's essentially the opposite of what we are led to believe our whole lives: our dream job, salary, partner, body, stuff, and grades do not actually boost our baseline happiness levels.

In other words, according to science, we are wasting precious time striving for and chasing after things that don't even make us happy. All while spending a lot less time on things that research proves *do* make us happy, like meditation, exercise, sleep, savoring and gratitude, kindness, doing things for others, social connection, time affluence, and a favorite practice of mine — building strong mental and emotional muscles. (Don't worry: I'll show you how to do this throughout this book because these practices work!)

But the truth is, I didn't need a Yale course to tell me all that. I'd already exhausted myself and experienced deep unhappiness proving this theory through my own life, over a course of many years. Since that time, I learned to tap into my innate knowledge that our well-being is truly an inside job — which is why I created the Full Spirit Workout.

Build Your Psychological Immunity

What the Science of Well-being course did teach me, however, was about a concept called "miswanting," which is the act of being mistaken about what and how much you will like something in the future. How can we fundamentally misjudge our own reactions and desires? Researchers Dan Gilbert and Tim Wilson argue that it's all about our reference points and that, unfortunately, we don't control them.

Reference points explain why a bronze medal winner in the Olympics is actually happier than the silver medalist. Why? Because bronze medalists know they were close to not medaling at all, so making it to the podium greatly increases their happiness. Silver medalists, on the other hand, know how close they were to winning the gold medal and are therefore a bit unhappy about not being the champion. Research shows that "our minds don't think in terms of absolutes; our minds judge relative to reference points."

The scary (and sad) part of the research that really hit home for me was that our minds get used to stuff, and we eventually stop getting pleasure from the things that once brought us so much joy (unless we consistently practice gratitude and savoring, that is). Studies show not only that our minds get used to stuff but also that we don't even realize that our minds are built to get used to stuff!

So if our goal is to make $100,000 a year and we achieve that, eventually (and sooner rather than later) our mind will get used to that salary — and then studies indicate we won't experience happiness about our salary again unless we jump to $250,000 a year.

What about true love? Does our mind get used to this dream realized, as well? According to researchers, yes. In the first two years of marriage (provided it's a good, healthy marriage), baseline happiness increases, but after just two years, married couples' happiness levels drop back down to the baseline levels they were at before tying the knot. This is illustrated poignantly in a cartoon showing a couple celebrating under the caption, "Just married!" followed by an image of the same couple two years later, looking expressionless under a caption that reads, "Just married...."

The good news is that we each have what's called a "psychological immune system," which means we overestimate our emotional reactions to negative events. So that awful diagnosis or event you fear happening (global pandemic, anyone?) won't have nearly as great an impact on your well-being as you think it will.

And guess what! You can build up your psychological or spiritual resources and counter the trends described above. Just like exercise bolsters our physical immune system, spiritual exercise can bolster our psychological immune system.

Here are some tips for building your spirit's immunity:

- **Avoid that addictive stuff that starts with an S.** What's tempting to turn to for a quick boost but always leads to a crash? Sugar, yes, but I'm talking about social media. Just as sugar erodes our physical health and immune systems, social media erodes our spirits. Want to know how to double your sense of well-being? Stay off social media. No big shocker here, but this knowledge won't do us any good unless we act on it. I'm not saying you need to live in the Dark Ages (or the twentieth century), but limit yourself, and when you find it's not working for you — stop! Now, when I find myself thinking that I would be so much happier if I just made more money, or whatever, I log off Facebook and Instagram instead. The best part? It's free!

- **Take your vitamins.** Just as getting enough daily vitamins supports our physical resilience, engaging in daily spiritual practices supports our spiritual resilience and overall well-being. Think of these practices as your "spiritual vitamins." Let's delve into some of the key ones: gratitude, visualizing, and savoring.

Pay a Gratitude Visit (Even a Virtual One)

Most of us are familiar with the power of gratitude and have heard about the importance of writing down at least five things that we are grateful for every day. If you aren't already doing this, I invite you to make this a consistent practice in your daily routine and experience the many proven benefits that occur as a result.

I learned about one of the most profound gratitude exercises we can do from psychologist Martin Seligman, founder of "positive psychology," the study of states like happiness, strength of character, and optimism. This practice can not only boost our own happiness levels but those of another person as well. How cool is that?

In a 2004 TED Talk titled "The New Era of Positive Psychology," Seligman spoke about the concept of a "gratitude visit." He invited the audience to close their eyes and think of someone who did something "enormously important" that changed their lives for the better and whom they'd "never properly thanked."

Seligman said, "The person has to be alive. Once you've thought of the person you would like to thank, your assignment is to write a three hundred–word testimonial to that person, and then call them on the phone, ask if you can visit, and don't tell them why. Show up at their door, and read the testimonial.

"Everyone weeps when this happens," he said. "And what happens is, when psychologists test people one week later, a month later, and three months later, they're both happier and less depressed."

I did this exercise, and my friend Vanessa immediately

came to mind. I'd only known her a short time, but she'd had a profound impact on me. This is the letter that I wrote:

> Dear Vanessa,
>
> Thank you for your extreme bravery. Your courage inspires me in ways I cannot even explain, but let me try. I oftentimes feel like an alien here on Earth as a status quo disrupter. As an unmarried woman with no children, I don't fit into societal standards. I sometimes feel alone in my decisions, like people don't get me, or I guess it's that people don't take the time to truly SEE me. I think this is an epidemic in our world, and it saddens me deeply.
>
> But you, Vanessa, you SEE me. And I SEE you. And as psychologist Susan David would say, "By seeing me, you bring me into existence."
>
> Thank you for this beautiful gift. It is priceless, and no one can ever take it away from me.
>
> I think of the sheer bravery it takes for anyone to show up and be themselves authentically and unapologetically in the world today. I think what a miracle it is to love, cherish, and embrace ourselves in a society that tells us daily how we don't quite add up to enough, especially as women. When I think of the additional strength, courage, and integrity it takes for you, a transgender woman, to show up with so much love, joy, and confidence and be able to offer that pure love, joy, and confidence so freely to others, I am brought to my knees in prayer that you came into my life to show me how to love more fully and completely. Your heart is so stunning, and your kindness touches my heart deeply. Your mere presence makes me feel so loved, acknowledged, understood. I feel less alone because of you.

One of my favorite things to do is compliment others. It lights me up, and I see how much it lights others up as well. Yet, I rarely receive the genuine compliments I so freely give. After we completed our week-long coaching intensive at Columbia University, you sent me a text message that I will cherish forever. In it, you said: "Your beauty outside is striking but the depth of your love for others as they are, as they authentically need to be, shows the most beautiful person I have had the privilege to call a friend in a very long time. Stay in your beauty with honor, pride, and dignity."

Thank you for this gorgeous message, Vanessa, but more importantly, thank you for loving me as I am and as I authentically need to be. I love you.

When I read this letter to Vanessa, I cried, she cried, and she said, "I will cherish that forever. Those words will stay with me for the rest of my life. Thank you." We spoke for about an hour after I read the letter, and while I can't tell you the exact words we shared with one another, I can tell you that the sentiment was so sacred, so deep, so touching, that I almost had an out-of-body experience. It's so rare that we (meaning everybody) share such honest, heartfelt expressions of love and appreciation that it almost felt like a lot to take in. Emotions, even extremely pleasant ones, can feel overwhelming and exhausting. But the gifts contained in the expression of our emotions (from one heart to another) are invaluable, and my greatest wish is that each of us commit to these honest, soulful expressions much more often. I'm no doctor, but I think it's necessary for optimal health.

JOURNALING EXERCISE
Recognition Reps

Follow Dr. Seligman's advice and think of someone living who has changed your life for the good, then write them a testimonial about how they helped you.

Once you've completed this, ask to pay them a visit and then surprise them by reading your testimonial.

Visualize Your Miraculous Day

One of my favorite questions to ask myself, my friends, and my coaching clients is: If a miracle occurred tonight, what would your life look like when you wake up tomorrow?

It is helpful to explore best-case scenarios and let our minds visualize our desired outcomes. Once we envision our own "miracles," we can plan how to get there, thinking about what obstacles could present themselves along the way and what to do when that happens. These steps prompt action and joy and, when done consistently, yield measurable (and pleasurable) results.

I recently asked this question of a client who was struggling with work-life balance. I watched as she reflected deeply, and quite frankly I was waiting for her to give me an elaborate description of her new life on a yacht on Lake Como with George Clooney. But instead, she said, "I would set aside a half hour every day to meditate and do yoga."

Really? I thought. *That's it? That's your miracle? Wonderful! How easy! And inexpensive! And doable!* But for a mother of two young children juggling career demands and serious mom guilt to take consistent, guilt-free quiet time for herself *is* a miracle most mothers can relate to, I'd bet.

We came up with a strategy that I learned while receiving my advanced certification in executive and organizational coaching at Columbia University. To do what we say we want to, it's vital that we be specific with what we want to accomplish (thirty minutes of meditation and yoga each day, in this case) and set an exact time to accomplish it. Put it in your calendar the same way you would a business meeting, dentist appointment, kid's tennis lesson, and so forth. Block it off. It sounds so simple, but I often find when coaching high-performing leaders that this can be challenging. Like many of us, they talk about wanting to take the time to be mindful through meditation and by nurturing themselves in a meaningful way but don't schedule it in their calendars, and therefore they don't actually do it. Remember, it is not enough to just know something intellectually.

When I met with my client the following week, she was glowing. I asked if she'd been able to implement her thirty-minute meditation and yoga practice, and she reported that she'd been doing it every day because she'd marked off time for it in her calendar. And from the look on her face and the productivity level in her business that week, I could see how much this practice was benefiting her by providing the peace of mind that marks the work-life balance she said she desired.

I invite you to take this a step further and imagine for yourself an entire miraculous day — and then put your plan into action. What will you do, where will you go, and with whom? I know, I know: "Who has time for that?" you might ask. Well, who has time to be stressed, exhausted, and miserable? (In coaching, this is what we call an "honest labeling" response. I don't know about you, but sometimes I need plain and simple straight talk to get me out of an outdated thought pattern and into action.)

My miraculous days always involve exploring, for example. I go somewhere in nature, hike, breathe in the fresh air, discover something new (about the land and myself), smile at strangers, feel the sun on my heavily sunscreened face, and let my mind focus on being in the present moment. I like to put my phone on airplane mode so I can photograph the beauty around me as a way to savor the moment and refer back to it later, but I'm unavailable for anything else, including the radiation from my phone. Afterward, I take myself to a healthy restaurant or meet up with a friend and talk and laugh.

Your "miraculous" can be as simple or elaborate as you make it. Sometimes my miraculous days are at a five-star spa with a girlfriend, and sometimes they are at home in my pajamas reading, making tea, lighting candles, and calling a dear friend on the phone to catch up. Sometimes I am in one of my favorite places in the world, like Italy or Portugal. Other times, I am in my brother's backyard in Ohio with my niece and nephew before taking them for bowling, laser tag, pizza, and ice cream. (Nothing greater than being an auntie!) There's no right or wrong way to create your miraculous day.

I journal about my miraculous-day experiences and how I implemented them into my real life, then I share my reflections with friends in the hopes that it will inspire them to do the same. Then they share their experience with me and with others. It creates a ripple effect, and soon we are talking about what is bringing us joy rather than what is bringing us stress. We are also focusing on visualizing and then doing things that actually make us happy rather than packing our days with to-do lists of things that science shows won't increase our sense of well-being. This is also a great opportunity to let social media work for us rather than against us by sharing our miraculous day experiences with our connections online.

JOURNALING EXERCISE
Miraculous Mountain Climbers

Take some time to envision your miraculous day. What will it look like? What will you do? Go ahead and write about it in detail in your journal. Have fun and get creative!

Then, on your social media platform of choice, post photos of your miraculous day — either images that provide inspiration or actual photos of your experience after you've gone out and lived your vision. Tag friends and family members to join you in creating their miraculous days and plan to have one together. Try it out for yourself, and let me know what you come up with!

(Just remember not to get sucked into the social media rabbit hole. We're making social media work *for* us, not against us.)

Slow Down and Savor the Moment

Another way to enhance our enjoyment in life and feel happier in our day-to-day tasks is to practice the art of savoring. Savoring means stepping outside an experience to review and appreciate it. It's about staying present in the moment and truly enjoying it, not taking it for granted.

A simple pleasure that I've been savoring lately is my morning espresso. I discovered a meditation app called Plum Village, and it has a few eating meditations to help listeners practice mindful eating and drinking. I find that when I listen to it with my espresso each morning, it sets a peaceful, mindful tone for my day. The meditation asks me to consider all the energy and circumstances that had to occur to get these coffee beans to me. It talks about clouds and rainwater, telling me that I'm essentially drinking a cloud and to enjoy drinking my cloud. It makes me laugh a little. It's so comforting and ethereal, and it allows me to focus on feeling lucky to be drinking this drink rather than taking it for granted and focusing on all the work I have to do. Enjoy drinking your cloud; what a beautiful thing to think about — and savor.

 **JOURNALING EXERCISE**
Savoring Squats

Pick one experience to slow down and truly savor each day. Think about how fortunate you are to be having the experience. Take a photo or keep a souvenir to remember it. In your journal, write about the experience you savored today in sensory detail. Did you notice things about it that you hadn't noticed before? Describe how the art of savoring is adding value to your life. Next, share your experience with another: even if you savor an experience alone, tell someone about what you did later.

Make Space for Love

One area where we really test our spiritual immune systems and our spiritual strength is in the ups and downs of relationships.

There's nothing quite as electrifying and soul-satisfying as falling in love, but that euphoric feeling rarely lasts. Over and over, I've fallen in love only to discover that the relationship wasn't going to be what I'd imagined. As a result, I've come to believe that relationships are actually soul assignments — projects that are meant to teach us lessons and enable us to grow into a more enlightened version of ourselves. Yes, of course, relationships are also there to bring us joy and give joy to those we love, but whether or not they last forever isn't the point.

All our relationships, from parental to platonic to professional, can teach us things, but romantic relationships in particular bring up all our triggers and baggage. The way I see it, that's a big part of their purpose. When those old wounds open up, it's an opportunity, not a curse. It doesn't mean the other person is wrong for us (although they may be) but that our soul is calling on us to take this chance to heal those old wounds.

When we experience disappointment in any relationship, especially a romantic one, it is extremely tempting to slip into the blame game, focusing on everything the other person said or did wrong. When I recently went through a breakup, I received a lot of support from friends who subscribed to the "Kate's ex is a jerk" mentality.

But I found that judging, criticizing, and blaming my ex-boyfriend felt just as debilitating as the breakup itself. Getting over my heartache wasn't about convincing myself I was better off without that "jerk" but rather focusing on where I got it wrong and could improve. Even if the demise of a relationship is 90 percent the other person's fault, we still have to look at our 10 percent. This truth speaks to an important shift we need to make in the way we view our relationships.

Instead of making a laundry list of traits we want in an ideal mate, what if we spent our time and energy figuring out who we want to be in a relationship?

Doesn't that feel so much more empowering? After all, our thoughts, feelings, and actions are the only things we can control. When we practice being the people we want to be, the ideal partner will show up, and this time, we will be better able to share and receive a deeply nourishing, lasting love. We will be more aware of our triggers and how to better manage our emotions, and instead of focusing on what we can get, we will be generous with what we can give. We won't settle or expect someone to "complete" us, as our core belief system becomes "I am complete."

When we begin to look at our relationships as adventuresome assignments for personal development and soul growth, our desperate need to try to control our partner will shift. Instead of obsessing over why someone wasn't able to love us exactly as we wanted, we will understand we were brought together to learn from one another.

Sure, sometimes you really were mistreated in your relationship. But other times, the lesson is actually: "I haven't done the inner work required to allow the relationship to flourish."

From a spiritual perspective, if we can learn not to attack or defend and instead practice forgiveness and take responsibility for our wounds (which appear as character defects we are tempted to judge in ourselves and others), then we can heal these wounds, release the painful feelings associated with them, and show up for ourselves and others as happy, healthy partners.

Here are some of the practices I use daily to make sure my focus in my relationships, past and present, is less about assessing how good the other person is or was and more about how I'm showing up:

Give Your Partner Unconditional Acceptance

What I am about to say is one of the biggest challenges we face as human beings: forgive and accept people — in this case, your mate — exactly as they are. If you don't like a certain behavior, try changing your response to that behavior rather than trying to change your partner. Accepting a person for who they are sets us free — we don't feel the need to try to control them. Instead we can focus on controlling our emotions and decide whether to stay in or leave the relationship.

Surrender Your Grievances and Attachments to Anyone Who Has Done You Wrong

Getting angry at someone for not wanting to be with us is disempowering and takes away our dignity. In fact, it's self-sabotaging to lash out at, show our disapproval of, and condemn the other person for leaving — because when we attack another, we are also attacking ourselves. On a spiritual level, we are all connected. When we judge, blame, or condemn another, we may feel good for a few minutes, but either they will attack us back or, even if they don't, we will feel as though they did due to our own guilt. This is a universal law of cause and effect: what we give, we must get back. That's why it feels so good to give a gift or compliment and make someone smile or laugh.

It's easy to accept people who want us, but the challenge is to accept people who do not want us. The goal is to get to a place where we love people whether they want us or not.

Moreover, approving of people for who they are and their decision not to be with us creates the space for us to attract the right person.

Practice More Forgiveness —
the Answer to Everything

When someone hurts our feelings and we don't feel the need to cause any emotional harm back, we pass the test. When we are willing to take 100 percent responsibility for our lives (even though it can be challenging), we grow up faster and become emotionally stronger.

Instead of lashing out at people who have hurt us, take a deep breath and see that hurt as an opportunity to heal an old wound and to grow. With practice, you will become less and less reactive and feel a greater sense of peace and freedom. Sit in meditation with the awareness that nothing changes until it is accepted exactly as it is.

The point here isn't to accept people's mistreatment of us — rather, the point is to not allow their mistreatment to get the best of our emotions. We can respond to a negative situation appropriately by leaving when needed, but the ability to accept and forgive is what will ultimately set us free from those hurtful emotions that came from it.

Show Up Fully

Instead of asking yourself, *Is this person really good enough for me?* ask, *Am I really showing up for this person and creating a safe space for their transformation and enlightenment?* That's a big difference!

In creating the space for another's transformation, we allow them to be who they were not yesterday — we give them the freedom to get it right. As long as your partner is willing to work on themselves, the relationship can move forward.

Of course, if your partner demonstrates they aren't willing to grow or aren't taking the necessary steps to actualize that growth, it may be time to move on. We can't force anyone to change; they must choose to evolve of their own free will.

In the meantime, while they're sorting themselves out, pray for their happiness every day. Remind them how wonderful they are. Give support and be generous with your time, compliments, undivided attention, and so forth. Resist the temptation to project onto another that they complete you or to demand that they behave a certain way. It is easy to love someone when they are doing and saying everything we want them to. The challenge is loving someone when they aren't acting the way we want them to.

Take Inventory of Your Own Shortcomings and the Work You Still Need to Do

It's important to ask ourselves, *If my "ideal partner" showed up right now, would they want me?*

None of us is perfect. We all have childhood wounds and heartbreaks from previous relationships. But I've found that our willingness and commitment to change our thought patterns and behaviors can make us available and ready for lasting love.

Release Expectations

What would it feel like to stop expecting your partner to be more, better, or different?

Knowing what we want in a relationship is important, but that knowledge must be coupled with the desire to learn how to be a great or even better partner ourselves. Rather than looking for that one special person to complete you — or for completion from the lovable, imperfect human(s) already in your life — look for ways you could love, honor, and accept yourself and others more completely.

To start envisioning what this might look like, write down all the ways you can prepare your heart, body, personality, beliefs, and home for real love — the kind of love you seek and the kind of love your current or future partner deserves.

An Illuminating Thought Experiment

As a student of *A Course in Miracles* and a woman devoted to my spiritual growth, I'm always game for working through any difficult emotions or situations that might arise in a relationship. In the last failed relationship before my paradigm shift, my partner was not. But of course, it wasn't as easy as just cutting him loose as soon as I discovered that. At that point, we were already in love.

A friend gave me a piece of advice that really struck a chord with me. It resonated much more than the typical clichés we hear when our friends try to be supportive but aren't quite sure what we want to hear. (Tip: your best bet is always, no matter what, to tell the truth with love.)

My spiritually astute friend recognized the truth that I hadn't been willing to recognize on my own. I was basing my decision to stay in that relationship on my feelings rather than my values. I explained to her that I loved this man and wanted a future with him but had some major concerns — for example, he wasn't interested in a spiritual life, nor was he willing to work through any emotional baggage or issues stemming from his past divorce.

It seemed obvious to my friend that my then-partner was simply not ready for a serious relationship, despite how often or how fervently he told me otherwise. His decision to lie to me on more than one occasion came up as a character defect as well (something I had overlooked because I loved him). We both knew the right decision was to walk away from this relationship. So, why was it so difficult and painful to end it? The answer, I now know, is that I had the wrong perspective.

When I wrote down what I value in a romantic partner, I realized this man did not embody many of those qualities: he was unwilling or unable to support me emotionally, to share my spiritual commitment to a higher power, or to be fully committed to me.

My friend took me through an illuminating thought experiment. She asked me to pretend I was single. Then, she said she was going to tell me about someone and wanted to know if he was a man I would want to go out with as a single woman.

She said, "I know this guy you're going to find so charming, so attractive. Want me to hook you up with him?"

"Sure," I said, playing along.

My friend said, "Okay, great! But you should know up front he won't share your values. He's spiritually passive. He will refuse to work through any of his emotional baggage and instead project his pain onto you. He will talk about his ex-wife regularly. He won't support you emotionally. He won't celebrate your career accomplishments. And he will attack and criticize your feelings. But I think you'll fall in love with him. So, do you want to go out with him?"

Feeling repulsed, I said, "Um, no. Why would I want to do that?"

My friend then told me, "I just described your boyfriend."
Talk about a mic drop!

At that point, I couldn't remain in denial any longer.
I had to confront the fact that I was leading with my feelings…and not my values. And that wasn't landing me in the
kind of relationship my soul longed for. My attachment to
this man was getting in the way of what I truly desired in a
life partner. It was clouding my judgment.

*If we want to experience the nourishing, nurturing, fulfilling
relationships our souls crave, we have to follow our values — not
our hearts.*

While at first I was heartbroken at the thought of walking away from love, I eventually realized I was actually protecting and preserving my love by waiting for someone with
the character and values that align with my own.

When I explained to my then-boyfriend what I wanted
and needed, he agreed that he was not ready for this kind of
relationship. I said, "I hope you become ready. I want that
person to be you, but right now, I have to move on." It was a
mutually respectful, loving way to end a relationship. That's
all any of us can hope for when something isn't right.

I truly wish him the best on his journey, and I'm thankful for the soul growth I experienced while I was with him.
I learned what I want and, more importantly, what I do *not*
want in a relationship.

If you take anything away from my experiences, let it be
this: know what core values you need in a partner before you
begin a relationship.

If someone you're getting to know romantically is not
displaying those values, make a conscious decision to not
get involved. Hold out for the person who embodies those

cherished values. And spend the time before you find that person cultivating in yourself the characteristics that you value, so you'll be ready for them when you do.

A steadfast commitment to your values is ultimately the best way to protect yourself from a life that doesn't live up to your dreams. Lead with your values, and your values will lead you to the right person.

Guard your heart. It's worth protecting.

 **JOURNALING EXERCISE**
Relationship Rows

The goal of these journaling exercises is to help you get clear and focused, inspired and motivated, and to create a safe space for you to get real and honest with yourself. As you answer the questions below, please don't edit. Simply let your innermost thoughts, feelings, hopes, fears, insecurities, doubts, passion — anything you're experiencing — flow onto the page. Notice whatever comes up without judgment. Practice self-forgiveness and compassion while blessing any energy, person, or situation you're ready to leave behind.

1. Who do you want to be in a relationship? How can you practice being the ideal partner for your ideal mate (whether you are single or already attached)?
2. What are some of your emotional triggers? For example, maybe you were called "lazy" as a child, and when your partner asks why you always sleep in instead of getting up early to work out, you get upset. Or perhaps you are a sexual assault survivor and feel triggered by what you see and hear in the media and

social media. Take some time to go within and explore some of your triggers.

3. How can you better manage your emotions and, instead of focusing on what you can get, be generous with what you can give?

4. What is your core belief system when it comes to relationships? What do you want it to be? For example, mine is "I am complete."

5. When we begin to look at our relationships as adventuresome assignments for ultimate personal development and soul growth, we will understand we were brought together to learn from one another. Think of a past relationship. What did it teach you?

6. If you were mistreated in your last relationship, what are you ready to let go of? Commit to blessing and forgiving the person so you can detach energetically.

7. What inner work can you do to help your relationships flourish?

8. In what ways can you accept your mate exactly as they are?

9. How can you change your response to behaviors you haven't accepted in the past?

10. What are three specific ways you can surrender your grievances and attachments to anyone who has done you wrong?

11. How can you practice more forgiveness?

12. What are you willing to accept about yourself, your partner, your relationship, or past relationship experiences?

13. What core values do you need in a partner?

14. What do you value in a romantic partner?

15. How can you show up more fully for yourself and your current or future partner?

IF YOU'RE IN A ROMANTIC RELATIONSHIP:

As mentioned earlier, instead of asking yourself, *Is this person really good enough for me?* ask, *Am I really showing up for this person and creating a safe space for their transformation and enlightenment?*

16. Is your partner demonstrating that they are willing to grow and taking the necessary steps to actualize that growth?
17. If you had never met your significant other and someone told you their best and worst qualities, would they be someone you wanted to spend your life with?
18. Take five minutes to pray for your partner's happiness every day. Remind them how wonderful they are. How does this feel?

IF YOU'RE NOT IN A RELATIONSHIP BUT ARE SEEKING ONE:

19. Take inventory of your own shortcomings and the work you still need to do. It's important to ask ourselves, *If the "ideal" partner showed up right now, would they want me?*

 TRUE LOVE MEDITATION

As we settle in and get comfortable in our meditation space, let's take a moment to focus on our breath, gently breathing in through the nose and out through the mouth.

As we close our eyes, we open to the light that is within.

We are willing to open ourselves up to the truth, and the truth is, we are loved. We are love. And we don't need to do anything to be loved. We already are loved. May we now allow this truth to come forward.

We open ourselves up to the possibility that figuring out who we want to be in all our relationships, starting with ourselves, is the path to deep and lasting love. The kind of love that nourishes us from the inside out and fills us with a deep sense of awe and wonder, gratitude and joy.

We understand now that our thoughts, feelings, and actions are the only things we can control. We practice being the people we want to be, and we are ready to share and receive a deeply nourishing, lasting love.

We are more aware of our triggers and how to better manage our emotions. We are generous with what we can give. Our core belief is "I am complete."

We understand we are brought together to learn from one another.

May we learn not to attack or defend and instead practice forgiveness and take responsibility for our wounds (which appear as character defects we are tempted to judge in ourselves and others), so we can heal these wounds and release the painful feelings associated with them, thereby showing up for ourselves and others as happy, healthy partners.

We are willing to give our partners unconditional acceptance.

When we don't like a certain behavior, we try changing our response to that behavior rather than trying to change our partner. When we accept a person for who they are, it sets us free — we don't feel the need to try to control them. Instead, we can focus on controlling our emotions and decide whether to stay in or leave the relationship.

We now surrender our grievances and attachments to anyone who has done us wrong.

We practice more forgiveness, which is the answer to everything.

When someone hurts our feelings, and we don't feel the need to cause any emotional harm back, we pass the test. When we are willing to take 100 percent responsibility for our lives (even though it can be challenging), we grow up faster and become emotionally stronger.

Instead of lashing out against people who've hurt us, we now take a deep breath and see it as an opportunity to heal an old wound and grow. With practice, we become less and less reactive and feel a greater sense of peace and freedom.

We sit here in meditation with the awareness that nothing changes until first it is accepted exactly as it is.

May we commit to showing up fully for ourselves and in all our relationships, asking ourselves, Am I really showing up for this person and creating a safe space for their transformation and enlightenment?

In creating the space for another's transformation, we allow them to be who they were not yesterday — we give them the freedom to get it right.

We pray for our partner's happiness every day. We remind them how wonderful they are. We resist the temptation to project onto another that they somehow complete us and to demand that they behave a certain way.

We take inventory of our own shortcomings and the work we still need to do. We understand that our commitment to changing our thought patterns and behaviors can make us available and ready for lasting love.

May we now release expectations.

Take a moment to imagine what it would feel like to stop expecting your partner to be more, better, or different.

Rather than looking for or expecting one special person to complete us, we look for ways we can love, honor, and accept ourselves and others more completely.

To start envisioning what this might look like, we ask our highest self all the ways we can prepare our heart, body, personality, beliefs, and home for real love — the kind of love we seek and the kind of love our current or future partner deserves.

May we be willing to hear whatever we need to hear, taking our time, before slowly and gently coming back to the room.

 COACH KATE CHECK-IN

- What are you learning about yourself?
- What does feeling the burn mean to you?
- Who do you need to be in order to feel your best in your relationships with yourself and others?
- Why is this important to you right now?
- How can you use what you've discovered about yourself in this step and apply it to your daily life?
- When will you do this? What day and time? Can you add it to your calendar right now?

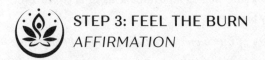 **STEP 3: FEEL THE BURN**
AFFIRMATION

I want to experience the nourishing, nurturing, fulfilling relationships my soul craves, so I choose to follow my values — not my heart. To start envisioning what this might look like, I write down all the ways I can prepare my heart, body, personality, beliefs, and home for real love — the kind of love I seek and the kind of love my current or future partner deserves.

STEP 4

Strengthen Your Core Confidence

*You gain strength, courage and confidence by every experience
in which you really stop to look fear in the face.
You must do the things you think you cannot do.*

— ELEANOR ROOSEVELT

"Let's start with failure," she said.

It was my first day working with my dance coach, Jess Grippo. Let me start by saying that it's hilarious that I have a dance coach, because I am not a dancer.

I'd met Jess about a month prior at a speaking event called Fearless Communicators. In just five days, all the participants — Jess, four other women, and me — created, wrote, and delivered fifteen-minute speeches in front of a packed audience. It was one of the most challenging, but rewarding, experiences of my life.

So when Jess, who's also a gorgeous professional dancer and coach, hit me up to take a dance lesson with her, I said,

"Sure!" I didn't fully know what I was getting myself into, but I knew I wanted to just trust the process and go for it. I wanted to continue to embody the word "fearless" and also stay true to the principles expressed in step 1 by stretching my comfort zone beyond the point of no return.

Which is why I laughed out loud when Jess and I walked into a Midtown Manhattan dance studio and she said, "Let's start with failure." Jess explained to me that starting with failure means giving ourselves permission to mess up, so that perfectionism doesn't stop us from starting. There's actually gold in failure because we discover creative new things that may not have been accessible to us if we were only striving to do it "right" or "perfectly."

Starting with failure, to me, means showing up and being okay with whatever comes out of us in the moment. It could be a brilliant performance (Jess's dancing), or it could be an embarrassingly pitiful display of incompetence (my dancing, for example). The point is, it doesn't matter. Starting with failure means more fun and lightheartedness because it's not about impressing anyone or "being the best." Those things may happen, but the goal is authenticity and freedom. The goal is to be ourselves. It's about being comfortable being fully seen for who and where we are in life. It's accepting all that we are. And aren't.

My inner perfectionist was mortified, though! *You are quite accomplished at many things; why don't you spend your time and energy doing those things?* queried that inner perfectionist, who I like to call "Kim." (Naming my inner critics and the feelings that try to tear me down or hold me back is my tongue-in-cheek — but powerful — way to master them.) *You're wasting your time here,* Kim continued. She's a real pill, right? Starting with failure was the perfect way to hush Kim up.

And that's what this step is all about: letting go of limiting beliefs that are holding us back — such as my belief that I couldn't (and shouldn't) dance — so that instead we strengthen our core confidence.

"Starting with failure" immediately took all the pressure off. I mean, here I was, a woman with no dance experience in a dance class with someone who can keep up with J.Lo! Hello! But "fail"? I could do that!

I went on to take a few lessons with Jess and also booked solo studio time to practice moving and connecting with my body and getting lost in the music. I learned some simple choreography and signed up for Jess's dance-immersion weekend workshop.

The first day of the workshop, Jess turned down the lights and put on some music, and we let our bodies simply flow with the beats of the songs. Through the beauty of the music and the movement of my body (truly dancing like nobody was watching)...shaking out my long, usually perfectly coiffed blond hair...I experienced an intense release of energy and found myself beginning to cry. The tears flowed softly and gently, like my body. It was as if all the years of trying to keep it together emotionally while "looking perfect" to the outside world just went out the basement window of that Tribeca dance studio. I felt like a caged animal who was finally unleashed to run free.

But the tears didn't just flow from the release of stored or blocked energy. I also cried because I'd been feeling so uncomfortable and out of my element. I was experiencing the discomfort of vulnerability in a whole new way. I was putting myself out there for others to see and judge — people who actually knew what the heck to do in dance class, who knew how to move their bodies beautifully — in a space where I had zero expertise or experience. I didn't want to embarrass myself. As we discussed in step 1, stretching can be uncomfortable at times.

But the rewards are so worth it. I discovered something about myself that is so liberating: when I'm dancing, I'm thinking of nothing else. The world stands still for me. I am completely lost in the movement of my body and the music and how they become one. I am purely in flow, and I allow the rhythm and emotion of the music to carry me...oftentimes away from burdens (real or imagined). To carry me into the depths of *me*, where the good stuff is — truth, love, joy, wisdom, power, strength — even if it's painful there at times.

On Sunday afternoon, we performed the dances we'd created in front of the group. There were about ten of us. I danced to Usher's "Numb," which is a very meaningful song to me.

In a perfect world, my goal for my dance lessons and weekend intensive with Jess would be to learn to dance like Usher. I'd embody fluid, gorgeous dance moves and inspire audiences to feel their emotions deeply just through watching my body move so effortlessly to the music.

But let's get real. I'm never going to move like Usher. And you know what's brilliant about that? I'm going to move like *me*, express like me, entertain and inspire like me. Dancing is the ultimate rebellion against my obsession with performance and perfectionism. It will never be about striving for a "perfect" performance because dancing is not in my skill set. I'm learning that the "perfect" performance in dance and anything else I dare to try means being willing to show up, try my best, and not be great at first, or even ever. And there is so much freedom, beauty, and wonder in that.

When I danced in front of my classmates, I felt so powerful, so free, so connected to my emotions and my body. I was raw, messy, alive, exhilarated. In that sense, I became a dancer.

When we show up and do something, there's no longer this question of "Can I do this?" or "Who am I to do this?" because you *are* doing it! That's why getting into action is such a massive confidence booster. And the more you show up and just do the thing, whatever that is, the easier it gets, and then *you* get to be in charge of your life. Not your limiting beliefs. Not Kim.

The act of *doing* changes your core beliefs — you're not just rewiring your brain; you're also rewiring your heart, your inner "knowing," and that's a powerful force to be reckoned with.

Dare to (Not) Be Great...Yet

Let's go back to that Fearless Communicators course where I met Jess. For a program with "fearless" in the title, it sure induced a lot of fear! On day three of the five days we had to prepare our speeches, I voice-texted my friend and colleague Allison Davis in total panic mode, to which she replied, "Are you okay? You sound like you're trapped in a basement and need assistance!"

I wasn't trapped in a basement, but I did need assistance. I was freaking out! My inner perfectionist was screaming at the top of her lungs, *There's no way we can deliver a "perfect" performance in just five days!*

It simply isn't possible, I heard my inner Kim saying.

In addition to attempting to quiet the hysteria that is Kim, I also noticed that I was feeling terrified to share very personal stories in front of a crowd of strangers, which I guess is quite normal (though Kim doesn't care about normal; she expects perfection at all times). It's not like I was talking about how to make cupcakes or getting up and telling jokes and making people laugh like I would do at a party, or selling beauty products like I do on live television throughout the world.

No, I was going to talk about some of my darkest moments because in the process of writing this speech, these were the stories that emerged. These were the experiences that have had the greatest impact on me, shaping me into the woman I am today and forcing me to expand and grow in numerous ways.

This was also challenging because, even though I was delving into painful moments in my past, I was actually now in a great place in my life and wanted to celebrate that. I wanted to laugh with friends over wine and tell them about my recent trip to Portugal. I'd earned some fun, after all!

Despite my panic and the challenges, ultimately, the speaking event went swimmingly well. I was up first, and I got through my speech without crying. Not that there's anything wrong with crying, mind you, but it showcased tremendous inner growth for me that I was able to speak about these heart-wrenching events and not break down.

But even though it went so well, the second I finished the speech, my first thought was *I could have done better. I want to be better. I messed that one part up a little bit. I didn't nail it.*

Basically, I wanted to be where I knew I would be after delivering that speech dozens of times. This is a pattern for me; I always want to be a million steps ahead of where I am. (Sound familiar to any of you?) But that's not how it works.

I've learned that, like anything worthwhile in life, you have to put in the work. Even the most gifted athletes, artists, and musicians have several coaches and mentors they train with around the clock. No one gets a free pass to excellence.

When the videographer came over to remove my microphone after the speech, she greeted me with enthusiasm and praise for my performance, but sadly I couldn't accept it deep down. All I could do was obsess over how I could have done better. In my heart, I knew I did a good job. I was proud of myself for putting something meaningful together and delivering it, especially in such a short amount of time. But I also had to be mindful of the fact that I was still (and continue to be) overcoming an old, worn-out, limiting core belief that says, *I'm not good enough.*

This self-awareness slowly made room for compassion and curiosity as I asked myself, *Why can't you give yourself the love and acceptance you so freely give to others?* Truly, this was more of a question for Kim, the inner critic who doesn't speak the truth and is committed to keeping me small and stuck.

When the event was over, a woman in the audience approached me, and with her hand on her heart said, "You were incredible. Thank you for opening my heart."

I immediately put my hand on my heart and said, "Thank you so much." I was so touched and honored and wanted to weep because I realized something so powerful in that moment: I did my job.

Ultimately, it isn't about giving the perfect performance, because there's no such thing. My speaking coach, Eduardo Placer, hates the word "performance." As he always says, "Just be a f'ing person!"

This woman gave me such an invaluable gift. Sure, compliments are always nice to hear, especially if your love language is "words of affirmation" like me, but it wasn't about that. (If you're not familiar with Gary Chapman's book *The Five Love Languages: How to Express Heartfelt Commitment to Your Mate*, which explains the five ways we choose to express and receive love, I highly recommend it.) She reminded me that I'd done my job — because I believe my "original medicine" is opening people's hearts. "Original medicine" is a term I learned from speaking coach and author extraordinaire Gail Larsen. It refers to our unique expression to the world. As stated on Larsen's website, RealSpeaking.com:

> Indigenous cultures call this gift our Original Medicine. It is a teaching that has two distinct parts.
>
> • You come to this earth with gifts and talents nowhere else duplicated.
> • If you don't express these gifts, they are lost to the world for all time.
>
> In teaching this perennial wisdom, I've discovered a third truth:
>
> Original Medicine fulfills our deep longing to know and live our purpose. Without its expression, we never feel quite whole.

While training together with Larsen years ago, author Beth Kempton labeled me "the open heart surgeon" because she said I have an uncanny, magical way of opening up and healing people's hearts. This became my "original medicine."

And here was this woman standing before me using that exact same language. *You can't make this stuff up!* I thought to myself. I felt God and my angels up there winking at me, and my emotionally exhausted self took a deep exhale, knowing I did what I came there to do that night — I showed up, shared my truth, and opened at least one heart.

When I watched the video of my speech, there was no denying that it went well. There is video evidence of me actually having a blast! I was smiling, laughing, engaging with the audience, and completely in the moment. I appreciate that there is video evidence of the *truth*, to prove just how loony Kim can be and how debilitating a disempowering core belief can feel.

When we become aware of our limiting core beliefs, we can choose to do something about them. Taking action consistently silences the self-criticism that stems from a limiting belief. The "I'm not good enough" lie gets replaced by inspired actions that say, "Watch me!"

A week after the event, on a Zoom video conference with my fellow "fearless communicators," I shared with them: "After that experience, I can do anything."

A Weak Core Undermines Our Confidence

According to psychologists, "core beliefs" are our basic beliefs about ourselves, other people, and the world we live in. They are things we hold deep down to be absolute truths, underneath all our surface thoughts. Essentially, core beliefs determine how we perceive and interpret the world.

In coaching, we refer to core beliefs as "developmental frames." In other words, these represent your worldview, which is an indication of what you pay attention to. For example, if you have a worldview that says, "People aren't to be trusted," then you will set yourself up to be in situations where people exhibit untrustworthy behavior, in order to prove yourself (and your core belief) right.

If your worldview is that people are kind and generous, you will experience more life situations where people show you kindness and generosity. Chances are you will behave this way as well and naturally attract the same behavior. You'll most likely be on the lookout for these kinds of people and experiences, too, and notice them more frequently.

Some of the core beliefs that affect our lives and sense of fulfillment the most are our core beliefs about ourselves. Limiting core beliefs are like flab that hold us back from achieving full spiritual fitness and coming into our own potential. We can jettison these limiting beliefs through exercises that strengthen our core confidence in ourselves and the world around us. Examples of these limiting core beliefs could be: "I'm not good at dance, so I shouldn't even try." "I have to hide my true self in order to be accepted." "I'm not smart. I should keep my mouth shut." "I'm less than other people, so I have to constantly try to prove my worth." And on and on.

Our core beliefs dictate the kind of life we experience more than we realize. The good news is that we can change our core beliefs, and therefore our lives, in very profound and meaningful ways.

Clarify Your Core Beliefs

In order to replace limiting core beliefs with self-fulfilling breakthroughs that build confidence, we first have to be clear on what worldview we bring to the table. If we hold a belief that we must have twenty years of experience at a job to be effective and merit the salary and recognition we desire, then we need to do some work on how we define merit and success. Perhaps we need to create a new core belief that says: "I have everything it takes to feel confident and be effective in my role *now* and to ask for what I'm worth."

Soccer coach James Galanis trains several Olympians, like US Women's National Team (USWNT) star Carli Lloyd. He shared a story with me about another player he was coaching that he felt wasn't playing up to her full potential. When he went to her games, he said, he noticed she was warming up behind the team and didn't seem like she was a part of the squad. When he asked her about this, she said she was on the practice roster, being groomed to be a starter in the *next* Olympics. She also said that as a defender, the strikers (who were the faces of the team and considered celebrities, with big endorsement deals) didn't appreciate when she played "all out" in practice, slide tackling and making other aggressive moves against them that showcased her skills.

Galanis insisted to her that she was good enough to be in the starting lineup *already*. He encouraged her to play all out, at her full speed and ability, not just for herself but for the betterment of the team.

He worked to change her core belief from "I'm on the practice squad, and the stars of the team don't like it when I play aggressively" to "I'm good enough to be a starter right now, and I'm going to play from that mindset."

Once she changed her core belief — and lived and played from that belief — the results were almost immediate. She became a starter within a few games and a standout star in her own right, scoring the winning goal as a defender in a key game.

Go Slow to Go Fast

It's worth spending a good amount of time uncovering our developmental frames because doing so indicates the specific data that we pay attention to — consciously or unconsciously. To do that, you can ask yourself a few key questions in any situation you're facing. Here are the questions I assign my coaching clients, which you can ask yourself. As an example, I'll include the answers Galanis and his client might have given to each question.

What is my focus as I frame the situation? Do I see it as a problem or opportunity? Why?

Coach Galanis saw his player's situation as an opportunity to become a starter and key contributor on the team, which ultimately led her to a world championship.

What important values are being challenged or need to be maintained as I approach this situation?

His player's integrity was being challenged, and her talents needed to be maintained.

What aspects of my reputation or identity can be leveraged in service of the situation?

The player's identity as a talented world-class athlete was leveraged in service of the USWNT and a gold medal for the USA.

How can my preferred way of communicating be leveraged in the situation?

This player preferred to let her performance on the field do the talking, so she showed up ready to play her best.

What may need to be dialed up or down?

She needed to dial up her aggressive play and dial down her fear of not being liked because of it.

As an executive leadership coach, I see the value and importance of working through and spending proper time on developmental frames — it yields great results, and quickly! As Columbia coaching program facilitator John Schuster likes to say, "Go slow to go fast." I'm learning the importance of not being in such a rush to get to action solutions.

For example, I had a client who was experiencing a lot of mental blocks around money. She hadn't been able to earn a six-figure-a-year income in more than a decade and couldn't understand why. She expressed frustration. I went a little deeper with my questioning and asked if her money issues were a pattern. I asked about the first time she experienced lack around money. She told me about her childhood and things her father would often say, like, "Don't be greedy" and "Money doesn't grow on trees." She said her dad feared never having enough money.

As a young adult, my client had experienced great financial success as a Hollywood actress. I asked her what had changed and why she thinks she hasn't been able to earn as much as she wants and is capable of earning. I could see she was getting stuck in her thoughts, so I asked, "What fear does earning a lot of money bring up in you?"

Almost immediately, she blurted out, "I don't want to make a lot of money because when I do, my husband just blows it all gambling!"

There it was — the limiting belief that turned into limiting behaviors around earning the income she desired. I could see this huge revelation all over her face. She said she felt so free afterward. A few months later, after a dozen coaching sessions, my client was happy to report that she'd made more money in three months than she usually earned in an entire year. She'd also established firm boundaries with her husband around finances. It was like a huge light turned on for her, and she was no longer consciously or subconsciously being held back by a thought system based on fear and lack. She was now plugged into confidence and abundance and was committed to this new, empowered, consistent belief and practice.

Coach Galanis and the soccer player were able to experience so much success (and get desired results rather quickly) because his client was willing to change her worldview, plus uncover and lean into her values — integrity, freedom, truth — rather than her fears and limitations. She was willing to be open to new ideas and ways of thinking. To focus on creating new and more empowering belief patterns and behaviors. To commit to trust in herself and what she uniquely brings to the table, in order to embody confidence.

When she showed up as a confident player, she was able to impart this confidence to her teammates, which is a sign of a true leader — you make the people around you better, too.

How to Shift Perspective

According to researchers Kathleen Taylor and Catherine Marienau, who study how adult brains develop, learn, and perform more effectively in various settings, our emotions are essential to meaningful learning. In their book *Facilitating Learning with the Adult Brain in Mind*, the authors assert that our brain has two mind states: the anxious brain and the curious brain.

The anxious brain thinks things like: *What do I have to do to save myself? I have to know what's happening. I have to focus narrowly on the immediate. I have to be certain. I have to be right. I have to avoid threat.*

Think cortisol: the "stress hormone."

On the other hand, the curious brain thinks: *I seek novel experiences. I focus more widely. I categorize and associate by comparison. I construct elaborate patterns. I determine cause and effect. I reward myself for figuring things out.*

Think oxytocin: a hormone linked to decreasing fear and increasing trust and generosity.

Whenever we take on a new challenge or opportunity, or commit to embodying a new core belief, it is inevitable that our anxious brains will try to take over. When this happens, try not to resist the anxiety but to notice it, acknowledge it, and then make the conscious decision to switch into curious-brain mode. With every switch into a curious-brain outlook, we strengthen our core confidence.

 MANTRA: A SPIRIT OF CONFIDENCE

A spirit of confidence will change your life.
It will change the way you see yourself.
It will change the way you relate to others.
It will change the way you move in the world.
It will change everything.

And it takes a spirit of confidence to have the tough
*   conversation.*
To make the sale.
To create the vision.

To let go.
Or to go big.

It takes a spirit of confidence to find your voice.
To love your reflection.
To follow your dreams.
To get out of your own way.

And sometimes, it takes a confident spirit to help coach
you along the way.

Build Your Core Beliefs around Confidence

Once we uncover and recognize our core beliefs (or developmental frames), we can consciously work to shift them in more positive directions. A key element of this is to build confidence into our core beliefs.

Through my work in front of the camera as a TV personality and model, I learned what it truly means to be confident. (It's not what you think.) The truth is, you already have what it takes. You were born with it. You just need to remember what that feels like.

I hold space for my clients to awaken their inner wisdom to guide them back to their most confident self. I do this by allowing them to share their truth in a nonjudgmental, nourishing environment, while focusing on their agenda, not mine. I let them talk freely and come to their own conclusions while I listen deeply — both to what is said and not said. Recognizing that they have the ability to access the answers to their most probing questions makes my clients feel empowered and in control. I don't believe it serves any of us to coddle our weaknesses or neuroses when we can choose to honor our greatness instead.

It is our birthright to be unstoppable. We just have to rediscover what it means to be free of judgment, fear, doubt — of anything that weighs us down.

I know it can feel scary and overwhelming to put ourselves out there in a big way and actually do what our hearts are urging us to do. We think, *Who am I to start this business? What will people say? Am I smart, talented, or good enough?* and so on.

But whatever pain we may experience from another's judgment of us is nothing compared to the pain we will undoubtedly feel by playing small.

What does it mean to play small? It means shrinking so others won't feel insecure around us. But when we dare to write our book, leave the unhealthy relationship, quit a job to start our dream business, or whatever it is, we inspire others to do the same.

The real question then becomes: Who are you *not* to start your own business or whatever you feel called to do, not to show up fully for yourself and others? Who are you not to be gorgeous, brilliant, wildly successful, and joyful?

Expressing our full potential is not just our right; it's our responsibility. And it starts with confidence.

Defining Confidence

To have confidence, we first must define what it means for us. When I tackled this question, here is what I wrote:

- I believe confidence is remembering who we truly are (love) and owning that — each and every day. Confidence is honoring who we are — perceived flaws and all — and presenting our highest self to everyone we meet, with a smile.

- Confidence is making our own rules and refusing to settle for societal standards we don't believe in. It is forgiveness, kindness, grace, and the ability to laugh at ourselves. It is taking our lives seriously, so we don't have to take ourselves so seriously.
- Confidence is more than just knowing we deserve the best; it's making choices that reflect that. It is saying no when we want to say no and not feeling bad about it. It's staying in bed when we need to rest, without feeling guilty, and listening to and caring for our bodies.
- Confidence is choosing to be the victor, not the victim. It is admitting when we are wrong and sincerely apologizing. It is following our heart's desires and asking for help.
- Confidence is knowing we were created by the same loving force that created the sun, moon, and stars and living from that magnificent space. It is not needing anyone's approval, validation, or applause.
- Confidence is looking within and asking, *Who do I need to be, to transform this relationship/situation/society/ world?* It is the recognition that the peace, love, freedom, and abundance we wish to experience start with us. It's the willingness to show up fully, speak up passionately, and stand up straight.
- Confidence is the spark that lights up any room. It doesn't label, judge, shame, blame, condemn, or attack.

If you struggle with feeling confident, don't fret! You're normal! Start by giving yourself a hug. I think I'll do the same.

Now I'm curious to know how *you* define confidence. I also invite you to identify and write down your limiting core beliefs. You may have to go way back to your childhood memories to come up with some of them. This can be a painful experience, so please be gentle with yourself. You may find it helpful to work with a hypnotherapist or other trained professional to help uncover some of the subconscious limiting beliefs that you unknowingly carry around (as we all do) that sabotage you without your even realizing it.

Once you've identified these beliefs, take some time to define and then reflect on how you can embody more confident core beliefs to take their place.

Transcendent Self-Confidence

We've all felt the sting of being let down, frustrated, unfulfilled, or not quite good enough in our lives and relationships. I've been guilty of having unrealistic expectations of others and wanting them to shower me with compliments, approval, and validation. And I've sometimes been guilty of trying to control situations or outcomes in an attempt to get what I thought would make me feel good. It was a painful, exhausting way to live.

Remember: studies show that basing our self-worth on external factors is actually harmful to our mental health. One study at the University of Michigan found that college students who based their self-worth on external sources (including academic performance, appearance, and approval from others) reported more stress, anger, academic problems, and relationship conflicts. They also had higher levels of alcohol and drug use, as well as more symptoms of eating disorders. The same study found that students who based their self-worth on internal sources not only felt better but also received higher grades and were less likely to use drugs and alcohol or develop eating disorders.

Through the consistent practices of self-compassion and meditation, I've discovered a few perspective shifts that have transformed my sense of self-worth. I've found that when I base my self-worth on who I am and my inherent value as a human being, rather than what others think or how much I achieve, my confidence soars and my inner critic quiets.

Try these four sets of self-confidence step-ups to tone your core sense of self-worth and feel spiritually fit and healthy:

First Set: Develop Self-Sufficiency

For the majority of my life, I got my self-worth from the outside world — someone else's approval or validation dictated how I felt about myself. What a setup that is! As we've learned, when we base our self-worth on sources outside ourselves (such as career, money, material possessions, relationships, appearance, and so forth), we can never have enough or be enough.

Being independent from others' thoughts of me (both positive and negative) and instead trusting in the God of my own understanding for my value, I have become more self-sufficient and, as a result, experience more peace, freedom, and material success.

Sure, compliments are very nice to hear, but my mood and mental and physical health are no longer dependent on another's approval of me. As long as we are judging our worth on another's opinion of us or how people choose to treat us, we will never be able to live up to our full potential and experience true joy.

Second Set: Let People Off the Hook

Instead of looking to others for validation to make us feel worthy or "enough," how about reframing our thinking around the notion that nobody owes us anything?

When we are truly anchored in our own self-love and get our self-worth from the unique qualities that make us one of a kind, we become self-sufficient. We don't need to go to our partners, friends, work, food, alcohol, or social media for a quick ego boost. We can turn inward and look to a higher power for our value, knowing we are enough simply because we are alive.

Third Set: Accept That People Can't Give You What They Don't Have

I've looked to significant others, bosses, parents, or friends to tell me something to make me feel better or to treat me a certain way so I could feel valued, respected, and loved. To see why this is wrong, let's take an analogy from the world of work: if a client simply doesn't have any more money in their budget to pay you, they can't give it to you, and perhaps the solution is to find an opportunity where the compensation matches the value, skills, and experience you bring to the table. Similarly, if a customer service representative is frustrating you because they can't help with your request, maybe they lack proper training and thorough information. And in the same way, maybe your partner isn't respecting you because they lack self-respect.

I've learned that the people who have cheated us, hurt us, or done us wrong cannot necessarily make amends — either they are unwilling or unable. Waiting for and expecting others to apologize, make it up to us, or even admit they were wrong implies a belief that their actions can make us feel whole again. But when we are dependent on others to make us happy, we will always be disappointed on some level.

The good news is that if we put our faith in ourselves and in the God of our own understanding, we will never be let down. The universe is self-organizing and self-correcting.

Fourth Set: Remember, It's Not about Keeping Everyone Happy — It's about Fulfilling Your Life's Purpose

As long as we are doing our best, honoring ourselves and our purpose, we will feel less and less inclined to seek the approval of others. Instead of feeling offended when people fail to acknowledge us, what if we could see it as an opportunity to expand and grow? What if we embraced the fact that such experiences prepare us to take our lives to the next level and start fulfilling our mission?

The less I depend on people to validate me, the stronger my emotional muscles become and, in turn, the stronger my sense of self-worth. I have accomplished more both personally and professionally in less time — and need fewer compliments to keep me going strong — simply because of my faith in myself and in the universe. Focusing on the special characteristics that make me uniquely me is much easier and more rewarding than waiting for someone to say or do something that will make me feel good for a little while... until I need my next "fix."

Our lives truly become fuller when we turn our attention inward to the miracle that we are, release expectations, and stay detached from outcomes and other people's opinions. Try it out for yourself, and let me know how it goes!

The Building Blocks of Confidence

While completing my advanced certification in executive and organizational coaching from Columbia University, I conducted extensive research into how to leverage confidence to accelerate leadership development.

To that end, I interviewed dozens of leaders in business and sports, in addition to reviewing numerous articles and research studies on the topic. Several major themes emerged, allowing me to identify some key building blocks of confidence. These building blocks can boost your confidence, both personally and professionally, whether you're a college student, professional athlete, entrepreneur, secretary, stay-at-home mom leading your household day in and day out (with no days off, no less), or the CEO of a Fortune 500 company.

These key confidence building blocks are trust and what I call the five Ps: presence, patience, purpose, preparation, and practice.

- **Trust:** At its root, *confidence* means "to trust," "to do something with trust," or "to have full trust or reliance." Trust emerged throughout all my research as a major key to building confidence. The way I see it, trusting in this context is a spiritual practice with three key components: (1) surrender, (2) willingness to show up fully on a consistent basis and do the work, and (3) accepting the invitation to not be great...yet! Through all three components, we're trusting in the process and in ourselves. This is all about strengthening your core beliefs in the name of growth, wisdom, and learning.

- **Presence:** In a world of overstimulation and countless distractions, the art of being present has become a valuable skill in itself. This means bringing your whole self to the present moment and truly being there — not stuck in the past or future but being and embracing exactly where you are.

- **Patience:** When you are present, you can have patience and truly know (not just intellectually, but in your body, in your bones) that what's best for you is either already here or on its way. Create a new mantra or story for yourself. Mine is "Everything that could possibly contribute to my happiness is either already here or on its way." There is a spiritual principle that says, "Infinite patience produces immediate results." As I like to say, "Achieving a goal is like being pregnant: you can't rush it." Or as the 38 Special song says, "Hold on loosely."

- **Purpose:** Having a purpose greater than ourselves came up again and again in my research as a confidence booster. On the days we may lack inspiration or motivation and not be fully invested in showing up for ourselves in a meaningful way, we can choose to show up for our families, friends, colleagues, teams, organizations, or society and set a good example as a friend, colleague, and leader.

- **Preparation:** Being prepared both breeds confidence directly and leads to improved outcomes, which also boost confidence.

- **Practice:** Repetition builds confidence. Consistency of behavior builds new habits, which create new results, which again boost confidence. My friend Heather won three Olympic gold medals in soccer as a member of the USWNT. I went to many of her games over the years, and what inspired me the most was the fight in her. Heather admitted to me that she really had no business making the 2012 Olympic roster. She was plagued by injuries and considered an "older" player on the team at the ripe old age of thirty-four. A slew of fit, spunky twentysomethings were gunning for her spot on the team. They were faster, more skilled. But what these players didn't have was Heather's sheer determination and willingness to practice when no one else was practicing. They didn't have her mental toughness. They weren't willing to put in extra reps with an outside coach on their days off to build fitness. Heather's coach and Heather herself will tell you she wasn't the most talented player in her position. But she was the most relentless, and her consistency of behavior ultimately earned her a spot on the team.

Tighten Your Spiritual Flab

A major obstacle that's been shown to keep us stuck in limiting core beliefs and that stands in the way of our confidence is the trap of comparison. I don't know about you, but when I compare myself to others, I always feel drained, insecure, and unhappy. I find myself creating stories about how I'm not good enough. These feelings build stress in my body and leave me unable to operate from a creative, empowered place. When you're comparing yourself to someone else, you aren't focusing on yourself and everything *you* have to offer the world in your own unique way.

So it's time to make the sometimes difficult but necessary commitment to stop comparing yourself to others. The world needs your special gifts. Here are five steps to get you started:

1. **Recognize that you're comparing yourself to others.** The first step in letting go of comparison is to acknowledge you're doing it. It won't feel natural to focus only on yourself at first, as we're conditioned to compare ourselves and have others compare us to one another. But by being aware of what you're doing, you can quickly dissolve any negative thoughts or feelings that may arise. Nip them in the bud and go back to embracing all you can offer the world instead.

2. **Focus on all that you are rather than what you think you're lacking.** Focus on how you can serve yourself, others, and the world. Celebrate others rather than feeling jealous and attacking them (even if it's just in your own thoughts). We're each great in our own unique way. Celebrate the greatness in others and yourself.

   When I catch myself comparing, I quickly say to myself, *Comparison is the thief of joy.* I never want to feel joyless, so I immediately shift my thoughts and behavior. Try it!

3. **Keep everything in perspective.** Some may envy that I live in New York and used to work full-time as a model. But I bet they don't envy all the rejection I regularly endured. I could envy friends and relatives

for having wonderful spouses and adorable children. But I don't envy the lack of sleep or immense
sacrifices all parents must make.

We each have our own path, journey, unique personalities, and gifts to share with the world. If you're
busy comparing yourself to other people, you might
miss all the blessings put before you on your path.

4. **Limit your time on social media.** Have you ever been
having a perfectly great day only to scroll through
your social media feeds and almost instantly feel
horrible about yourself? I know I have, on numerous occasions. I remember sitting at the hair salon
feeling relaxed and pampered, casually browsing
my Instagram feed. Within seconds, I felt my energy
plummet — I was comparing myself to other women
who seemed to have it all (fancy careers, outfits, va-
cations).

These thoughts give rise to feelings that bring us
down! We feel as though we can never measure up as
people, parents, daughters or sons, friends, employees, and so on. The message you're sending yourself
is *I am not enough. I need to have more and be more to
compete with my social media feed.* But you know what?
That's a bunch of crap.

5. **Forgive yourself.** It's human nature to compare ourselves to other people. Forgive yourself for this nasty
habit we've all succumbed to, but stay committed to
the intention that you'll no longer do it.

The bottom line: someone is always going to be
more physically attractive, smarter, wealthier, fun-
nier — or seem that way in the fantasy worlds that

are social media, Hollywood, magazine covers, and our own imaginations. It doesn't matter. What's important are the unique gifts you and only you can bring to the table, and your special connections to others. Even the people you deem the most successful — with enviable careers, relationships, wardrobes, and homes — have bad days, trauma, and sadness in their lives.

REFLECTION EXERCISE
Tone Your Trust Muscles

Building trust in ourselves and the world takes time. Here are some practices that help build the kind of trust you need to develop true confidence. Consider each one, and take time to think about ways you can put it into practice in your life. In these ways, you'll build a fit, toned, and confident spiritual core.

1. Walk the walk. Is there a goal you're talking about but not taking action toward?
2. Be kind, generous, and reassuring; focus on being a trustworthy person. Working to inspire and merit trust helps us trust ourselves.
3. Pay attention to details, and trust in the process. My beloved swim coach Larry Lyons always used to tell us, "If you pay attention to the little things, the big things will take care of themselves." Little things — like not breathing in and out of your turns, practicing fingertip finishes every single time you come to the wall, and using proper stroke technique — lead

to the big things, like winning state and national championships, which my team did consecutively for more than a decade under his leadership.

4. Practice accepting that you will not be great at something at first — that's how you learn, grow, challenge yourself, and become better. Trust in your ability to grow if you give yourself room to develop new competencies.

Foam-Rolling for Forgiveness

Stress, anger, unhappiness, and feelings of lack or unworthiness are reminders that we need to get toned on the inside, that we need to focus again on strengthening our core (core confidence, that is). One big way to do that is to practice forgiveness.

So let's do this now. Engaging in forgiveness has this magical way of transforming pain and suffering into peace, whether we're forgiving a loved one, a major player in our lives, a stranger who somehow offended us, or even political or societal leaders. When we forgive, we get to be in control of our thoughts and feelings, which is empowering, rather than feeling victimized by the actions of others or by world events — anything outside our control. And feeling genuinely and positively empowered is the bedrock of confidence.

I recently had a moment when I thought, *Our world is so unsafe right now. I'm scared.* I quickly shifted my perspective to a much more loving one: *I trust I am safe and always protected.*

See how much better that feels? We can choose to unsubscribe from fearful thoughts and replace them with loving ones. Our thoughts will then be reflected back to us, and we will collect more and more evidence that the world is a safe place to live and that we are surrounded by love.

Peace begins with you and me. If we want to live in a peaceful, loving, kind, compassionate world, we must first embody those characteristics ourselves and share them with everyone we meet.

We can't control others, but by being kind, first and foremost to ourselves, we spread kindness into the world instead of more anger, hatred, and fear. I see so many people on Facebook outraged by political happenings, and they have every right to be, but then they treat themselves and others the same way that the leaders they are criticizing behave. When I ask if they're voting, donating money, or volunteering their time, they say no.

It is easy to point fingers and blame laws and politicians, or bosses, or anyone we feel has power in our lives — and you will be justified in your anger and opinions in many instances, but you will not be happy or at peace. In fact, when we carry resentment toward another, it actually bonds us to that person energetically. Forgiveness then becomes an effective tool for detachment and liberation.

How empowering to know that one decision can make you free right now. To forgive.

 CONFIDENT CORE BELIEFS MEDITATION

Get comfortable in your meditation space. Begin your meditative breathing, taking deep breaths in through your nose and out through your mouth. Continue this cycle of breath throughout your meditation. Allow your awareness to move as you breathe, noticing the rise and fall of your chest and stomach. Let any outside noises

allow you to go even deeper into your meditation as you focus on your breath. Notice any sensations throughout your body. Go ahead and scan both your physical and emotional body. Release any tension, stress, anxiety, fears, or concerns. Allow yourself to become more deeply relaxed.

As you breathe, take a moment to think about a time when you didn't feel confident. You may have been filled with insecurity, self-doubt, fear, judgment, or worry. Give yourself permission to access those painful or unwanted emotions now.

Take a deep breath in, and as you exhale, see and feel yourself releasing every emotion you no longer wish to carry. Good. Take another deep, cleansing breath in, and as you exhale, gently release any remaining emotion you still need to let go of. Sometimes our emotions are just trying to protect us from a perceived threat, but really they are standing in the way of our most actualized self, hurting us in the process.

Forgive your emotions. Forgive yourself. It is safe to let go now.

Become aware of your experience of these feelings. Try not to deny or judge them. Just be present. As you continue to deepen your breath, ask these emotions why they are here. What are they trying to tell you?

Take a moment to listen for the answer. When you are ready, kindly ask them to leave. Now invite in an image of what confidence means to you. Notice any feelings, images, or colors that come up. How does confidence make you feel? Ask your higher, ideal self how you can incorporate more confidence into your life to help you achieve your ultimate healthy self-image.

When you're ready, begin to explore the ways in which you can incorporate the building blocks of self-confidence into your daily life.

Ask yourself:

How can I trust more?

How can I be more present?

How can I exercise more patience?

How can I truly live my purpose?

How can I prepare myself each day to embody confidence?

How can I practice being more confident on a consistent basis?

Take as much time as you need. Be willing to experience all you need to experience . . . trusting that whatever comes up for you is perfect. . . . Then, when you are ready, slowly and gently open your eyes and come back to the room.

 ## COACH KATE CHECK-IN

- What is one baby step you could take to strengthen your core confidence?
- Who do you have to be in order to create this vision, achieve these goals?
- Why is this important to you right now?
- How can you eliminate life-draining habits while implementing sustaining, life-giving practices?
- How will you know when you have achieved the result you want?

 ## STEP 4: STRENGTHEN YOUR CORE CONFIDENCE *AFFIRMATION*

I am willing to trust myself and others more fully. I lead with my values. I am confident exactly as I am right now, and I leverage that confidence in service of others. I open myself up to a worldview with endless possibilities and opportunities for learning, growth, connection, and community. I look forward to sharing my unique gifts with everyone I meet.

STEP 5

Build Your
Emotional Muscles

Wisdom is always an overmatch for strength.

— PHIL JACKSON

We all know that if we want to be physically fit, we have to train our physical muscles through cardiovascular exercise, strength training, and stretching. We also know this takes discipline. We won't see any benefits unless we exercise regularly. The same is true of our emotional muscles. We have to spend the time, energy, and money to build strong mental "muscles" to combat *emotional* gravity, like anxiety, fear, self-doubt, external pressures and expectations, judgment — anything that weighs us down. That's why self-awareness, self-confidence, and the willingness to take inspired action consistently are key.

As a huge sports fan, I found it thrilling to live in Los

Angeles at the same time the Lakers won back-to-back-to-back NBA championships. I absolutely loved going to the games and watching the chemistry and magic (and sometimes discord) between megastars Shaquille O'Neal and Kobe Bryant. There wasn't and probably never will be a more electrifying duo in any sport.

But what I found even more fascinating as I cheered on the Lakers both in person and on TV was the sheer calmness of their head coach, Phil Jackson. I'm used to seeing head coaches marching up and down the court sweating, with beet-red faces, screaming and yelling at referees and players, arms flailing in the air in frustration, and throwing tantrums that often led to ejections.

Phil Jackson, on the other hand, was ultracool, calm, and collected. Regardless of what was going on in the game and around him, he sat in his seat completely unbothered, expressionless, grounded. He reminded me of Buddha sitting on the mountaintop — a vision of pure transcendence and enlightenment. I find this demeanor impressive in any life situation, but in an NBA coach, with all the stress and pressure, demands and chaos, that come with it, I found it mesmerizing. It made me curious. I often thought to myself, *How can I be more like that?*

It reminds me of that infamous scene in the classic romantic comedy *When Harry Met Sally,* when Meg Ryan's character fakes an orgasm in the middle of a crowded New York City restaurant, and a fellow patron says to her waiter, "I'll have what she's having."

I would watch Jackson and think just that: *I'll have what he's having.* But what *is* it?

In this spirit, I did what any good journalist would do:

I googled Phil Jackson. I discovered he is referred to as the "Zen master" because he integrates meditation, Buddhism, and other spiritual traditions into his coaching practice. I read about his use of mindfulness and integrating Zen practices into his training sessions, blending the physical, mental, and spiritual aspects of each player into one.

In his book *Sacred Hoops: Spiritual Lessons of a Hardwood Warrior*, Jackson wrote, "There's more to life than basketball — and more to basketball than basketball." He revealed the importance of directing his players to live in the moment and to stay calmly focused in the midst of chaos — something he demonstrates so effortlessly. This is what I refer to as having strong emotional muscles.

What I learned from Jackson is that the discipline of being able to return to our center gives us power. This is exactly what I experienced watching him coach; he was the most centered, grounded, present — and powerful — human being I had even seen.

This was the beginning of my study of meditation and mindfulness practices. I saw firsthand the impact it could have on performance and overall well-being. And I couldn't help but think that if he could ease the egos of legends like Michael Jordan (he coached the Chicago Bulls to NBA championships as well) and Kobe Bryant and could get players to see their oneness and work together as a team to make each other better, I wanted a piece of that. In the sports world, where it's all about the physical, I saw clearly that the winning edge wasn't about building stronger physical muscles; it was about developing strong attitudinal muscles — mental, emotional, spiritual.

Why Does Emotional Fitness Matter?

Were you ever doing perfectly well (even wonderfully!), only to have an upsetting interaction, phone call, or email that instantly "ruined" your day? I know I have. I recently received a phone call from my agent telling me that a client was refusing to pay me for a job I had already performed, making all kinds of excuses and trying to justify withholding payment.

I found myself getting irate — taking their unprofessionalism personally and feeling attacked, saying, "How dare they mess with my money?" While I had a valid reason to be upset, nothing is worth getting that worked up over.

It's one thing for someone to go back on a commitment. It is another to allow that person to steal our joy. I literally gave away my good mood for free, and there is no price tag we can put on our peace and happiness. It is invaluable.

I learned a huge lesson that day. I saw how little control I had over my well-being. I gave someone else the keys. I knew I never wanted to feel this way again. While none of us will go through life without experiencing hurts and frustrations, it's important to embrace the fact that we are responsible for our reactions to upsetting events. In other words, most of us need to bulk up our emotional muscles and emotional fitness. Here's how:

How to Build Strong Emotional Muscles

- **Give yourself emotional timeouts.** If you're a parent, you're familiar with giving your children a "time-out." Sometimes adults need a timeout, too. Rather than acting on emotional impulses and saying or doing something we will later regret, we can resist the temptation and see our reaction as an opportunity to grow and develop character.

There will always be opportunities to lose our temper and get upset, but when we feel our emotions rising, we can choose not to act on them and to stay calm instead. It's like going to the gym when you don't want to, just because you know how good you'll feel afterward.

- **Take the high road. Forgive.** When someone is rude to us and we don't engage, we pass the test. When we are willing to take responsibility even though it's hard, we grow up faster and build strong character that attracts abundance into our lives.

   We will always be tempted to overreact in the areas where we are the weakest. These situations shine a light on our own limitations. It is easy to love people who are loving, but the challenge is to love those who are not. They teach us how to love better and be stronger. Forgive them. They are building your character.

- **Don't get on board.** It's hard to overlook an insult, keep a positive attitude, and be patient when nothing seems to be going our way. We think if those rude people would just stop being rude, everything would be great. But when we allow ourselves to realize that a rude person or upsetting situation is perfect for us because it allows us to change for the better, we take back our power.

   It may not feel very pleasant to do one hundred burpees at the gym with your personal trainer, but think how strong your body will look and feel if you commit to exercising your physical muscles this way regularly. You know when you're sweating to death and out of breath during your workout and not really enjoying it that much, but afterward you feel great? The same applies to our emotional workouts, too.

So, the next time somebody does you wrong and you want to get upset, send an unloving text or email, scream at the top of your lungs, or completely shut down, try instead to take a deep breath and see it as an opportunity to heal an old wound and grow. With practice, you will begin to become less and less reactive and feel a greater sense of peace and freedom.

As I like to say, "When you see the anger train coming, don't get on board!"

Emotional Fitness for Mindful Eating and Stress Reduction

Improving our emotional fitness also combats the habit of regulating difficult feelings with food. Discovering how to overcome emotional eating is important to me because I love to eat and usually do so in a noisy, crowded New York City restaurant or at home in front of the television.

I'm also a recovering emotional eater known to put away five or more slices of pizza in one sitting, especially when triggered by an unsettling event or memory. My habits have been the opposite of "mindful eating," and I can easily consume a tidy amount of food without really noticing.

I've noticed I'm not alone in this. As we become busier and busier in a society bombarded with electronic devices and social media updates, it's no wonder many of us feel increasingly distracted. We rush through our meals so we can get back to work, our favorite TV show, or Instagram.

I had never heard of mindful eating until I went on a weeklong spiritual retreat at Kripalu in Stockbridge, Massachusetts. Kripalu Center for Yoga and Health implements a silent breakfast every morning, where guests are requested to stay quiet while eating. (That's right, no chatting with your friend or neighbor.)

At first I thought, *How am I going to do that?* I'm extremely outgoing and love getting to know people, and sharing a meal is a perfect time to socialize. What I found, however, is that practicing the art of silent breakfast is not only doable but completely enjoyable! The added health benefits could also make distraction-free silent eating a little more enticing.

MINDFUL EATING BENEFITS

- **Weight loss.** When I practice mindful eating, I consume about a third of what I normally eat. I enjoy my food more and notice instantly when I'm full. I stop eating rather than being distracted and stuffing myself. I find it is much easier to control the amount of food I am eating, and I feel more satisfied. Recent studies show that people who eat mindlessly (or while highly distracted) tend to overeat and consume more calories than they realize.
- **Peace of mind.** I find myself at ease and stress-free while eating in silence. It gives me the opportunity to deeply relax into my dining space and engage all my senses with each bite. The intention of eating in silence is to center you for a day of calm and peace — a day where you can be more clear, focused, creative, and cheerful.
- **Healthy digestion.** I also noticed something very profound: my stomach doesn't hurt after eating

mindfully, which is quite rare for me. I learned that
healthy digestion happens when meals are taken
while relaxed, in a calm environment, either alone
or with good company.

- **Proper nourishment.** Savor the moment. We are
conditioned to talk, swipe, text, and email on our
phones while eating (I know I am), but truly nourishing yourself is more than just what you eat. Nourishment is about sustenance — not just what you
feed your body but also how you fuel your soul. Nurture yourself during meals by being fully present and
truly enjoying your food — the textures, aromas,
and unique flavors.

SIMPLE WAYS TO PRACTICE MINDFUL EATING

- Relax the body and mind with a few deep breaths
before eating.
- Notice any sensations within the body.
- Think about all the energy that was expended from
people, plants, animals, and machinery in order to
get this food to your door.
- Send gratitude to everyone who prepared your food.
- Admire your food; notice all the shapes and colors.
- Breathe in all the wonderful aromas of the meal.
- Chew thoroughly, delighting in the depths of the
flavors.
- Take a pause in between bites.
- Relax for a few minutes before moving to your next
activity.
- Say "thank you" for the nourishment you received,
which will enable you to live your best day.

Mindful eating is a daily commitment and may take some practice. The keys are being aware and nonjudgmental and understanding what you're feeding yourself.

Begin to notice if you're physically hungry for food or hungry for something else, like love or comfort. When you aren't distracted, it's much easier to differentiate between the two, and when you are aware, you can make healthier choices.

A SIMPLE BREATHWORK EXERCISE TO RETURN TO JOY

If you're feeling out of alignment, allow yourself to feel this way completely. In other words, don't self-medicate with food, alcohol, shopping, mindless TV, or social media scrolling.

It is vital that we fully recognize our pain; otherwise, it will just resurface later with a vengeance. When we raise our vibration — we're more in tune, elevated, have higher energy — we raise the vibration of the world. And the world could certainly use our radiance right now!

Give yourself sufficient time to work through whatever negative emotions come up, then start the journey back to gratitude with a breathwork exercise.

I learned about the power of focusing on our breath in my meditation practice and Reiki master certification training. Not only is breathing a vital part of life, delivering oxygen into our bloodstream while removing carbon dioxide, but focusing on our breath forces us to slow down and, in turn, breathe more deeply.

Try this quick breathwork exercise to connect to your power — your truth and spirit.

1. Find a comfortable place to sit. Welcome your journey into the present. Tell your muscles to let go and relax. Close your eyes and place your hands on your heart. Breathe slowly and deeply into your heart. Let your breath carry you deeper into yourself. The more relaxed you become the more powerful your experience will be. Focus on the strength and beauty of your breath and your heart. Feel appreciation.

2. Now, think of the situation that is causing you pain, suffering, frustration, or grief — something you wish to change. Be specific. Whatever just came up for you is perfect.

3. Keep breathing into your heart. Feel it become full and heavy and ripe with love. Allow its light to shine out into the world. As the light shines from your heart in every direction, listen carefully to it. What guidance is it giving you? If you're having difficulty tuning in, shift into observation mode and simply notice what images, messages, textures, or colors are making their way to you.

4. With your mind relaxed and eyes still closed, breathe deeper into your heart and ask it to connect to the power of your spirit. Allow each cleansing breath to center you into your inner wisdom, relaxing you to your core. You are now deep in your spirit. Keep breathing while you allow the truth to sink into all parts of your being.

5. Fill in the blanks for the phrases below. Take as long as you need. There are no right or wrong answers. The important thing is to simply let yourself feel and be open to the truth pouring from your spirit.

In this moment, the truth is _____.
I trust that _____.
I'm free from _____.
I'm ready for _____.
All I need to do is _____.

Our Heart Always Knows the Answer

Many of us spend our lives overstimulated and exhausted, just trying to keep up. We forget to return to our breath, slow down, and listen to our inner knowledge. Our spirit always knows the answer. We just have to give it the time and space to speak our truth to us.

I find the breathwork exercise to be a quick and powerful way to ground myself and acknowledge why I feel out of sorts. It's free, relaxing, quick, and can be done again and again. I also love this exercise because it builds strong attitudinal musculature. It's a great reminder that we are 100 percent responsible for our life experiences. What an empowered place to live from!

Certainly, setbacks and disappointments, trauma and tragedy can and will still arise, but we don't have to stay stuck in a low-vibe state of despair. Our hearts and minds and emotional muscles want to work together to bring us a fulfilling, meaningful life that lights us up.

Spiritual Practices to Center and Ground Ourselves

Learning how to center and ground ourselves spiritually means that we are building the inner musculature to be able to withstand any storm. Think of this as your core foundation, which you choose to build on solid rock rather than sand. When we center ourselves in this way, we become stronger, more present, aware, and balanced. Life flows more naturally without force or strain. We experience our minds as clear rather than cluttered, and our spirit feels free and certain rather than restricted and confused. Here are some practices to get to that elevated state.

Reframe What It Means to "Let It Go"

When we're feeling out of sorts and confide in a trusted friend or family member about something that's bothering us, they'll often try to help by advising us to just "let it go." But it's not that easy. *Yes, great, I would love that,* we may think, *but how exactly do I do that?*

We usually know when we need to "let it go," but what if we aren't quite ready or we are really stinking mad and need to sit with those feelings for a minute? Sometimes someone suggesting we just "let it go" seems a little harsh and angers us even more.

Being human means people will annoy and upset us, circumstances and situations will disappoint us, and we will be left feeling powerless at times. But we don't have to stay stuck. We can lean back into a more elevated, empowered state. We can feel calm and tranquil. We can trust we are on the right path and everything is happening for the greatest good for all.

When something upsets me, instead of telling myself to let it go, I now say, *Please take this from me.* This phrase means surrendering our stress, frustration, disappointment, or whatever is troubling us to the God of our own understanding. This may look something like, *Wow, I am really judging this person; please take this from me.* Or, *I am freaking out about whether I am going to get this job/relationship/money; please take this from me.*

Acknowledging the presence of a higher power reminds us that we are never alone and are always being guided and protected. When we are fearful, we have forgotten this and are relying on our strength alone. Let the universe assist you. It's a simple way to take back *your* power.

Working as a freelancer, I often live in limbo. I'm constantly between jobs and vying for big projects. I used to be in a constant state of fear, desperately trying to control outcomes. Stress and anxiety led the way. This is what I call a low vibration. It didn't feel good at all because I was giving all my power away.

When I find myself getting caught up in why I didn't get the job, why so-and-so didn't call me back or support me, how I am going to pay off my credit card, lose the weight, or find a worthy life partner or even a parking spot in New York City, I stop, take a step back, and ask the universe to lead the way and work out all the details.

"Let it go" has new meaning to me. It isn't about trying to pretend something doesn't bother us. It isn't about trying to control someone with our behavior. It isn't fear or not caring. It is doing nothing and everything all at once: surrendering.

Acknowledge Your Resistance and Attachments

Some time ago, I received feedback from a potential client that initially felt disappointing. My knee-jerk reaction was, *I don't want to do it that way. I shouldn't have to jump through these hoops.* When I stepped back from the experience and realized how resistant I was to this expert's feedback, I felt a big shift. I was then able to interpret the feedback as a valuable gift — information that could be used to my advantage to make me a more attractive candidate, not just to this client but to all clients. It also motivated me to take inspired action and create a series of online courses designed to help others create more fulfilling and purpose-driven lives.

I also recognized that I was resisting the spiritual principle listed above and trusting solely in myself, instead of allowing a higher power to guide me. I needed to trust that this "rejection" was actually a good thing, leading me to an even better opportunity.

Having a forward-facing career certainly means experiencing more than the average share of rejection, and through these challenges I've learned that the "road closures" of our lives are not by accident. The failure, the rejection, the loss of a job are all big detour signs with flashing lights saying, "Stop! You're going the wrong way! Turn around!"

Sometimes we are forced down a new road. We may not know exactly where we are going at first. We resist the unfamiliar terrain. But we must face the fact that we can't drive on autopilot. We have to wake up and pay attention to what's going on around us and *within* us to stay safe.

Fortunately, the newly paved road will feel significantly smoother. You will discover new opportunities, beauty, and adventure, and if you listen to your internal GPS, you will rediscover... *you!*

So buckle up and drive safely, my friend. Take the scenic route that leads you away from who you *aren't,* so you can embrace who you really *are.* And remember, nothing is ever really taken away from us. It's simply the universe forcing you to see its lack of value, for you, at this time.

Oftentimes we are so attached to wanting to work with a particular client or be in a relationship with a certain person that we cause ourselves unnecessary pain. As Buddha said, "All suffering comes from attachment."

A big step in "letting it go" is becoming detached rather than grasping onto a person, job, or situation that we think will make us happy. When we become aware we are behaving this way, we can adjust our thoughts and release expectations. We are all going to fall off the path — that's a given — but what matters is how quickly we come back to center. Let yourself off the hook.

Choose Stillness

Our willingness to see things differently is everything. When we are willing to choose love instead of fear, peace instead of chaos, and stillness and nonreactivity instead of anger and attack, we will create the space to become more deeply fulfilled people.

When we are triggered, it can be very painful, but it is also a beautiful opportunity to expand and grow into more enlightened people. We do this by disciplining our minds and choosing stillness, peace, love, forgiveness, and compassion even when we feel tempted to judge, blame, criticize, attack, or feel unworthy.

Sometimes that means admitting to ourselves that we are not enlightened enough to not feel angry or insulted, but we are enlightened enough to know not to send that text or email or make a phone call when we are in that place.

I ask the God of my own understanding, "How would you have me serve today?" As a *Course in Miracles* student, I take it a step further and ask for specifics:

"Where would you have me go?"

"What would you have me do?"

"What would you have me say and to whom?"

I ask that His will be done. I trust. I surrender my career and personal goals and struggles to Him and ask that it all be used as an instrument of peace. I pray that my fearful perceptions be healed and transformed into more loving ones.

The sooner we can acknowledge that life isn't all about us, and we don't have to go it alone, the better. We can choose to surrender our thoughts and fears about money, career, family, love, children — you name it — to a power greater than us.

It's taken me years, but I've learned to see feelings as less threatening and more like temporary breezes or storms. As long as we don't contract and fear our feelings, we stay emotionally flexible so that the storms can pass by quickly.

Whenever we hold on to feelings like anger, judgment, or resentment, we block blessings from flowing to us. So even if you're not fully ready to surrender your annoyance, for example, try to remember you're closing yourself off to receiving miracles from the universe, and commit to shifting your perspective. A quick way to do this is to think of someone experiencing a true setback like a cancer diagnosis, the loss of a loved one, or another tragedy.

Instead of wallowing in our wounds and triggers, why don't we think about the person we wish to be instead? What a perfect opportunity to decide who we want to be and not let outside sources dictate how we feel.

Being annoyed is a great opportunity to practice being the men and women we are capable of being. What a gift! It doesn't matter who or what annoys us, and it is inevitable we will all be irritated from time to time. What matters is who we choose to be in those frustrating moments. We can choose stillness and nonreactivity.

When we slow down and are still, it is easier to receive divine guidance. We realize the entire universe is set up for our good. So keep your eyes and your heart open. The person, money, opportunity, or experience you desire is on its way or probably standing right next to you. Let your annoyance open you up to new possibilities. I love this beautiful quote from *A Course in Miracles*: "In my defenselessness my safety lies."

In every moment, we get to choose who we want to be, and the best part is, we can always change our minds.

I invite you to reflect upon or journal about what you are willing to surrender today.

The Art of Doing Absolutely Nothing: Exercising Our Days Off

You know the drill: every January we are bombarded with messages like "Make it happen!" and "Grab the bull by the horns!" everywhere we turn. I don't know about you, but these messages don't inspire me to do anything but take a nap. It's like all those at-home video workouts I see on Instagram that make me want to do *anything* but work out.

My first thought is always that something is wrong with me for not wanting to achieve a new goal, get killer abs, or make anything "happen." Some days, I simply want to do nothing, and a part of me still judges myself for it. A practice I like to do is to go to my meditation pillow for some guidance, asking my higher self for some insight.

The first time I did this, the response I received was "Do nothing. You need to rest. Take a moment to reflect and honor yourself for everything you achieved just last year alone. No wonder you are exhausted."

As a type A, overachieving go-getter, the notion of doing nothing feels like death to the ego. Much of my life (like many other people's) has been defined by what I accomplish in the material world and by proving my worth to myself and others. I know I am not alone in feeling guilt and self-judgment for wanting to slow down and just be. But I decided to try something new: surrender to my inner wisdom and truth.

Now, anytime my work schedule is slow, I take it as a sign and signal to ask myself who I am without all my achievements and accomplishments in the outside world. Who am I without my career, looks, money, fancy clothes, car, and condo? What does it really mean to live a "good life"?

Not so long ago, if I had some time without work, I would go into panic mode about how my bills would get paid and why I wasn't booking more jobs. I finally decided I was tired of that way of thinking. It's exhausting and doesn't attract anything positive into my life. Instead of pushing, forcing, or trying to "make things happen," I'm consciously choosing to do less and let go of trying to control the situation.

As a suicide prevention awareness advocate, one of my core messages is "Never give up." But when it comes to trying to control and manipulate outcomes in our lives, I'm discovering that "giving up" is necessary. "Giving up" isn't throwing in the towel; it's an act of faith. It's a powerful devotion to a higher power.

Speaking of faith, I'm not talking about religion here. Everyone has faith. Let me say that again: *everyone has faith.* It's just that some people have faith that everything is going to work out, and others have faith that the whole world is against them. Either way, everyone has faith. Some people have conviction in their hate; others have conviction in their love. Some have faith in their greatness; others have faith in their unworthiness. You get the picture. And it's a choice we make daily.

Giving up or surrendering as an act of faith is a whole new way of problem-solving. It is a more grounding and peaceful approach to getting what we want more easily. It is the opposite of rushing around or forcing; it is about letting ourselves and our lives unfold more naturally, piece by piece, layer by layer.

It reminds me of nature. Nature does not struggle to express its beauty and glory. Flowers weren't created to struggle, and neither are we as human beings. That's just a lie we've been told in a "Be productive and make it happen!" society. But we don't have to subscribe to the struggle. That's why it was so important for each of us to sign the contract in the introduction to *unsubscribe* from the struggle!

It is easier to give up the struggle when we realize our lives are about so much more than what we achieve materially. What if we could begin to see ourselves and our lives with fresh eyes and focus more on our emotional journey home to our true selves?

My goals are no longer wrapped up in a dream job or relationship — both of which are still fantastic, of course, but nothing outside ourselves can give us lasting happiness. I've proven that theory dozens of times, and I'm sure you have, too. My new goals are radical self-acceptance, inner peace, and deep, fulfilling joy. Some days, that looks like doing hard work in the outside world, and other days, it means staying home in my pajamas taking care of my inner child, feeling my feelings, giving myself empathy, and conserving energy.

Society tells us how acceptable it is to work ourselves to exhaustion in the name of making "it" happen — a career, relationship, family, business — but not nearly enough time and attention is paid to our emotional journey (aka our emotional muscles).

I used to really berate myself for not feeling like doing anything for days. As it turns out, "not doing anything" is achieving something extraordinary — a beautiful, healthy, kind, and loving relationship with myself. When we learn to stop pushing and accept the perfection of what is, we can enjoy the perfect place we are in.

Sometimes, "giving up" as an act of faith is all we need.

Emotional Muscles on Drugs: There Is No Quick Fix

When I was twenty-nine years old, I went to see a new doctor for my yearly exam. At the time, I was working as a TV news reporter, covering disturbing, crime-filled stories. The long hours and the job itself were taxing physically and emotionally, leaving me so exhausted that I'd often cry as I drove home from work.

My new doctor immediately recognized me from the news. He also noted that I seemed on edge as I sat in his office that day. His comments on my demeanor made me feel like there was something wrong with me, like working long days interviewing grieving parents about the murders of their children shouldn't overwhelm me. "It is stressful," I said. "Isn't it appropriate I am stressed?"

But the doctor wanted to. "fix" my stress. When I con-
fessed that work had sometimes brought me to tears, he
urged me to try medication. "You're a strong, brilliant career woman. You can't be crying at work," I remember him
saying.

At the time, I was so desperate to feel "normal" that I let
this stranger convince me that I needed drugs to numb me
to my surroundings. I walked out of his office that day with a
prescription for Lexapro — a drug used to treat anxiety and
major depressive disorder. After a ten-minute consultation, I
became part of the statistics on the overmedication of Americans, and looking back on that is terrifying.

A recent study published in the *Journal of Clinical Psychiatry* reports that antidepressant use has skyrocketed over the
last two decades, up nearly 400 percent. Statistics show that
one in ten Americans now take such medication. Among
women in their forties and fifties, the figure is one in four.

Yet 69 percent of people taking the most common type
of antidepressants (selective serotonin reuptake inhibitors, or
SSRIs) have *never suffered from major depressive disorder* (MDD).
Even more shocking, 38 percent have not only never suffered
from MMD but also have never in their lifetime met the cri-
teria for another disorder, like obsessive-compulsive disorder,
panic disorder, social phobia, or generalized anxiety disorder. Yet still they take the pills that treat these conditions.

I stayed on Lexapro for several years — even after I left
the TV news business. I was changing careers, moving, and
breaking up with a serious boyfriend, and I thought that the
medication would take the edge off my life's uncertainties.

It wasn't until I attended a lecture by bestselling author
Marianne Williamson that I had my wake-up call. I listened

as Marianne talked about her latest book, *Tears to Triumph*, and about how moving "with the edge" is our life's work, spiritually speaking. The "edge" is made up of those sleepless nights, those cries, those uncomfortable conversations.

She told me that heartbreak is nothing new. Has anyone not had their heart broken? Has anyone not suffered a professional failure? Has anyone not experienced the loss of a loved one?

These things may be painful, but they are not mental illness. As I look back on that day in the doctor's office, I want to pull my twenty-nine-year-old self aside and hug her. I want to tell her, "You don't need an antidepressant; you need to find a new station to work for, a new boss, a new job, or even a new career. You need to sit in meditation twenty minutes a day, twice a day, reconnect with your spirit, and pray. You need to surrender your life to a higher power, eat healthier food, rest, and connect with your friends and family in a meaningful way."

After just a few months of weaning myself off Lexapro with the guidance of my doctor, I felt like myself again. I had a hundred times more energy. I was clear. I was joyful and alive. That lethargic, dark cloud that had followed me everywhere had lifted.

Since becoming more conscious and awake, I've discovered that our society seems to promote self-medicating and numbing ourselves out. I can't tell you how many times I've said and heard, "I need a drink." I've rarely heard, "Let's pray. Time to meditate. I need to feel my feelings so I can release this pain once and for all."

I am in no way saying that my story holds true for everyone. I'm not saying that anyone who has been diagnosed with a mental illness should give up their medications cold turkey, or at all. I'm simply suggesting that we all take a deeper look into our choices, do our research, ask our health-care providers and drug companies tough questions, and explore our options for treating anxiety and depression.

Feeling sad, out of sorts, anxious, or depressed at times is part of what it means to be human. My hope is that anyone who is considering taking antidepressants will at least also consider looking into other forms of relief. Your brain and heart will thank you.

Freedom from Fear

If you ask most people what they want from life, they will probably tell you they want to be happy — they want to be loved. Success, fame, and fortune might come up, too. But I think what we ultimately yearn for is freedom. The freedom to be ourselves, especially in a world that is constantly telling us not to. The freedom of inner peace and feeling at home and being able to take that feeling with us everywhere we go.

For me, the one thing that gets in the way of feeling free is fear. Fear keeps us small and stuck in self-limiting beliefs that don't serve us. As with most behaviors we want to change, the first step in overcoming fear is acknowledging it.

Tell Yourself the Truth

A big reason it is so difficult to release fear is we have to be brutally honest with ourselves. We have to get real and look deep within to discover how fear has been holding us back. The key is to confront our fears rather than ignoring them.

I invite you to reflect on what fears are coming up for you regularly:

- Is it the fear of being seen? The fear of being yourself? Being alone? Being judged? Not feeling like enough?
- Are you noticing that you're angry? Sad? Frustrated? Over it? Why?
- Or are you immensely happy? Reflect on ways to continue this feeling if that feels right.
- Do you ask yourself things like: Am I attractive enough? Smart enough? Am I lovable? Have I accomplished enough? Will I make enough money this year to live the kind of life I desire?

For years, I ruminated on these fear-based stories that I wasn't good enough. I constantly strove for something that doesn't exist — perfection — and it was making me physically sick. The stress and anxiety this story created in my life crippled me at times with meltdowns and panic attacks.

Remember, You Are Not Your Ego

Reflect on ways your ego, which is constructed out of fear-based thinking that is not based on the truth, is blocking your blessings and keeping you from living your truth — your best possible life as your best possible self.

My life shifted dramatically the moment I realized that my ego is just this silly, fear-based voice in my head that feeds off my insecurities and likes to keep me in a state of worry and disempowerment. What a jerk!

By identifying my ego for what it is (a jerk!), I am able to laugh at it and see the absurdity in my fearful thoughts, from *I'm not thin enough to date him* to *I'm too old to book this job.*

Saying these words out loud shows me just how ridiculous my fearful thoughts are. They serve no other purpose than to make me feel small and unworthy.

Witness Your Fear

Once you are able to get real with yourself about what scares you, write it down and say it out loud to yourself, a friend, a therapist, or a support group. I promise you, your fears will lose power over you.

It was extremely embarrassing to admit to myself — let alone say out loud to my therapist — that I believed that if I were a size 2, I would probably be married to my dream man right now. The instant I muttered this lie I wanted to vomit, but it was eye-opening (and heart opening) to hear myself say it out loud. Once I could really "see" this hidden fear, I could laugh at it because I knew it wasn't the truth. It's transformative to witness our lies by writing them down or saying them out loud with someone to witness it. It's hard to lie to ourselves out loud in a room full of people. That's why support groups are so powerful as well.

Laugh at Your Fear

By speaking my truth to a friend (and now all of you), I am able to laugh at it. The absurdity of my fear-based story is hilarious.

Your truth is your power. Your willingness to be honest with yourself and not take these fear-based thoughts so seriously will set you free down a much more pleasant path.

What fear-based story can you laugh at (and release) today?

Write a New Story

One of my favorite quotes is from author Mike Dooley: "Thoughts become things...choose the good ones."

The new story I've created for myself is "I am good enough and worthy of everything my heart desires and more."

And more: After a hypnotherapy session, a new mantra emerged for me that filled me with much joy, certainty, and confidence: "I am the sunshine."

When I think of sunshine, I think of the joy it brings to the world simply by being itself. The sun doesn't have to try to be cool, smart, funny, beautiful, or awesome — it just is. It simply gets to *be*. It gets to shine brightly and light up the world. The sun isn't trying to be the moon. The sun isn't worried about what the clouds think of it. The sun isn't jealous of a rainbow, and the sun isn't worried if it's bright enough or hot enough. When I live my life from the place of *I am the sunshine*, I let go of what others think, don't worry about being good enough, and simply rise up as my sunny self each day. It's liberating.

We can choose to see and create a new vision for ourselves rooted in serenity and love. How do we do this? By making the conscious choice to see ourselves in a new light. We can look in the mirror and choose to see strength and beauty or choose to see something unattractive. We can be the sun or a destructive storm.

Either way, there we are in the mirror. How do we want to see ourselves? Powerful or powerless? It is a choice, and our thoughts are extremely potent in creating our reality.

When I was in my thirties and a healthy size 12, I started working full-time as a model all over the world. If I chose to listen to society or anyone else's opinion or my own inner critic telling me I was too old, too big, too *something* to work as a model, I would never have had this exciting career, which allowed me to blossom in numerous ways.

You created a form of mantra for yourself during the breathwork exercise. What's another new story and mantra you can create for yourself? I find it helpful to have more than one!

Release Your Fears Rather Than Holding On to Them So Tightly

I do this through meditation — twice a day, every day. I know what you're thinking: *I don't have time to meditate! I don't know how to meditate,* That's what I used to think and say, until one day I had a panic attack and could barely breathe. That is why I include a meditation in each step that you can refer back to again and again.

I recommend not waiting until you become physically ill to make some simple changes to your life that will yield huge, positive benefits. Learning through pleasure feels much better than learning from pain. Remember to laugh!

Trust

Trust was a major theme in step 4, and it's a concept that we can never refer back to enough. It's that important! We live in uncertain times, and if you watch the news, I can see why you'd be extremely fearful. The truth is, there really is no place completely safe from fear, except within ourselves. Try to stay focused on what you can control: your thoughts. Connect to your inner wisdom and intuition, what many refer to as their gut reaction.

Your fear-based ego might say, *You have to take this job, you need the money, otherwise you won't be able to pay your bills, and you'll be out on the street.* Yikes, that feels icky.

Your intuition, higher self, gut, whatever you want to call it, knows you will be okay if you don't take this job that doesn't feel right to you. Your inner wisdom knows that something more suitable for you is just around the corner, and if you stay true to yourself and your values, you will get it. You don't need to settle.

As my mentor Marianne likes to say, "The Holy Spirit knows how much your rent is each month."

While I have struggled for years with overcoming fearful thoughts and battling anxiety, I've discovered that what scared me the most — not being good enough — has been my greatest opportunity for deep healing and personal growth.

When fearful thoughts come up now, I trust that I am on the right path, and I out my ego with a deep, hearty laugh.

How can you lean into trust this week?

JOURNALING EXERCISE
Flex Your Feelings

Think of a topic that is important to you right now that you view as a problem, challenge, or opportunity. Write it at the top of a page in your journal, and answer the following questions about it.

1. How do you feel about the situation?
2. What would it feel like to reach your goal?
3. When you tune in to your heart, what does it tell you?
4. What is standing in your way?

5. What pressure are you willing to let go of now?
6. What's the most courageous step you can take?
7. How ready are you to take this step?
8. On a scale of 1 to 10, how much do you want this change?
9. On a scale of 1 to 10, how willing are you to do the work?
10. What's one word to describe the transformation that would occur if you did this work and made the change?
11. What do you *really* want?

 ## SHED YOUR EMOTIONAL SKIN MEDITATION

You've done so much incredible work, and I honor your commitment to exercising your spiritual muscles so you can be fit, healthy, and strong on the inside. I hope you are starting to notice some results. Give yourself a big hug and high five for all your effort. I also hope you're having fun along the way. You might even consider teaming up with a spiritual workout buddy to help hold you accountable and keep you motivated. Of course, I'm always right there beside you in spirit, coaching and cheering you along! I believe in you!

I admire you for taking the time to create new core beliefs for yourself while strengthening your core confidence in turn. It's a strenuous but empowering practice worth its weight in gold! Take a break when you need to rest, but please don't give up! You're nearly halfway finished with the Full Spirit Workout.

It's now time to shed your emotional skin, releasing the outer layers and paving the way for the fresh, glowing, authentic person you are. (I'm a big skin-care junkie, so I love this visual. It reminds me of how good it feels to give yourself a facial at home or let an aesthetician steam, exfoliate, deeply hydrate, and polish your skin! Ahhhh!)

We are going to shed our emotional skin by reflecting deeply in meditation on the answers that emerged in the journaling exercise above.

As you find a comfortable seated position, quietly focus on your breath, gently breathing in through your nose and out through your mouth. Good. Continue this relaxed pattern of breathing throughout your meditation. Keep your eyes softly closed while you gently quiet your mind and relax your body. Affirm to yourself that the entire universe is set up for your good. Be aware and in awe of the blessings and miracles all around you, knowing that the person, situation, or experience you desire is on its way to you now. It could even be standing right next to you, and you just need to open yourself up to that possibility. Take a moment to see your heart, your mind, and your arms open wide to receive this blessing now. Imagine it coming to you in the form of a ball of golden light, ready to transform you and your entire world. Hold that ball of golden light in your hands now.

With that awareness, think about what you wrote for the last question above, "What do you really want?" Invite that truth to come forward now as you repeat it to yourself silently or out loud as many times as you need. Sense how this truth feels in your body. Place this feeling in your heart along with that ball of golden light as you continue to breathe slowly in and out. As you breathe out, allow this truth, and this light to release into the room and into the world, making it your ultimate truth and guide.

Now ask yourself what strengths you can leverage

to bring this desired feeling, situation, or outcome into existence. We will explore how to uncover and use our strengths in a deeper way in the next step. Right now, simply allow any divine guidance to pour through you, washing away any lingering fears or concerns. It is safe to use this wisdom for your highest good and in service of others. Take as much time as you need before gently opening your eyes and returning to the room.

 COACH KATE CHECK-IN

Not feeling up for a workout one day? I get it! We all need days off to rest, rejuvenate, restore, and reset. Find a cozy, comfortable place to relax, and recall moments when you felt strong, fit, energized, and kind to yourself after exercising. Reflect on those moments to inspire you to take baby steps toward getting in some stillness today, whether it's just five minutes spent sitting alone reflecting on your state of being or a whole day to refresh and honor your spirit. I see you! I'm so proud of you! You're doing a great job!

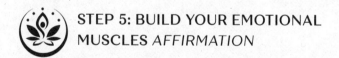 STEP 5: BUILD YOUR EMOTIONAL MUSCLES *AFFIRMATION*

The truth is, I am safe, and all I need to do is trust and focus on doing my best. I have the emotional flexibility to withstand any life stretch. I surrender any stress, fear, or worry and let the universe work out all the details while I relax and stay at peace. My heart, mind, and emotional muscles are working together seamlessly to bring me a fulfilling, joyful life that lights me up! And so it is!

STEP 6

Boost Your
Mental Metabolism

*Watch your thoughts, they become your words; watch your words,
they become your actions; watch your actions, they become your
habits; watch your habits, they become your character;
watch your character, it becomes your destiny.*

— LAO TZU

"Keep the hammer down!"

I was in the seventh grade, splashing up and down the
lanes of a Cincinnati swimming pool. The voice was that of
swim coach extraordinaire Larry Lyons. That year, I'd begun
training alongside high school kids on a nationally ranked
swim team (a big step up in my swimming career).

What did he mean? "Keep the hammer down" means
don't let up, keep working with that same intensity or push
even harder — challenge yourself! If it sounds intense, it is.
And training with Larry was definitely challenging; he was a
top-notch swim coach.

But what I liked most about swimming for Larry was the

life lessons he taught us, oftentimes in the middle of practice. He would stop us between sets and give these inspira-
tional talks from the side of the pool as we all stood quietly
in our lanes listening. Sometimes he would make us laugh,
like when he said there are thoroughbreds and plow horses,
and thoroughbreds who trained like thoroughbreds would
always be the champions. But a plow horse who trained like
a thoroughbred would beat the thoroughbred who trained
like a plow horse. The wisdom hit home: natural talent matters, and you can't control what you're born with, but you
can control how hard you work, and that "thoroughbred"
mentality can make you a champion. This kind of wisdom
urged us to avoid focusing on how much natural talent we
had (or our competitor had) and instead concentrate on
maximizing our own strengths.

Even at a young age, Larry helped us see that swimming
was about a lot more than just swimming. This is true of anything we want to excel at and give our all to. Picture an ice-
berg. All we see is the tip of it, but it's so massive underneath
the surface. For me, that mass underneath the surface is our
mind and our spirit. There's no denying how powerful they
are and how much they affect what we actually see — the
physical.

Larry was like a father figure to all of us. He made sure
that we were well equipped to excel not just in swimming
but in life. Ultimately, he instilled in me the drive to embody
what I call a "spirit of excellence" — and this is what I consider to be the winning edge in life.

Swimming (and Larry) set me up for life in terms of
work ethic, dedication, and discipline. Every competitive
athlete knows the importance of discipline. We need to

discipline not only our bodies but also our minds and spirits. All that getting up at 4 a.m. to dive into a cold pool, swim for two hours, go to school all day, and then return to the pool to swim for another two and a half hours? Not to mention all those push-ups, pull-ups, sit-ups, and medicine ball exercises before practice! *Phew!* To this day, nothing has ever been more challenging than seventeen years of competitive swimming. Even my rigorous, intensive master's programs at Northwestern University and Columbia University, which required the very best of me mentally, couldn't compete with the mental and physical demands of competitive swimming, and I'm thankful for that.

The benefits to my physical metabolism of athletic training were wonderful, but the benefits to my *mental metabolism* have been the most lasting gift.

Physical metabolism is how our bodies convert what we eat and drink into energy. Our mental metabolism is how we convert thought patterns into energy. If our thoughts are constantly negative and we are blindly leading with bad habits, we're squandering our precious energy. On the other hand, if we recognize our strengths, lead with those, and work to build good habits and positive mindsets, we boost our positive energy. That's why it's imperative we examine our thought habits and mental metabolism every day.

How can we improve our mental metabolism? The key is identifying, leveraging, and building on our strengths. This is a key part of spiritual fitness.

Lead with Your Signature Strengths

A lesson that has stuck with me through the years is the importance of being on time. Larry had a military background and was, well, militant about punctuality. Practice began at 2:30 p.m. sharp. *Sharp.* So if you rolled in at 2:32 p.m. and the team was 200 yards into a 300-yard warm-up, Larry would say, "Hurry up and catch up!" It makes me laugh to type this because I can hear him saying it now, but these are five words you never wanted to hear! *Hurry up and catch up* meant you had to practically sprint warm-up to make up how many laps behind you were due to your tardiness. You'd be awkwardly doing flip-turns on top of your teammates and setting yourself up to be exhausted long before getting to the main set. Quite simply put: it was awful.

Hurry up and catch up ingrained in me that to compete with the best, to be a leader and show respect for yourself and others, you must be *on time!* Larry didn't care if you got caught in traffic, couldn't find your goggles, or your carpool ride was late to pick you up. Practice began at 2:30 p.m. with or without you. Being late had consequences. And in a sport where you can lose a gold medal by one one-hundredth of a second, I'd say being two minutes late is in fact a huge deal!

I knew I had chosen the right executive coaching master's program at Columbia because the head of the program, Terry Maltbia, ran the program the exact same way. We started promptly on time and ended each session exactly on time, and it set the tone for excellence and the most effective learning environment. I believe that my punctuality demonstrates the high level of respect I have for myself and my time, as well as for others and their time, and I believe respect is a fundamental principle of excellence. Like all strengths, punctuality is a mindset and way of being. It is a learned behavior and can be easily improved upon, provided we are willing to improve!

So why am I talking about punctuality in a step on mental metabolism? Well, for me, being on time is one of my signature strengths and virtues. A "signature strength" means a strength that is dominant in your personality and is expressed authentically. Identifying your own signature strengths and learning to lead with those puts you in a much more powerful place to engage from — even when your goal is to work on improving one of your areas of weakness. So spotting and respecting your signature strengths is absolutely key to boosting your mental metabolism.

Because we are gorgeously flawed humans, it's inevitable that we are going to feel insecure either consciously or subconsciously from time to time. It's part of what it means to live an awakened life. We combat this by identifying and building on our strengths. I've seen firsthand the transformation that occurs within organizations when leaders focus on their strengths and the strengths of their team members. I spend a lot of time helping individuals identify and leverage their strengths rather than fretting over their real or perceived weaknesses and limitations. Let me show you how.

Identify Your Strengths

Some of our strengths are easy to identify, but others can be harder to recognize.

Reflection is key to recognizing your own strengths, but there's also a great online tool that can help you identify your strengths: the VIA (Values in Action) Signature Strengths Finder from the Institute on Character. You can take the free assessment here: www.viacharacter.org. This survey will ask you a series of questions and then rank your character strengths out of a list of twenty-four traits. The idea is to show us who we are at our best and help us bring our character strengths to life in order to live more fully.

If you're struggling to identify your strengths, ask other people what they think you do well. (Tip: tell them what you think they do well to give them an example and help build their confidence in the process.)

Another great way to reflect on your signature strengths is to ask yourself what energizes you. I asked a client of mine this question, and he said his work energizes him. "*What about your work?*" I asked.

He said, "I like helping people reach their full potential."

"How do you help people do that?" I probed.

His reply: "By creating the space and asking the questions that allow them to feel safe enough to tell the truth."

Truth-telling emerged as a signature strength for this client, and we explored ways in which he could leverage truth-telling to help draw the truth out of his clients, so they could tell powerful and impactful stories as keynote speakers and inspire audiences to share their truths as well.

You Are Unique, but It May Be Up to You to Recognize It

I remember going to a TV-host audition in Los Angeles in my early twenties and listening in dismay as the casting director told a room full of young women who looked similar to me, "Right now I could call every agent in town, and in an hour hundreds of women who look and sound just like you could show up here."

Yikes! I guess his point was to let us know we aren't that special, that we're very replaceable? That we're essentially blow-up dolls or talking hairdos to him? That's a conversation for another book, but do you think I wanted to do my best for this guy? Do you think I was inspired to embody my signature strengths?

No. I instantly felt insecure and judged, questioning why I would even want this part. Yet I still wanted him to pick me (a sign of needing acceptance to validate our self-worth), and I acted from a place of desperation. I didn't have the spiritual fitness back then that I've now been working for years to build. If I were faced with a similar situation today, knowing for certain that I would never want to work for someone like that, I would immediately conclude that I was not a fit, leave the casting, and tell my agent, "No, thank you, next!" (my own little spin on Ariana Grande's hit song, "Thank U, Next").

This incident, however, like many icky incidents, contains authentic wisdom, and it offered me the opportunity to reflect more deeply about what makes me uniquely *me*. If so many women look and sound "just like me," how can I differentiate myself? And even if we're not at a silly on-camera casting, which is so much about the externals, at some point in our lives we are going to be up against people who share our same level of education, experience, talent, or whatever. What will help us stand out? How can we be more uniquely ourselves? I call these primary signature strengths our "heart talent," "spirit strength," or "special sauce." (Hint: it always comes from within.)

When I was a junior at Penn State University, my swim coach spoke about my "infectious enthusiasm" in the athletic media guide. I had never heard that phrase before, and I loved it. It resonated with me. It was much more meaningful and poetic than "Kate was an Ohio high school state champion" or "Kate has beautiful stroke technique and is a strong kicker."

Infectious enthusiasm felt unique to *me*. It's about my character and who I am at my core. I could list one hundred ways I exercised that signature strength not just for the betterment of myself but for the betterment of my team. I genuinely cared about my teammates both in and out of the pool. I pushed them to practice harder and consistently cheered them on. I would entertain them by singing and acting out a terrible rendition of "Hopelessly Devoted to You" and other songs from the *Grease* soundtrack on the team bus or on the side of the pool after practice. I exercised my signature strengths of humor and being quirky and playful to lift the mood and build camaraderie, and my coach saw that.

In college, I was never the fastest swimmer on the team, but I always brought the best energy to practice and meets. When I think about my career and relationships, this same energy or infectious enthusiasm is my special sauce.

When Doris Dalton, the creator and owner of Doll 10 Beauty, hired me to be her international spokesperson, she said, "You can teach anyone how to be a product expert, but you can't teach personality. You have personality. You have that special sparkle. I would buy anything from you."

When you recognize and honor your signature strengths, you can let the other things go, whether it's not being the fastest swimmer on the team or not being an extrovert like I am. Your strengths are what make you special, and learning to build on them through mental metabolism workouts will help *you* shine.

Exercise Your Strengths

Once we identify our unique character strengths, the challenge then is to use them in new ways. For instance, if your strength is kindness and you're great at extending that kindness to others, perhaps the challenge is to extend that kindness inward — to be more empathetic to yourself, doing more small favors for yourself on a regular basis. It could also be that while you find it easy to be kind to people who are acting kindly, your challenge is to keep your cool and still extend kindness to people who are not.

Regardless of what your signature strengths are, there are several tried-and-true methods to boost your mental metabolism by exercising your strength muscles regularly, with intention.

Reframe

Let's explore an extraordinarily effective way to give up habitual negative thinking or negative self-talk, through a powerful tool known as reframing. When we reframe a situation, we can quickly jump into a much more empowering mindset. This helps boost our mental metabolism so that our energy level rises in jubilation, self-assurance, and motivation.

If you have friends who help you become better, more evolved versions of yourself, consider yourself fortunate. While opening up to my friend Natasha, I told her how my obsession with perfectionism was getting in my way, making me feel less productive, overwhelmed, and stressed-out. It was sucking the joy out of things I enjoy doing. I had placed this label of perfectionist on myself and was embodying the negative qualities derived from the meaning of that word.

Natasha said, "You want to do well and strive for perfection because you care. That's a good thing. What if you could release this label (and limitation) of referring to yourself as a perfectionist and embrace the fact that you have a great respect for mastery?"

Respect for mastery. What an incredible reframe! I remember shifting my perspective completely the moment Natasha uttered these three powerful words. I felt a major burden lift as I traded in my perfectionist label and all its negative connotations for my new and improved "respect for mastery" framework and the empowering meaning I took from that terminology. It's incredible how different we can feel simply by referring to ourselves using different language. For me, *perfectionist* creates heavy, negative, binding, constrictive feelings. *Respect for mastery* feels energizing, uplifting, strong, capable.

When we can shed a limiting label, belief, or habit and strengthen ourselves by adopting a new and improved perspective, our sense of well-being can shift dramatically, that quickly. This is a high mental metabolism, and what's awesome is that we aren't at the mercy of our genetics to have access to this. We can speed up our mental metabolism and access our power with two simple words: "What if?"

Let's say you feel stuck in some area of your life and find yourself saying, "This is so hard." The statement "This is hard" feels disempowering, right? What if (see what I did there?) you instead asked yourself, *What if this could be easy, fun, even pleasurable? What if I asked for help? What if I stopped trying to figure it all out by myself? What if this were an opportunity to grow? What if I could learn something new that could help me become more skilled and valuable in my job or relationship? What if this were actually a blessing? What if I could really have everything I desire? What if I could feel relaxed instead? What if this were actually true? What if...?*

Do you see how much more empowering and freeing that feels? Asking ourselves *What if...?* changes our consciousness. I love how quickly it works and how we can access this empowered state anytime, anywhere, in our minds silently, out loud, or in our journals. You can take it a step further and explore what your life would be like if all your "What if?" statements were the truth. (Hint: this *can* be your truth.) This conscious connection to your truth, which you can activate at any time, is what I refer to as connecting to our "full spirit." Our full spirit is our truth, our light, our power, our connection to self and others, and the epicenter of love. I invite you to set aside time each day to boost your mental metabolism by sitting in the silence and sacredness of your full spirit.

Of course, "emotional gravity," like fear and self-doubt, will inevitably creep up from time to time; that's why we have to keep working out our spiritual muscles. Reframing a problem or challenge into an opportunity or solution is one of my all-time favorite ways to boost my mental metabolism! Have fun and get creative with reframing and asking yourself, *What if...?*

Design Your Day

Sticking to a routine and setting ourselves up for success creates an environment that makes it easier to exercise our strengths rather than fall back into areas where we are weaker. And remember: leveraging our strengths is what boosting our mental metabolism is all about — it's how we develop positive thought patterns that can convert into energy (and replace negative thought patterns that sap our energy).

Every day I write, I set the mood for myself in order to bring about clarity and calm, deep focus, and a little fun. I make my espresso and breakfast, take my vitamins, make myself a green drink (I'm better at drinking vegetables than eating them), light my lovely, scented candles, turn off my phone, meditate, get out my pink llama notebook, and have endless sparkling waters on hand.

This routine ensures I have the best chance of doing my best work and doing it with pleasure rather than frustration. I am in the flow rather than trying to force anything. Regardless of what is going on in the world, I feel safe and secure in my morning espresso routine. It is one thing I can always count on to start my day out right.

For someone else, setting positive routines that emphasize their strengths might involve planning to take a certain bus to work each day so they can exercise their strengths of teamwork and interacting with others and sidestep their punctuality weakness; selecting a distraction-free workspace so they can exercise their strength of creativity; adapting their work schedule so they can capitalize on their strength of morning energy; and so on.

Keep a "Most Improved" Mindset

For swim team, there would always be a banquet at the end of each season, where coaches would give out trophies in each age group for things like "Most Valuable" and "Most Improved" swimmer.

Of course, I always wanted MVP, which was all about how many points you scored, how many records you broke, and so forth — basically, how fast you could swim. I think being a good teammate also played a factor, but ultimately it went to the most decorated performer.

Now, though, I see more clearly how much value is in the "Most Improved" award. I've learned that when we focus on how much we are learning and how much progress we are making, rather than on performance alone, we feel so much better. Stress and anxiety are replaced by grace and gratitude.

It feels so rewarding to learn and grow, whereas the thrill of "winning" is so fleeting. We are almost always on to the next meet, performance, task, or challenge so quickly that we barely even celebrate any of our wins. And even if we win, there's the nagging ego that still criticizes, *You could have done better* or *How did you miss that shot?*

When we place our energy and attention on our progress and honor the fact that we showed up, had fun, and tried our best, it feels much more fulfilling. We are much more present to life and appreciative of our efforts.

One of my favorite ways to exercise my "Most Improved" mindset is a trick I learned from one of my best friends, Justin Clynes. He's an accomplished photographer and model and has shot so many of my favorite portfolio images over the years. He was instrumental in helping me book and keep solid clients over the course of my modeling career, and he told me something early on that I will never forget: "Don't point out your flaws!" I was so used to doing this from years of castings when we were told what was "wrong" with us. But Justin would remind me time and time again to turn my focus around. Rather than praying the client would like and hire me, he said, I should believe, "The client is lucky to have *me*."

In addition to being an awesome reframe, this tip also supported me to approach new opportunities with a "Most Improved" mentality of willingness to show up and do my best. Having conscious awareness around *this* truth gave me renewed energy to shine my strengths. Think of boosting your mental metabolism like putting on your most comfortable pair of pj's. Simply put: you feel comforted, cozy, real — you feel like *you*!

Take 100 Percent Responsibility

I'll keep this simple because it is that simple. Not easy, but simple — much like the truth. It's vital that we take full responsibility for our lives because then we can do something about them. We can only change what we are first willing to accept and take ownership of. Which is why a lot of people talk about doing great things or having quality relationships but oftentimes don't reach their goals: they aren't willing to take responsibility for behaviors that need to be cleaned up or own how much work it will take to get there.

Don't Argue with Reality

I absolutely love this quote by author Byron Katie: "I am a lover of what is, not because I am a spiritual person, but because it hurts when I argue with reality. No thinking in the world can change it. What is is. Everything I need is already here now. How do I know I don't need what I think I need? I don't have it. So everything I need is always supplied."

That is one of the most powerful things I've ever read, because I think we spend at least half our lives arguing with reality and wanting people and situations to be different than they are. Her words give me so much freedom and really help bulk up my strength muscles.

We may wish to have the strengths of our colleague, competitor, neighbor, or celebrity idol. But the strengths *we* have are our reality. Don't argue with it; rock it!

Another tip? Notice someone's behavior rather than react to it. As my friend Deb says, "Observe, don't absorb."

Know It Isn't about You

Many years ago, I had a heart-to-heart conversation with an ex-boyfriend who I felt had blown me off. We would get really close, and then he would push me away. I always thought his rejection meant I wasn't good enough for him, but he communicated to me that *he* didn't feel worthy of me and my love. He said he always feared I would leave him, so he "rejected" me first in order to protect himself.

I was blown away! Not only did I appreciate his honesty, but all these years I'd carried around the belief of not being "good enough" only to discover he felt the exact same way.

I think this is often the case in relationships when two imperfect people come together with unresolved childhood wounds and don't speak candidly about their true feelings — oftentimes because it is too painful or difficult to even admit to ourselves, let alone others.

It is more difficult to see at the time, but with practice, I am able to look back at jobs I didn't get and men who never called again and see how perfect it all has been — because much more appropriate opportunities, experiences, and people have come into my life as a result.

When I hear "no" now, I get excited because I know a much more suitable "yes!" is right around the corner.

I no longer subscribe to the notion that an opportunity was unfairly taken away from me or is being withheld. I choose to believe that potential heartaches and roadblocks are being removed from my path when I avoid a wrong situation.

My life has shifted dramatically since I stopped taking rejection personally. I've given up the constant obsession of "What did I do wrong?" The truth is, there is nothing wrong with us. Sometimes someone or something is simply not a good fit, that's all.

I've decided it isn't my job to analyze why I was rejected, but it is my responsibility to remind myself of my inherent worthiness. To recognize and lead with my strengths.

Empower Others

"Choose to see what's right about people. A whole shift happens when we treat people this way."

My friend Heidi Guest said this to me when I asked her how she's managed to be such a strong, effective (and kind) leader in the beauty industry for decades. She emphasized the importance of empowering the people who work for and with you. She said, "Give people a standard to live in to, not a standard to live up to."

Or as I like to say, "Let people be who they were not yesterday." In other words, give people the space and freedom to want to show up as the best version of themselves. This empowers you, and it empowers them, too. Talk about a mental metabolism supercharge!

A lovely example of this is when I met and worked with QVC program host Jane Treacy. Jane is my kind of woman: genuine, kind, outgoing, personable, friendly, authentic, and empowered. She does my absolute favorite thing effortlessly and with ease — she compliments other women!

This may not sound like a big deal, but it is, especially in my line of work. I can't even say Jane went out of her way to make me feel comfortable and at home, because that's just who she is. It's a refreshing quality in a world where words like "threatened," "jealous," "catty," "competition," and "bitchy" are frequently used to describe female interactions. When I worked as a TV news reporter, I had a news director who would pit women against each other, creating a hostile work environment of backstabbing and fear-based sabotage. Gross!

Empowered people, on the other hand, support one another. They know there is plenty to go around, and one person's beauty and success do not dampen another's. In fact, when working together, you actually make each other better and more powerful.

When you shine brightly, you allow others to shine brightly, too.

We are each unique and gifted in our own special way, which means competition is an illusion. If you feel jealousy toward another person, just know the light you see in them is also in you; otherwise, you wouldn't see it. And remember, on a spiritual level, jealousy blocks blessings. If you feel threatened by a quality or characteristic you don't think you possess, be grateful and honor that person for showing you what you are capable of becoming or achieving as well.

Women are natural nurturers, designed to love and support others. Lifting other women up and helping them discover their greatest potential creates endless possibilities for personal and professional growth, connection, and community.

Working with Jane Treacy on QVC felt magical. We sold

a ton of product together, but more importantly, we sold the power of authenticity, stepping into your power, genuinely loving and supporting one another, and having fun. There is no room for envy, competition, anger, or insecurities when you give yourself and others permission to be themselves.

When you celebrate another's success, it automatically brings you more success. That's the law of attraction, which is always at work, whether we believe it or not. Keep this in mind the next time you are feeling threatened or jealous. It's a quick way to turn your mood around and attract more goodness into your life instantly.

Take Yourself on a Strengths Date

My love-of-learning strength takes me out of the country a lot because I love to travel, explore, and learn about different cultures. I think we can learn so much from people who are different than us. Living in New York City, I can take myself to different parts of town and experience various cultures, and I absolutely take advantage of that, but I feel especially stretched and strengthened when I take myself to foreign lands. I almost always travel the world solo in what I call an extended "strengths date." I invite you to come up with a creative way to exercise your strengths and "date yourself" for an afternoon or evening — or a whole trip. It's an opportunity of a lifetime to truly get to know ourselves.

An Example: One of My Favorite Reframes

Earlier in this step, I talked about some useful reframes I learned earlier in life. I'd like to take a moment now to look at another example, which I learned much later on.

There was a time when I tried every fad diet and trendy

workout New York City had to offer. I counted calories strictly, obsessed about everything I ate, juice-cleansed, cycled, and did hours of Pilates, personal training, sweaty dance classes, you name it. None of that helped me lose weight. I've discovered why: I wasn't listening to my body.

Learning to honor and listen to our bodies with respect and appreciation is an incredibly important reframe for many people, including those who worry their bodies are unattractive (overweight, underweight, or whatever!), those who push their bodies to tackle physical challenges, those living with physical limitations or illnesses, and those struggling against the ways their bodies change as they grow older. Developing a new attitude in which we're thankful to our bodies for all they do for us — their strengths — is such an empowering reframe for people in any of these or similar situations.

So, back to my story: I wasn't being loving and nurturing. I was being harsh, critical, and extremely judgmental. *Why can't you do anymore jump squats?* (I had just done 120 reps, maybe that was why!) *Why aren't you losing weight? Why do your knees hurt when you run? Why are you so tired? Ugh, what's wrong with you?*

Wow! With that sort of self-talk, I'm amazed my body did anything for me! No wonder I wasn't feeling like my best self, physically or otherwise.

Listening to my body was the opposite of what I was doing. When my body told me, *Hey, I'm exhausted,* I ignored it and pounded away at the gym anyway. When I wasn't hungry for food but really yearned for love and needed to do something nice for myself — like sleep, take a bubble bath, read a good book, or have lunch with a nurturing friend — I ordered pizza instead (and ate the entire pie by myself, sending shame through my entire being). When my body was craving physical activity, I lay on the couch.

Our bodies are constantly sending signals. The problem is, many of us aren't listening to our greatest ally. Our minds, picking up on many self-limiting messages and images from the media, think they know best. The key is to have our minds and bodies in sync with one another. Our bodies need to talk to us, and we need to hear them.

All the things you can do to find inner happiness require the body; the mind isn't living in a separate house. I could never fully commit to the best regime of diet, exercise, stress reduction, and meditation until I got my body on board and comfortable with it. That meant loving, honoring, and respecting my body for all it does for me rather than criticizing it for not being superhuman. It is vital to work with your body and not against it.

Turning away from our demands or criticisms of our bodies and instead embracing them with gratitude and working *with* them is powerful. And tuning in to their messages is key. Just as we have signature personality strengths, our bodies have their own signature strengths. If you're reading this book right now, your body is letting you breathe and absorb new ideas. Leading with your physical strengths, rather than focusing on your body's weaknesses or challenges or imperfections, boosts your mental metabolism just as surely as focusing on any of your other strengths.

Look Differently at Your Body to Strengthen Your Mind

Here's how to start listening to your body so you can boost your mental metabolism, increasing your energy and positivity (not to mention starting a positive feedback loop with your body).

- **Feel what you feel.** Simply ask yourself, *How do I feel right now?* Sometimes you're feeling something you don't want to feel. Instead of self-medicating, try being emotionally available to yourself. Through the practice of checking in with and nurturing yourself, you will eventually stop feeling the need to comfort yourself by satisfying cravings. Journaling has helped me open up and be honest about what I'm really experiencing.

   Now, when I crave my go-to comfort food (pizza), I ask myself why I feel the need to be comforted in the moment. Recently, for example, I felt lonesome. Instead of ordering pizza to comfort me, I called a dear friend on the phone to connect, and Face-Timed with my niece and nephew. Afterward, I felt nourished and realized I was no longer hungry. I made myself some white tea and curled up with a good book.

- **Accept what you feel.** Don't judge or criticize what you're feeling. Practice radical self-compassion. Instead of beating yourself up for wanting a cheeseburger and fries instead of salad and shaming yourself with thoughts like *I should eat this and not that,* compromise with yourself. I will order crab cakes, for example: something satisfying that is neither super healthy nor super unhealthy. Instead of being angry with your body for any weaknesses, real or perceived, for limitations, or for aging and changing, give yourself and your body a break; focus on all your body is doing for you and how you can help and support your body.

- **Be open to your body.** It's always speaking, so be willing to listen. I do this through prayer and meditation to give my body a deep sense of peace, relaxation, ease, calmness, lightness, alertness, and energy. When you are open to your body's needs, you are less likely to pollute it with food, drugs, or alcohol you know doesn't agree with you. Your mind and body work together as a team with the common goal of feeling good rather than ignoring each other.

- **Trust your body.** Every cell is on your side, which means you have hundreds of billions of allies. Ground yourself by turning inward and feeling the sensations of your body. Take deep breaths; be aware of your body. I recommend trying Pilates or yoga. When you are connected to all the ways your body is working *for* you, you will make healthier choices that support you.

- **Live your life.** Before I eat, I ask myself if I am hungry for food or hungry for something else like love, comfort, stability, validation, and so on. I shed unnecessary weight when I stopped obsessing over everything I was putting in my body and rigidly counting calories. When I stopped labeling myself and my food as "good" or "bad" and enduring the shameful feelings and emotions that accompany that way of thinking, weight literally melted off my body.

I now share this with people I care about: the next time you feel tempted to indulge in any kind of craving you feel is wrong for you, try to stop focusing on the craving and listen to what your body is telling

you instead. For example, healer Johanne Picard-
Scott says that a craving for a cigarette can be our
brain's subconscious way of asking us to slow down,
take a break, and breathe deeply to calm ourselves.
"Wrong remedy, but right instinct," she writes.

When out with friends and tempted to order
a beer like everyone else, I can now hear my body
gently remind me that beer makes "us" extremely
bloated and sick for hours. I order a glass of wine or
iced tea instead. (If I only want to drink water when
I'm in a social setting and don't want to deal with
any pushback from partygoers, I ask the bartender
to put a slice of lime in my drink. People think I'm
sipping on vodka and leave me alone.)

- **Enjoy what your body wants to do.** I choose to ask
my body what it needs and follow its advice without
judging, whether it's sleep, rest, nourishment, physical activity, or time spent in nature. If you can barely
keep your eyes open, it's probably best to go home
and go to sleep and skip spin class.

The Shadow Side of Our Character Strengths

Chances are you're familiar with the saying "There's a time
and place for everything" or, conversely, "Wrong place,
wrong time." Psychologist Karen Reivich says sometimes the
best of who we are is also capable of causing harm to ourselves and others.

This resonates with my life experience. My number one
character strength, love, not only can but did cause me great
harm when I became seriously involved with a man who has
narcissistic personality disorder. Because I love so hard and

desire to connect deeply with others, being love-bombed in the beginning of our relationship felt euphoric enough that I overlooked red flags and fell for someone who became emotionally abusive. (Love-bombing, a tactic used by a narcissist early in the relationship to "bomb" you with affection, flattery, gifts, and praise in an attempt to control you, is in itself a huge red flag.)

Similarly, I can think of a time when my strength of humor got me into trouble as well. It was the morning of my grandmother's funeral, and my mom and her two sisters, my dad, my brother, and I were all staying in my grandmother's home. You could cut the heaviness and sadness in the air with a knife, so I thought it would be a great idea to lighten the mood and start singing really loudly and terribly to make everyone laugh. My brother gave me a half-amused, embarrassed-for-me laugh before my mom quickly snapped at me, "Stop it, Kate!" My attempt at humor was not well received and actually offended the people I was trying to comfort.

Sometimes our strengths may prohibit us from being properly attuned to other people, stopping us from considering how they may deal with life's situations differently than us. It's important that we are aware of how our strengths could potentially overwhelm others, especially at the wrong place and time.

In this instance, boosting our mental metabolism means becoming aware of our unhelpful habits, some of which we perceived as strengths, and developing a new pattern of behavior instead. It's being willing to become so self-aware that we can tune in to the energies around us and try on other, less-developed strengths that can help shift the well-being of others while uplifting the energy in the room. While I'm not suggesting you become someone else to accommodate others, I am inviting you to dial up or down certain habits to strengthen your overall spiritual fitness and, in turn, help others do the same.

Reivich also talks about the importance of refraining from judging ourselves because we don't have someone else's strengths. She says we can elevate rather than diminish ourselves by appreciating the greatness of others while learning how to engage with people who possess different strengths than we do.

When you think about your own strengths, take a moment to recognize that they can also have pitfalls and to forgive yourself for not having all twenty-four strengths in equal degrees. That will not only help you build your own strengths but also allow you to value the strengths of others without negativity. A common pitfall I see in myself and others is judgment. I see judging ourselves and others as an invitation. It's an invitation showing us what's ready to be healed, released, and transformed. An antidote to judgment is being in the energy of willingness. I often say out loud, "I am willing to think differently about this person or issue." The challenge, and opportunity, is to make peace with what is and then be willing to interpret the situation differently. How we choose to interpret what happens to us is like a tall glass of potent green tea to the mind and spirit — it boosts our mental metabolism! "She is difficult to work with" becomes "I can set a good example!" And if we are open and willing, the divine guidance in terms of what next steps to take — big or small — will arrive in the form of inspiration, a phone call, an email, or a person we meet. Stay open.

This takes practice! And as with anything else, some days

will go smoothly and seem easy, and other days or instances will seem like an uphill battle. Past mistakes or belief patterns will creep up and try to take over. I get it! I've been there. But we get to choose who we want to be *now*, and the more we practice, the more our desired thoughts, behaviors, and patterns become our default setting rather than ideals we strive for but ultimately miss.

Aligning Goals with Strengths, Values, and Priorities

Besides understanding our strengths, we should be clear on what we value and prioritize. Oftentimes, I hear clients talk about the stress of working for an organization that doesn't share their values. Or I hear nearly everyone I know complain that they don't have time for this, that, and the other — and, sometimes (sadly), *this, that, and the other* are people they care about.

In these cases, I ask them a question aimed at accomplishing what in coaching we refer to as "honest labeling": "May I ask whether it was about not having time, or might you have put other things in the way to avoid having to do this?" In other words, do we not have enough time, or do we not have clear priorities?

I can think of several instances when I felt I didn't have enough time, but when I honestly took stock, I saw that I was wasting two hours a day mindlessly scrolling on Instagram. I know this because I began setting time limits on my social media apps (two hours a day total across all social media apps), and I was a bit traumatized to find there were days I reached my daily time limit at 10 a.m. I had no idea I might have been scrolling for almost two hours!

Mindfully setting priorities and finding ways to integrate

what's important to us into our lives help ensure we're making space for what matters most to us. For example, one of my *strengths* is love of learning; I *value* authenticity, integrity, and freedom; and I want to *prioritize* spending quality time with loved ones. Getting clear on that can help me envision ways to integrate these: I could invite a best friend or family member to Portugal to learn about the people and culture and discover the best restaurants and wineries together. Workwise, I could ask one of my favorite colleagues to get certified in a new assessment with me, so we could spend quality time together learning something new, simultaneously building my coaching business's authenticity.

Make a Plan

I'm definitely a fly-by-the-seat-of-my-pants, spontaneous type of gal, but professionally speaking, I'm a big fan of making a plan because it gives us a road map of how to get from where we are to where we want to be. We aren't driving blindly or directionless. It also brings in the aspect of accountability — it's like having someone waiting for you at your final destination. You need to show up like you said you would, and if you're anything like me, you'll want to show up early or at least on time.

Once we have a plan in place, the next step is to ask ourselves, are we actually acting on what we've planned? If we aren't acting, why not? A clarity of purpose arises. This is the perfect opportunity to connect or reconnect to our *why*. What is our priority, and *why*? What do we hope for, and *why*?

Establishing priorities, setting and achieving goals, and getting clear on critical success factors (what success looks like to you) are effective ways to leverage our strengths to reach our desired outcomes.

I do this through encouraging clients to find a range of choices, develop a vision, and devise a plan to make the vision real. What is their ideal option? What goals would they like to establish and explore within this ideal option?

I also find it can be helpful when the client makes their fears the agenda. Sometimes knowing what we don't want helps us clarify what's important to us right now. I then invite clients to summarize and interpret the work we have done together. It's not enough to just know what we want; we have to reflect on why it's important to us (studies show this is where change and motivation take place) and take even the smallest of actions to help bring our desires to life in a practical, tangible way.

Making a plan in order to achieve our goals is smart, literally. SMART goals are specific, measurable, attainable, relevant, and time-based. As with any plan, there are benefits and costs. It's important to ask ourselves, *How do these options hold me back or move me forward?*

True strength comes from gaining mastery through action, changing belief patterns and self-talk, and learning to embrace failure while avoiding rumination on weaknesses and doubts. We are stronger when we act authentically from our values. How and when could you experiment with this concept? What could you do differently? What behaviors are holding you back? What's a current example? Is this a pattern you need to explore? What made you successful in the past? Anything else?

Identifying, reinforcing, and building your strengths will help you keep your mental metabolism running at peak performance, giving you the energy to support the spiritual fitness you seek, need, and deserve.

JOURNALING EXERCISE
Resiliency Reps

Resilience is our ability to spring back and recover quickly from life's challenges, disruptions, uncertainties, and misfortunes. The ability to react with resilience builds optimism and hope. I like to think of resilience as the motivation muscle that comes from within and starts with our mindset. In terms of boosting our mental metabolism, resilience means staying committed to the new and improved perspectives we've chosen for ourselves even when it is tempting to fall back into old thought patterns and behaviors. It is choosing to learn from our mistakes rather than throwing in the towel when we have a human moment and step off track. It is choosing to be so committed to our well-being and the well-being of others that we make decisions from that space rather than giving in to the stress and chaos of the situation. Instead of "acting out," we "act in" and connect with our power and spirit.

There is great value in being intentional with our choices. Our consistent choices become our daily habits, which become the default setting to who we are at our core. For me, the key to achieving what I say I wish to achieve is to have a disciplined mind.

The point of this journaling exercise is to challenge yourself to think more productively in real time by quieting mental chatter and combating counterproductive thoughts — replacing them with a more optimistic and empowering perspective. I learned this technique while earning my positive psychology certification from the University of Pennsylvania on Coursera.

To begin, identify a situation where a counterproductive thought arises. Maybe you're about to take the stage to make a speech and the voice in your head says, *You're not qualified to speak at this event.* Perhaps you're stepping into the batter's box and your mind says, *You always strike out against this pitcher.* Or you could be getting dressed and hear, *You know you can't wear that! Your thighs are too big!*

Once you've identified your counterproductive thought, I'd like you to write it down and then replace it with at least one positive statement. Let's say your counterproductive thought is *I don't have enough credentials or qualifications to earn the kind of money I'd like to earn.* Now write down some reasons why this statement isn't true. For example, "That's not true, because I see people all over the internet with absolutely no formal training or higher education making seven figures. That's not true, because I have a ton of life and professional experience, which adds immeasurable value to my clients and allows me to charge the kind of rates I deserve."

Next, I'd like you to practice the tool of reframing, like I did with my colleague Natasha. Remember, I reframed being a perfectionist to "I have a respect for mastery." For our example above, I could say, "A more thoughtful and beneficial way to see this is that I already have everything it takes to earn the income I desire. I'm also open to exploring courses or programs that could give me an additional advantage to earn more money."

Finally, I invite you to have a contingency plan. In other words, if *X* happens, you will do *Y*: "If I discover through self-reflection or valued feedback from a trusted source that earning additional credentials or qualifications will make me an even more ideal candidate to earn the income I desire, then I will take the necessary action steps."

Again, have fun with these exercises. Get creative. Play around. Pretend you're a movie director plotting alternative endings to your romantic comedy or sci-fi thriller. There are never any right or wrong answers, just different perspectives to try on like clothing. Some ideas fit and feel great, others are comfortable but not your style, some are too tight and feel restrictive, and others are just hideous. Like when you put on your favorite T-shirt, pajamas, or jeans, you will know when you've gotten it just right. And as always, feel free to choose again and again. As you grow, your ideas and desires will grow with you.

EXERCISE
The Mindset Mirror

In this step, we've explored an extraordinarily effective way to give up our habitual negative self-talk through a powerful tool known as reframing. When we reframe a situation, we can quickly jump into a growth mindset. This helps boost our mental metabolism and gives us upbeat energy. Yippee!

In the "mindset mirror" exercise, I'd like us to move beyond a fixed way of thinking in order to accomplish goals with greater ease and effectiveness.

Choose a mindset you can take with you everywhere you go, so when you look in the mirror you can smile and feel confident. This may sound silly or even feel a bit uncomfortable, especially at first. I've spent a lot of time in green rooms and on set listening to countless women (and men) look in the mirror and complain, saying something negative about themselves. I've also seen this mindset spread like wildfire. It goes something like this:

CEO of a global beauty brand: "Ugh, I look so tired. I'm going to bomb this presentation."

Self-made millionaire entrepreneur and mother of four: "I know. I shouldn't even be allowed on-air tonight. I'm so stressed-out."

Gorgeous model: "Why did they even hire me? I don't have enough experience."

Award-winning makeup artist: "I'm filled with anxiety and self-doubt."

Well-known TV host: "I don't even know what I'm doing half the time."

Celebrity: "I've never felt more insecure in my life."

These are all things I've heard firsthand. I've certainly been guilty of looking in the mirror and having a critical thought before a complimentary one. Insults and unhealed insecurities add up and stay ingrained in our subconscious. Then we unknowingly live our lives from this space rather than from our truth and our magnificence.

Starting today, I challenge you to be extra aware of what you think and say to yourself when you look in the mirror, and then treat yourself with compassion. If the truth is that you look tired, maybe you need more sleep and perhaps it's because you're a spouse and parent juggling a full-time career.

I often joke that all I want is for someone to hug me and tell me I'm amazing. Sometimes that comfort and validation just feel so nourishing. But when I get real with myself, I ask, *How often do you tell yourself that you're amazing?*

Again, I know it seems counterintuitive to compliment ourselves, because society sets us up to do just the opposite. That's why this is a practice, and an important one at that. Here are some mindset mirror mantras you could try on for size and make your own:

I look amazing.

I feel amazing.

I am amazing.

I'm so proud of myself.

It's going to be a great day!

I have so much energy!

I'm going to nail this presentation!

I feel so prepared.

I feel so rested.

Life is good.

Everything is going to work out!

I trust myself.

I love you!

I'm doing a great job!

I may look or feel a little [fill in negative here], but it's because... [Examples: "I may feel like I don't have what it takes right now, but I trust that if I stay present and focused on my best qualities, I can do a great job and even have fun doing so!" Or "I may feel insecure, but I'm willing not to be. In fact, I've got this!" Or "I may have lines on my face, but they represent all the experience that's made me unique."]

THE ART OF SURRENDER MEDITATION

Go ahead and get comfortable in your meditation space.

Feel the support of your meditation cushion, sofa, or whatever you are sitting on. Notice how supported you are.

With your eyes gently closed, start by taking a few deep, letting-go breaths as you relax into your body and focus on your breath.

Good. Continue this relaxed style of breathing throughout your meditation practice.

Now choose a color that you love. Run this color in through the top of your head, all the way through your body, and out the bottom of your feet. Watch as this color cleanses your entire mind and your entire body. Continue to run this color through the top of your head, through your body, and out the bottom of your feet, relaxing and releasing with each breath.

When you're ready, think of something you'd like to change. It could be something you'd like to change about yourself, your relationship, your career.... Whatever just came to your mind is perfect.

Maybe you have the power to change this, or maybe it is out of your control.

If you're struggling to let go of negative thoughts or emotions that are threatening to eat you up inside, it is safe to release them now.

Go ahead and watch in your mind as you write down all these thoughts and feelings.

Take a moment to really get honest with yourself while you're in this calm, safe, relaxed space.

When you're ready, take everything you've written down and place it in an imaginary box. Notice what this box looks like. Maybe it's smooth and shiny. Notice its color and how big or small it is. Is it heavy or lightweight? Feel the texture. Is it soft? Really see yourself putting the paper with the thoughts you no longer need into this special, sacred box.

This is your "surrender box," and it is available to you anytime. You can envision yourself writing down any thoughts you don't need, at any time, and placing them into the box.

You can even create your own real-life surrender box at home and add to it regularly. When you place the thoughts you no longer need into the surrender box, ask that the God of your own understanding take these troubles or worries from you. You can even say out loud or silently to yourself: "Please take this from me. Thank you."

This isn't about pretending that something doesn't bother us. It's about expressing it in our mind or on paper and then surrendering it in a sacred letting-go ritual. Do this as often as you need. You may need to do this more than once with life's biggest challenges, but each time, you will release more and more of your most painful experiences, boosting your mental metabolism and becoming more spiritually fit in the process. Take as much time as you need to fully let go. When you are ready, slowly open your eyes, and return to your day. Travel softly.

 ## COACH KATE CHECK-IN

How are you doing? Remember, the Full Spirit Workout is a new regimen for life. There's no one to compete against, and you get to go at a pace that feels comfortable for you. If you're feeling tired, rest. If you're feeling energized, try an additional journaling exercise, reflect on other ways to answer the questions, or discuss your insights with a trusted friend or partner. By the way, there are no right or wrong answers, and you don't need a study guide or cheat sheet, because you have all the answers inside you. It's my job to ask the questions that will allow the answers to pour out of you. I invite you to journal like no one will ever read the answers so you can be as open and honest, raw, and vulnerable as possible. It's your time to discover and embrace all your unique strengths! Have fun with it!

STEP 6: BOOST YOUR MENTAL METABOLISM *AFFIRMATION*

I don't need to obsess or judge. The right people and experiences will show up. My job is to stay open to the endless possibilities that surround me. I no longer compete with anyone. When I bring my full spirit to whatever I'm doing, I've already won. I've stopped worrying about what others think and can focus on the unique blend of strengths that I bring to the world so naturally. I feel so spiritually fit!

STEP 7
Step Up Your Spiritual Stamina

Being okay if it happens and okay if it doesn't
is a very powerful place to be.

— KATE ECKMAN

It feels funny to quote yourself, right?

I share this quote because when I posted it on Instagram and Pinterest, it went viral. These words got more than two and a half million views and forty-seven thousand saves on my Pinterest account in three days! I can't even give you the numbers from Instagram because it got shared so many times (oftentimes without attributing it to me, so now I put it in quotes, which is a good tip for anyone who posts their original work online).

But this isn't about celebrating likes and views but rather about illustrating how much these words resonate with *a lot* of people all over the world. They highlight the importance of practicing the art of surrender and staying detached from outcomes. It's a challenge of a lifetime and takes practice. That's why I am writing this book — to help each of us develop empowered, consistent practices that become our default setting — something we begin to enjoy doing that yields countless benefits.

The Full Spirit Workout isn't a fad or a boot camp. It's a regimen for life that requires spiritual stamina. But that isn't like other kinds of stamina, which are about self-determination, will, or gritting our teeth. Spiritual stamina is about constantly returning to vulnerability. It's about choosing to be open and tender. As we do this, we make ourselves available for transformation and renewal over and over, yielding to a higher perspective.

In this step, we'll explore what this new type of stamina really means in practical terms and how we can learn to trust ourselves and the universe so we can remain open and vulnerable, so we can "be okay if it happens and okay if it doesn't."

In many ways, I feel silly taking credit for this quote because it was God, or unconditional love, speaking through me. And clearly, millions of people needed to hear this message about having the courage to put ourselves out there and be seen while opening up to possibilities and opportunities that we desire — all while being willing to be judged, hurt, or rejected, or even to fail altogether.

Stepping up our spiritual stamina means we keep going no matter what, even when we have no control over the outcome. It means being who we really are rather than hiding behind a veil of protection. It's owning every piece of ourselves with pride rather than disowning less favorable aspects or characteristics. It's about letting our guard down rather than putting a wall up. It's not about success or failure. Advanced spiritual stamina is keeping a glorious sense of humor even when nothing seems to be going our way, and trusting that eventually it will. (Spoiler alert: things *will* go your way when you consistently strengthen your spirit with the exercises in this book — although not always in the way you envisioned.)

The words quoted above came to me on a beautiful fall afternoon while I was sitting outside at my favorite Italian place in my neighborhood, enjoying a Naples-style Margherita pizza and a glass of Montepulciano red wine — my go-to comfort meal that makes me feel like (or at least pretend) I am blissed out in Italy.

I love coming to this restaurant because the staff knows not just my name but my order, and I can show up in the middle of the day in my workout clothes and no one cares. You know those places you can go where you just feel so welcomed, safe, and cozy? I often hear the theme song from *Cheers* playing in my mind as I walk in, and I am always greeted with a hug from one of the servers-turned-friends.

I needed a bit of comforting that day. I had just received another rejection notice from my agent about a huge opportunity I was being seriously considered for. It was the second time in a month that my agent, who sounded just as deflated as I felt, called to deliver such news.

When I hung up the phone, I remember saying out loud in my apartment to myself, "I don't even have time for this project right now! My life is full and fabulous as it is! I don't need this!" Then I looked up at God and my angels and said, "This is a divine assignment I took on for you! Why would you have me do all this work if you're not going to help me see it through? If you really want me to do this project, I'll let you figure it out. I'm done!"

A few hours later, as I felt the warm sun and gentle breeze from underneath a patio table umbrella, while listening to a live band, sipping my decadent Italian red wine, and savoring every bite of my Margherita pizza, I slipped into a state of deep reflection. I had just had some choice words for God, so I was open to listening for His response. The truth is, God or our divine wisdom is always speaking to us; we just aren't practiced at listening. This is a skill I have learned to develop over the years because I know this is the voice of truth — the voice of love, not fear and ego. The voice that will lead me back home to myself, where I make choices for my greatest benefit and the collective well-being as well.

I can still picture exactly where I was sitting when I heard a divine voice download to my mind that said, "Being okay if it happens and okay if it doesn't is a very powerful place to be."

Those words hit home in a very profound way for me. This is vulnerability and openness, a resolve to face the world with this attitude of trust. This is the heart of spiritual stamina.

Surrender for Spiritual Stamina

When I heard that divine sentence, I immediately thought of my mom. She is one of those women who, unlike me, always wanted to be a mom more than anything. I have always loved children but could go either way when it came to being a mother. Maybe it's because I haven't met the "right" person, but I also think some women absolutely *have* to be mothers, and others, like me, are better off as fun aunties. My favorite role in life is being Ross and Melia's Aunt Kate and playing auntie to every child I meet. My mom, on the other hand, is a bona fide mom. Being an aunt was not going to cut it for her.

Right after my parents married, my dad left to serve in the Vietnam War. It's a miracle he survived and returned home safely, as so many men who served with him did not. My parents then tried to have a baby for seven years with no luck. It got to the point where my mom's doctor said, "If you really want to have a child, you're going to have to adopt."

My mom was devastated. It was the seventies and nearly every woman she knew had a child and seemed to have gotten pregnant so easily. She was also now in her thirties, and back then you were considered a dinosaur when it came to having children at that age.

When I asked my mom how she was finally able to get pregnant with my older brother, John, she said, "I gave up." She didn't mean she gave up, quit trying, and felt sorry for herself; she meant she gave the situation up to God as an act of surrender. By placing trust in herself, her body, and God, she remained open and vulnerable. Accessing our vulnerability and its hidden strengths steps up our spiritual stamina, aligning us with our life purpose. A month after she "gave up," she got pregnant with my brother, and within two years, she had a healthy little boy and a baby girl — miracle children, as she likes to call us.

I think of this story often because it explains why and how I am alive. It also illustrates advanced spiritual stamina because we all want who and what we want, when we want it, and usually we want it *right now!*

I've learned that our desire to try to control others or outcomes actually acts as a repellent to achieving our goals. The alternative? Exercising complete surrender to what is, and fully trusting that there is a plan far greater than ours working overtime behind the scenes, even while we are sleeping.

Before I made my way to the pizza place that day, I was putting away clothes in my bedroom, and I heard my intuition or inner wisdom laughing at me and saying, *If everything you wanted happened on your timeline, you would be so overwhelmed and exhausted. You would not be able to give 100 percent to it all (which is the only way you roll), and you wouldn't be enjoying your life or the gift of achieving your goals. You would probably be miserable, actually.*

Wow.

That's cause for a pause.

I truly believe in divine timing. I had been so close to crossing the finish line of a cherished goal for about a year and a half. There were three or four instances where I thought it was finally my time.

In full disclosure, though, when I received that latest "no," I sobbed to my friend Josh for a good ten minutes. It was only after that release that I received the major revelation that I didn't care *when* reaching my cherished goal happened anymore because I knew it *would* happen. In the meantime, my life was full of so many wonderful things, opportunities, and people that I truly didn't care. What a beautiful place to be.

That patience and surrender paid off. Just weeks after I sat blissfully with my pizza and wine and heard this now "viral" message of relief and peace, I had a phone meeting with my literary agent, Wendy, and my now-editor, Georgia. A book deal with a dream publisher, New World Library, and their world-class team followed soon after. The divine project and cherished goal I've been referring to is this book you are reading now.

These exercises truly work if you commit to them. It's not just about posting a quote or understanding a spiritual principle or universal truth intellectually; we have to put it into practice consistently. We have to actually believe the words we are reading, saying, and posting. My story and this book are the proof.

I invite you to "give it up" and loosen your grip. Sometimes the best thing we can do is give up — when giving up is an act of faith. "Giving it up" again and again is spiritual stamina because we are choosing to constantly return to vulnerability, get honest with ourselves, and act from faith, not fear.

Giving Vulnerability a Chance

The Full Spirit Workout is, of course, a play on the expression "full body workout," which you often hear advertised at the gym. But it's also about bringing your full spirit to everything you do and everyone you meet.

Spiritual stamina involves accepting what our spirit is trying to tell us (something we often ignore because we don't like what it's trying to tell us or we don't want to do the work that will be required as a result). Spiritual stamina is how we achieve intimacy and experience a meaningful connection with ourselves and others. And just like training for and running a marathon, it takes courage. We have to be willing to be truly seen, and we have to be courageous enough to be imperfect or, in other words, be ourselves — the put-together person we present to the world *and* the messy person trying to keep it all together behind the scenes. (Gotta love him or her! As my friend in Atlanta would say, "Bless her heart.")

Several years ago, I attended a personal development seminar to work through some relationship blocks that were getting in the way of my overall sense of well-being. I felt like I was dating the same man over and over again. Sure, they had different names and professions, but one thing that they all had in common was me. I remember complaining to a participant I was partnered up with that I was sick of dealing with all these emotionally unavailable jerks. (I used a different word besides *jerks*, but you get the idea.) At the time, I thought the guys were the problem. "Why do I have to be attracted to them?" I lamented. "I shouldn't have to be dealing with them, especially since I'm so emotionally *available*."

A few self-exploration exercises later, frustrations about my relationship with my mom began to emerge as well. I was angry at her, and we weren't getting along. I noticed how much resentment I was feeling toward her. The seminar leader suggested I call my mom and tell her how I was feeling and how much I would like to mend our fractured relationship.

But I didn't want to call her. At all. I was filled with un-comfortable emotions ranging from deep sadness to mild rage. I did not want to feel or deal with any of this. I couldn't believe how much resistance I was experiencing over a simple phone call to my mother.

During the lunch break I ate alone, attempting to have

a conversation with my emotions instead of other people. *What are you trying to tell me?* I inquired. After break, participants were invited to come up to the microphone in the front of the conference room to share what they were feeling. As I listened to each person share their story, I felt as though a light bulb exploded in my mind. I suddenly felt like my head was going to pop off! It felt like an aha moment on ten shots of espresso.

I stood up from my chair, my body shaking and sweating with adrenaline. I approached the microphone and began telling around one hundred strangers how I'd been so sick of dealing with all these emotionally unavailable jerks, and then I blurted out, "But what I'm discovering is that *I'm* the emotionally unavailable jerk!"

The room erupted in laughter, cheers, and applause. Not because I had delivered some epic speech but because I had told the truth so vulnerably — I took responsibility for myself and my life experiences. That accountability and acceptance are what moves the needle and begins the change process toward becoming more self-actualized. That acknowledgment and understanding transformed the energy in the room. Participants told me they felt like they now had permission to dramatically take ownership of their thoughts and shift their perspectives, too. It was as if I had said, "If I can do it, so can you." And Lord knows, we've all been a jerk at one time or another!

Vulnerability is tough and oftentimes extremely painful to navigate. There's no instructor's manual; there's no looking cool or feeling like you've got it all figured out. (None of us do, by the way.) When we are willing to consider new ideas or ways of being with an open heart, we are performing an act of courage. We are daring to go *there*. This is the opposite of numbing ourselves with food, alcohol, shopping, or "busyness" or pretending we don't care. We are hardwired to care. It's like standing onstage fully clothed but feeling completely naked. People see us. There is no hiding.

But this is the gold. This is where our life starts to have true meaning, genuine connection, and deeper value. Vulnerability is like upgrading from a flip phone to a smartphone in terms of benefits and possibilities, or being able to connect to Wi-Fi in order to make an emergency phone call in the middle of a jungle — it's definitely life-giving, but it can also be lifesaving.

With this new revelation, I saw very clearly why I had chosen many of the men I dated, and I had compassion for them and myself. We were all trying to work out our "stuff" with one another, whether we realized it at the time or not.

I think I was scared to call my mom and talk about our relationship at that point because I didn't have all the tools to have the kind of calm, honest, vulnerable conversation I really wanted to have with her — to create the loving, respectful relationship we both wanted and deserved. My anger owned me at times, and I felt powerless to it. I wasn't able to communicate my feelings without getting upset, because I didn't feel truly seen or heard in her presence. I felt judged. And I think she felt the same way. But I was willing to work on myself to try to improve our relationship. I guess I didn't know if she was willing to do the same. But I had to find out.

While I was terrified to make this call and put myself out there, I dared to dial her number. I explained to her that I was at this seminar and what was coming up for me emotionally. She was sweet and open, listening as I expressed my frustrations with our relationship but also my desire for it to improve. I don't remember exactly what she said, as it's been years now, and we are in a much happier and healthier place (thanks to the Full Spirit Workout and therapy), but it was such a healing conversation, and I know it's because I set the tone by calling her and leading with vulnerability. Our willingness to be vulnerable paves the way for us to set our weapons down. (Judgment and resistance, shame and blame, for example, can be weapons of mass destruction.) Spiritual stamina is choosing to be open and tender again and again, even when it doesn't make sense or feel safe, or when we're really stinking mad.

Miracles occur when we do this — it's a spiritual truce, and both sides win. Even if the person you're opening up to chooses to leave or respond in an undesirable way, you still win. The peace of mind I experience when I share my truth (kindly) is the prize. Oftentimes we think we want someone to act a specific way or something to be a certain way and then we will be happy, but really our goal is inner peace, and that can only come from within, as we've discovered. One of my favorite mantras is "Peace begins with me." This mantra will help you feel more resilient and flexible.

Stop Pretending

Another exercise I practice is about pretending. Pretending is the opposite of our good friend vulnerability. Pretending looks like this: I pretend I'm comfortable being the only minority in this entire office, but what I *really* want is to work at a company that values diversity and inclusion and hires people with diverse backgrounds, so we can all learn from each other's unique perspectives and be a stronger, more well-rounded team and organization.

Something I find myself saying a lot is "I pretend I'm completely cool doing everything on my own and being a strong, independent, single woman," but what I *really* want is to share my life with an incredible, equal partner. As I like to say, "I'd like to share my completeness with another complete person."

We can't change something (including ourselves) until we first accept it exactly as it is. Then we have to *believe* we are worthy of the change we desire. These sound like simple truths to execute, but, at least for me, it takes a lot of practice. We are unlearning a lot of societal beliefs that we've adopted as our own, and it takes time and discipline to develop and execute new belief systems. But the results are so worth it! Keep going!

Emotional Bypassing

Bypassing hurtful emotions is a theme that comes up often in my daily conversations. For example, I might be talking about how hurtful it feels that a friend or relative is not emotionally supportive and shows little concern for what I am doing. I will express my feelings and then say something like, "But I guess she is doing the best she can," or "It's okay, there are people starving in the world. I'm so lucky."

Have you undermined your own feelings and made them no big deal when really you were suffering? Spiritual stamina is owning the fact that someone can love us but also choose not to support us, and it makes sense that this would bother us.

There is such freedom in admitting we are hurt (returning to vulnerability and thereby stepping up our spiritual stamina) and in choosing not to bypass hurtful emotions. For one, we get to feel our feelings authentically and then move through the discomfort rather quickly. We also take ownership of our feelings without making the other person wrong. We begin to understand the other person is behaving from their own reality that ultimately has very little to do with us.

In a personal interview, Boston-based psychologist Chris Tecce, PhD, said, "Emotional bypassing is quite helpful for people in acute and immediate post-trauma situations to prevent being overwhelmed. For the long term, though, I've found that it's important for the underlying emotions to be gradually processed at some point to prevent subconscious compensatory behaviors like eating disorders or other addictions or self-harm."

One of my best friends was telling me that she pulled a muscle in her neck and was in excruciating pain to the point that it woke her up throughout the night. She told me about how much her body ached and then said, "But it's nothing compared to what others are going through. I guess it's really not that bad."

Um, what?! You just said you were in excruciating pain, and in the twenty years I've known you, I don't ever remember you complaining about physical pain ever (which tells me this must be really bad).

I noticed her emotional bypassing immediately. I shared with her my observation, inviting her to not minimize her pain. I told her, "Yes, you don't have a deadly disease, but you are in pain. It's not a competition. You're allowed to not feel well and express it without the disclaimer that your life is more privileged than many others on the planet."

When I offered this to her, she began to cry. It's as if I

had given her permission to feel the full extent of what she was experiencing without comparing it to what others may be going through. I know for myself how important it is to process our emotions, especially in a safe environment with a trusted friend or professional coach or therapist. It's not a pass to complain and feel sorry for ourselves but rather an invitation to be real, to acknowledge our truth apart from the truth of others — it's an invitation to heal.

I invite you to become aware of this habit if it's something you recognize in yourself. Minimizing our feelings in the name of "Well, I still have it better" doesn't serve anyone. The quicker we come to terms with the full scope of our emotions and pain and what they are here to teach us, the quicker we return home to our healthiest selves, and the easier it is for us to be a force of healing love to others.

Don't Force It, Explore It!

My colleague Margaret McLean Walsh once advised me, "Don't force it, explore it!" and it really resonated. Have you ever been in conversation with someone and they simply remained quiet, giving you the time and space to come to your own conclusions? That's an example of exploring, not forcing.

Coaches call this WAIT! (Why Am I Talking!). We can use this technique with ourselves, too. We may struggle with opening up emotionally and allowing ourselves to be vulnerable. We want certainty and comfort. We fear failure. We want to look good and appear confident and competent at all times — even (or sometimes most of all) to ourselves. We tell ourselves everything is fine, but we sense there are other, more uncomfortable feelings underneath the surface.

But when we explore our emotions and get curious about what they can teach us, slowing down and not forcing but instead exploring, we begin to actually feel what is going on inside our minds and bodies. Then we are able to recognize and name our emotions and spend some time getting to know them without being distracted, interrupted, shamed, blamed, or criticized.

Many of us struggle with being very hard on ourselves. Rather than going down the rabbit hole of why we're so hard on ourselves or trying to force ourselves out of these patterns, I've found it more effective to explore alternatives. We can do this by asking ourselves, *What would it look like if I was being kind to myself?*

To me, this exploration is like going shopping and trying on a ton of beautiful outfits just for fun. You may purchase some of them and not others, but you get to explore what "fits." Exploring what fits mentally and spiritually is a powerful tool to get us out of our heads, out of the past, and into the present moment, where we are positioned to make a plan and take action. It is in implementing our plan that we become more energized and more comfortable with whatever emotions are brought to the surface.

Giving ourselves kindness instead of criticism takes practice. It opens us up to new possibilities for meaning in life. Criticism is like throwing salt on our wounded hearts. Kindness, on the other hand, shines a light on the wound, allowing us to see it more clearly and this time with a more compassionate frame of mind. It allows us to open our full selves to the world, with vulnerability, building our spiritual stamina.

Win Anyway

My friend Maya is married to a well-known college basketball coach. I've sat next to her at countless games and often heard her yell to her husband's players, "Win anyway!"

She does this after there's been a bad call by the refs or a player has turned the ball over, for example. Every time she says it, I think, *Yes!*

You've probably had many "win anyway" moments in your life, and now I want you to pay attention to them. Some may be small, like when I got my hair done to go to an important audition and then walked outside to discover pouring rain — despite predictions of sunshine — and I had no umbrella. So I thought, *Well, take a forty-dollar cab ride a few blocks in rush-hour traffic in this storm, run into the building while trying to keep dry, and win anyway!*

I think of the time I was stuck in my car on the New Jersey Turnpike for six hours, not moving, having to go to the bathroom so badly and saying to myself, *Wow, the world is really trying to keep me from being great today, but I'm going to be great anyway!* I kept my wits about me, called a friend, and reminded myself that I was safe in the comfort of my own car.

Then there are big examples, like unexpected events that change the course of our lives forever, be it a pandemic or loss of a loved one. Even in the direst of circumstances, we can still find a way to win anyway. It's a choice we make from the strength of vulnerability. When was the last time you chose to "win anyway"? What did you do?

Your Thoughts Matter Most

In 2001, I was a die-hard Lakers fan, like many Los Angeles residents. All these years later, I can still remember one game in particular from the NBA Finals, where the Lakers were taking on the Philadelphia 76ers in Philly. Lakers star Kobe Bryant, who grew up in the Philadelphia area, was being heckled and harassed by fans like I have never seen before — in his hometown, no less! He was being booed so loudly you couldn't even hear the announcers. I was nervous for him, as this was a huge game. It's typical that there is little fan support at away games, but this was such a monumental display of negative commotion — something Philadelphia fans are known for — that it was on another level, even for Philly.

While the screaming fans managed to negatively affect me, sitting comfortably at home eating popcorn and watching the game, Kobe was completely unaffected. It was like he had some superhuman power that kept him not only completely focused and unbothered but actually fueled by the jeers! You may call it being one of the greatest athletes of all time, and there's some truth to that, but Kobe had this aura of "I don't care what anyone thinks" that was so inspiring to someone like me — someone who used to invest so heavily in what others thought about me.

I watched in awe as Kobe went on to play one of the best games of his career, knocking down six three-pointers in a row, teaching a clinic to players and fans alike that night. He would smile and laugh every time he knocked down another heroic shot despite the deafening boos. I'll never forget that performance because it taught me such a great lesson: don't allow any outside noise or the opinions of others (especially those who aren't even playing in the actual game with you) to disrupt your greatness and the gifts you are destined to share with the world.

If you're brave enough to put yourself out there and be vulnerable, whether it's as a public figure giving a speech, writing a book, playing in a big game, telling someone "I love you," having a difficult conversation — you name it — and someone who doesn't have the courage to do what you're doing says something nasty about you or your work, continue to hold your head high, play like a champion, and don't concern yourself with any outside noise.

Think of your favorite performer in athletics or the arts. Do you think Beyoncé is concerned with what a drunk fan in the cheap seats says about her performance? No. Embody your inner Beyoncé, Kobe, or whoever inspires you with their audacity to put it all out there for the world to see. Talent and accolades aside, "winning" and "wealth" are about showing up and giving it your all. As I like to tell my friends, "Be Seabiscuit," the champion thoroughbred racehorse. Put your blinders on and run your own race! Stay focused. Keep putting one foot in front of the other until you cross the finish line. Don't concern yourself with the other horses on the track or the fans in the crowd. Run free!

An Inner Game

Playing and watching sports my entire life have taught me so many invaluable lessons. A huge takeaway is the mental toughness it takes to win a physical competition. Time and time again, I have seen that the winning edge is inner stamina, not outer strength.

The power of spiritual stamina was on full display during one of the greatest sports upsets we have ever seen. At the 2015 US Open tennis championship, no one gave Roberta Vinci, an unseeded Italian ranked number 43 in the world, a chance against number 1–ranked superstar Serena Williams, who was just two set wins away from a calendar-year Grand Slam for the first time since 1988.

Williams was aiming for her twenty-second major title, which would have tied her with Steffi Graf for the most in the Open Era. She had won the Australian Open, the French Open, and Wimbledon and needed only the US Open to clinch the Grand Slam.

Vinci was a three-hundred-to-one underdog to Williams. She had never made it past the quarterfinals of a Grand Slam tournament. In four previous matches against Williams, she had never even won a set. And yet, that day, she defeated Williams.

Stunning upset and statistics aside, I learned a lot about spiritual stamina while watching this match:

- **Be ready for anything.** Before the match, Serena was asked how the rain delay affected her (they'd been scheduled to play the night before but got rained out). She calmly and quietly stated it didn't affect her at all because, in tennis, you have to be ready for anything. I loved that simple sentiment and confidence. As we would see later in the match, you have to be ready for people to play or act out of character, too. In this case, her opponent "played out of her mind" and shocked everybody, even herself.
- **It's okay to be nervous.** Serena is a champion. We all know that. She's my favorite athlete, and I consider her one of the greatest of all time. I think sometimes we are guilty of placing sports stars like her on a pedestal. She plays tennis like a superhuman, but ultimately Serena Williams is a human being like you and me. (Well, maybe a little bit more superhuman than you and me.) She has good days, challenging days, and a range of emotions.

I found it interesting that someone like her, with

all her accolades and experience, could be nervous. But that's what I love about Serena — her humanity, her fight, the beautiful way she wears her emotions on her face for everyone to see. Her vulnerability is what makes her so relatable and so real and is why she has a loyal fan following both on and off the court. She's just like us — except a much, much better tennis player.

- **Mistakes are part of the game; keep playing.** This is an important concept for me because I used to carry around the self-limiting belief that I had to be "perfect" in order to succeed. But here was one of the greatest sports champions ever making unforced errors and hitting shots long and wide. This is part of life. We all make mistakes. We can blame it on nerves, fatigue, stress, anxiety, others, the weather, you name it, but ultimately mistakes are part of what it means to be human and can be our greatest teachers.

- **Change your racket/mind.** We always have the opportunity to choose again, whether it's our tennis racket or our mind. After Serena changed her racket in the first set, she won the next several games. We can choose to change our minds at any given moment, too. For example, if you're holding a grudge against someone, you can choose to forgive that person, choose love, let it go, and move on. Or you can hold on to anger and frustration and feel lousy. Either way, you get to choose, and you decide how you want your game of life to play out.

- **Don't overthink it. Use your instincts.** Stay present and stay out of your head. Don't give in to negative self-talk. Deep down or in your heart, you always know what to do and what would serve you and others the best. Trust your gut.

- **Don't give up.** Be relentless in pursuit of your goals. Like Vinci, just keep trying to return everything that comes your way. Points add up, and before you know it, you may just upset the world champ in front of her home crowd. Keep the hammer down!

- **Anything is possible.** Even Roberta Vinci herself said she didn't think she had a chance to beat Williams. Her nothing-to-lose-just-enjoy-yourself, go-out-there-and-play attitude paid off. Big time.

- **Rise up.** Vinci embodied this notion. As Serena said in an interview post-match, "She played out of her mind." Vinci rose to the playing level of her opponent and then some. How did she do it?

- **Have fun.** Vinci told a reporter her game plan was just to have fun and not think about the fact that she was playing Serena Williams, the number one player in the world. She said she didn't want to overthink the match; her goal was to just keep the ball within the lines on the court.

- **Enjoy the moment.** Vinci could not believe she beat Serena Williams, calling the victory "the greatest moment of my life." It was clear how present and focused she was throughout the match, returning nearly everything Serena slammed her way.

The present moment is all we have. When the last point is over, it's over. We may not get to play another set. All that matters is what's in front of us right now, and we can only control what we're doing, nothing else. Be ready!

- **When it's your time, it's your time.** As Vinci said, "Today's my day!" It certainly is. What's meant for you will always be yours. So relax, work hard, stay focused, and most importantly, have fun!

Give Yourself Credit

When was the last time you told yourself, *Good job! I'm so proud of you!*

Reinventing our definition of success and exploring the passion of purpose in our lives will help us maintain our spiritual stamina better than anything.

I used to define success by such high standards that I pushed myself to exhaustion more than once. I'd like to encourage you to ask yourself the same question I ask myself:

What does it really mean to be successful?

I came to terms with the truth that success is not what we do. It's who we are. In my experience, when we "get over ourselves" and find a higher purpose through serving others, we naturally attract what we desire, including many of the outer manifestations of success. We also attract success when we tend to our current garden with gratitude. As they say, what we appreciate, appreciates. So the universe will give us an even bigger, better garden to nurture once we're grateful for the one we have now.

Cultivating an Appreciator Mindset

One way to develop an attitude of gratitude and step up our spiritual stamina is to adopt an appreciator, rather than criticizer, mindset. This table I created has been helpful for my clients and me.

CRITICIZER VS. APPRECIATOR MINDSET

Function	Criticizer Mindset	Appreciator Mindset
Head/Thinking	Why am I not good enough?	How can I acknowledge and validate myself?
	How can I prove myself?	How can I focus on my gifts and strengths?
	Why isn't anything going my way?	What is going right?
Heart/Feeling	How can I numb myself to avoid feeling?	How can I better tap into my feelings and use them as a superpower?
	What will others think if I allow myself to be who I really am and stop hiding?	What's one thing I can do right now to accept and embrace my unique feelings?
	Why do I feel like I have to go it alone?	How can I use my feelings as data to learn, grow, and support myself? Who is available to support me?

Function	Criticizer Mindset	Appreciator Mindset
Hand/Doing	What can I do to make myself look better to others?	What steps can I take to be more authentic and approachable?
	How can I manipulate others to get my way?	What can I do to connect more deeply with myself and others?
	Who can I control?	Who can I collaborate with?
Spirit/Being	In what ways am I more worthy, valuable, and loved than others?	In what ways are we all connected as one?
	Why can't I be perfect?	How can I celebrate my imperfections?
	How can I be more special?	How can I serve my community and make it a more special place?

Turn Off Your Autopilot

Another way to cultivate appreciation and gratitude and step up your spiritual stamina is to turn off your autopilot. You know when you've lived in the same house and worked at the same office for years, and you can drive to and from work without really thinking at all? That's how many of us go through life.

But then think of when you're in a foreign city, have no idea where you're going, and need to pay careful attention, so you will reach your desired destination and also stay safe and respect the safety of those around you. What do you have to do then? For starters, you have to pay attention to the present moment with purpose and intention because more focus and clarity are required.

It's nice to have familiarity with a region and a map to help us get where we are going, but don't forget to slow down and tune in to your own inner GPS as well. We tune in by practicing being intentional, which means we actively interact and engage with our lives.

Thrust into Vulnerability

Sometimes life doesn't care if we are ready to lean into vulnerability and be open and tender. There are instances when we have no choice but to step up our spiritual stamina.

Between October 2014 and October 2015, I lost two dear friends, who had also been two of the great loves of my life, to suicide. Their deaths came as a complete shock to all of us who loved them. There were no warning signs, no drugs involved, and no indications of unhappiness, let alone depression or other mental illness.

"I can't believe this," I kept saying over and over again. "No, not Sam, not Raf; they were so happy. They loved life. They had so much to live for. They were so close to their families, had so many friends. I can't believe this. This can't be real."

But according to the American Foundation for Suicide

Prevention, there actually are almost always warning signs. Research shows that 90 percent of people who die by suicide suffer from mental disorders or substance abuse. In most cases, the condition is untreated.

I believe these two men, like most men, were taught not to express their deepest fears or emotions and to keep their pain hidden inside. And people like me who were close to them and loved them didn't know what signs and symptoms to look for.

What is clear is how much these men were loved and adored by family, friends, and coworkers. Both had pure, gentle hearts, life-of-the-party personalities, and kind dispositions. I never heard either of them say one bad thing about another person.

Despite not being romantically involved with either of them at the times of their deaths, they always occupied a special place in my heart. They are in my bones. They quite literally are a part of me, of my spirit.

I am haunted by the way they chose to end their lives, leaving me and many others with questions that will never be answered, heartache that will forever be part of our existence, and pain that we must accept will never fully go away. In a way, I don't want it to. It reminds me of how much they meant to me, how their love and presence in my life affected me in such a profound way.

I've learned that surviving the suicide of a loved one means accepting a new normal — the normal being your heart is always a little heavy — it's raw, it bleeds, and that's okay.

According to the Centers for Disease Control and Prevention, nearly fifty thousand Americans die by suicide every year. Globally the number is one million, with suicide taking more lives than war, murder, and natural disaster combined. It is something we are all familiar with, yet very few of us actually talk about it.

The media speaks of the event itself, especially in cases like that of my friend Sam, who was a public figure. But I've found that most people don't want to speak of suicide at all. It's unfortunately a taboo subject, leaving the people left behind, like me, feeling isolated, angry, alone. Even mentioning that someone incredibly close to me jumped off a bridge out of nowhere caused some people to completely shut down, some even walking away from me, unable to give me even a simple hug — something I craved and still crave every day.

When I returned home from Sam's funeral in Los Angeles, my mom told me she was happy I could go to the service for closure. But I didn't feel any closure after the funeral. All I felt was more confusion, sadness, anger, and guilt. My mind still couldn't comprehend that he was gone.

It's hard to celebrate the life of someone who chose to end theirs, right? But the thing is, I don't think Sam or Raf killed themselves. I think whatever demons they were silently battling killed them. They clearly weren't in their right minds when they decided to leave us so soon. How could they be? These are the questions I'm learning to let go of. When I am overwhelmed with grief, I tell myself, *I surrender it all.*

I think one of the hardest things about losing a loved one to suicide is that I will never truly know why they chose to end their lives. It hurts me to accept that I couldn't heal, help, or solve their problems and prevent the act itself — none of us could.

Some days I begin to feel a bit better, remembering all

the good times we shared together. But just when I think I am over the hump, I realize there will always be another hump.

I will experience waves of uncontrollable anger and sadness, or I will hear a song, see a photo, or have a dream about them. Sometimes during a meditation or even walking down the street, they will come to me and hold my hand. It is comforting but also makes me miss them terribly, desperately wanting to see and talk to them again and remind them how much I love them. They let me know that they know. They are always with me now.

As many gifts, lessons, and memories as they gave me in life, they continue to send me gifts and blessings in their deaths — sending people and circumstances to help me heal and grow. I smile and say thank you.

To some, suicide is viewed as a selfish act. I don't think these men were selfish, and they definitely didn't want to cause any of us pain. They just needed to escape their own suffering. At Sam's funeral, we were given a message from him from heaven, one that came to his father in a dream. Sam said, "I'm sorry I didn't give you more notice I was leaving. I just couldn't stay another day."

Sam and Raf may be gone from this earth, but they will never leave my heart or my side. I take them with me everywhere I go. In that way, I don't have to get over their deaths, because I've accepted I never will, but I get to be with them in spirit for the rest of my life here and beyond.

My hope is that sharing my story will bring awareness to suicide and suicide prevention, and others will feel more comfortable talking about the subject. I hope my broken heart can help others heal theirs as well. It's time we start talking about it and taking care of each other, before we lose the chance. Remember, when we open ourselves up and allow ourselves to be vulnerable, we build our spiritual stamina and make ourselves available for renewal.

If you are in a crisis, please call a friend or family member — we want to listen and help! Or you can call the National Suicide Prevention Lifeline: 1-800-273-TALK.

Making Friends with Our Uncomfortable Feelings

"Can we be friends?"

"I see you've come to visit and want to connect with me. What would you like me to know?"

This is the conversation I've learned to have with difficult emotions like grief, anger, and despair. Part of building our spiritual stamina is learning to accept all our feelings, including the uncomfortable ones.

Luckily, grief is a wise old friend, here to teach us lessons we may not have had the capacity to understand until now. She carries with her the gift of deep appreciation. When she leaves, our lives appear more meaningful and fulfilling — it's like we have a new set of eyes and an even bigger heart. Yielding to a higher perspective steps up our spiritual stamina.

Here's what your friend grief would like you to know:

You are not going crazy. You are recovering.

Intense, uncontrollable feelings of pain, confusion, shock, fatigue, and exhaustion may feel foreign to us at first. I remember leaving work one evening, walking into a coffee shop, ordering my drink, and sitting down at a table to relax. Seemingly out of nowhere, I started sobbing. There was no stopping my tears.

I missed Sam. I didn't understand why. I couldn't bear to think of the amount of pain he must have been in to end his beautiful life, unknowingly transferring his pain on to those of us who loved him so much. I cried knowing I would never see him again, touch him, look into his eyes and smile, hear his voice, hold his hand.

It was all too much. And there I was, sitting by myself in a coffee shop in the middle of Manhattan, surrounded by people, feeling isolated and alone — that same feeling my two friends must have felt when they took their own lives at such a young age.

When I reached out to friends and family, I got the "I'm sorry; you'll be okay" response. I felt more alone. They couldn't feel my pain. I wouldn't wish it upon anybody, but was it normal to be feeling this sad?

When you go through a trauma, it's key to understand that whatever feelings are coming up for you are "normal" and are there to help you heal. As the saying goes, "You have to feel it to heal it." Try to embrace your emotions rather than fight or control them. Find a friend or support group that can understand what you are going through.

Here are some tips for making friends with uncomfortable feelings.

Stop Judging

Some days I would think to myself, *Shouldn't I be feeling better by now?* Even though it had only been a few months, I got irritated that all my body wanted to do was rest. *Really, another nap? I have things I want and need to do! How much time is it going to take to get over this?*

The answer is that it will take as long as it takes.

It isn't about getting over something; it is about creating a new way of being with yourself and others in the world. Surviving a tragedy, trauma, loss, or any experience that brings up big, uncomfortable feelings isn't something to "get over." We may have to accept that we will never be the same person, and that's okay. Opening up and sharing your story will help you and others heal. You can choose to turn your pain into your purpose and offer some sort of peace and comfort to others.

Easy Does It

Be extremely gentle with yourself. If this means not getting out of your pajamas and staying home all day doing nothing, then so be it. No judgment. Radical self-care goes a long way when it comes to healing and dealing with grief. Bubble baths, nutritious meals, walks in nature, journaling, spa treatments, and naps are always on my agenda.

If we want to be supported, we must learn to support ourselves first. Check in with your body, head, heart, and soul, and ask, *What do you need to feel better/great/happy/cared for?*

Difficult Emotions Are Different for Everyone

Comparison is never a good idea, but it's especially harmful to those healing from grief, anger, or despair. One person may deal with their pain by staying extremely busy and active, while another may need to stay in bed for a week. There is no right or wrong, good or bad when it comes to healing, unless you are causing harm to yourself or others.

You Are Not Alone

Dozens of professional organizations are available to those who need counseling to get through difficult feelings and help recovering from damaging experiences. All it takes is asking for help. People want to assist us in our recovery.

JOURNALING EXERCISE
Vulnerability V-Ups

1. When was the last time someone triggered you? Can you think of a few reasons they may have acted the way they did that have nothing to do with you?
2. Bring to mind a somewhat difficult person in your life. What might you have in common with them as a human being?
3. What would you offer a friend at the end of a hard day that you could offer yourself now?
4. If a child told you they were a failure because of some small mistake, how might you respond? Can you try the same words and tone for yourself?
5. If compassion could speak, what would it say to you right now to comfort you?
6. Ask yourself if there is any part of you that resists self-compassion. If so, ask that part, *How are you try-ing to keep me safe?*
7. Can you think of a small, painful experience that can be transformed into purpose or growth to heal yourself or others?
8. Is there some part of you that hides from the world?

Write a short note to that part of you from the perspective of a best friend.

9. What old story do you tell about yourself over and over again? Could you take a moment and write down the more helpful version?

10. Write down one small way you can wish yourself well today.

 ## LOVING COMPASSION MEDITATION

Find a comfortable seated position in your meditation space. Gently close your eyes, and as you breathe in and out, see if you can let yourself enjoy the sensations of simply breathing. Allow it to be a life-giving sensation and enjoy it as deeply as you can. Repeat this cycle of breathing as you continue to relax into your body.

Good.

Now bring to mind a small frustration or irritation you've had with yourself. Observe the energy of these difficult emotions as they rise to the surface of your consciousness. They may have a color, shape, size, or image associated with them. Take a deep, letting-go breath, and then notice if any other emotions may also be present and in need of some kind, loving attention.

Allow any unpleasant emotions to simply be for a few moments. And then watch as they disappear into the air. You may wish to envision yourself putting these emotions into a hot air balloon basket, for example, and watch them take flight and fly away. Smile as you wave goodbye.

If you are experiencing any emotions that don't feel like your own and belong to someone else, be it a spouse, friend, relative, coworker, or stranger you passed by during your day, go ahead and pack up those emotions in a beautiful box and give them back to their owner. Maybe you need to give your friend her grief back. Perhaps your coworker passed his frustration on to you. Now's the time to give everyone back their "stuff." Watch in your mind's eye as you present everyone with their neatly wrapped packages containing their emotions that were never yours to carry.

This is also a perfect time to give your inner critic their emotions back as well. You can calmly say, I know you are criticizing me because you are suffering. I want to care for you.

Send yourself and your inner critic compassion for three breaths, and notice if there is a shift.

Now take a deep breath in, and as you exhale, breathe into your heart center. If it's comfortable for you, place your hand on your heart. As you continue to take deep breaths in and out, consciously exhale any tension in your mind and body. Take as much time as you need to do this. This is not a time to rush or force; simply allow yourself to be still in the present moment. Whatever comes up mentally, physically, or emotionally for you is perfect. Notice that in this moment, as you are still and breathing, all is well. Life is beautiful. Life supports you. Life is like art, and you are the artist.

Now that you've had a moment to tune in to your heart, your breath, and the present moment, notice any sensations in your body. Ask your heart if it has any messages for you. You may hear something right away. Or it may take a moment. Tune in and listen. Receive what your heart is trying to tell you.

(Pause)

Now ask your heart how you can give yourself even more loving compassion.

(Pause)

Keep track of the number of self-criticisms and the number of compassionate encouragements you give yourself. Set an intention to shift that ratio toward compassion.

Continue to breathe in compassionate thoughts and breathe out any leftover criticism. When you are ready, start to wiggle your fingers and toes and gently come back to the room.

 COACH KATE CHECK-IN

How are you feeling?! You're doing such a great job! I want to pass along a checklist that I use to keep my spiritual stamina high. You may find it helpful to write your answers down on Post-it notes to keep handy by your desk, refrigerator, or vanity. It's inevitable that we will have "off days," so I find this check-in to be a good reminder of how we can come back home to our center and feel more grounded. This checklist ties together some of the skills from the various steps leading up to this point.

Make a list of the following:

1. Things that will support you.
2. Ways that you can rely on others to help you. What resources do you have?
3. Uplifting and energizing phrases you can say to yourself when you're being hard on yourself.
4. People and behaviors to avoid when you are struggling.
5. Actions you will take when you feel like giving up.

STEP 7: STEP UP YOUR SPIRITUAL STAMINA *AFFIRMATION*

I am okay if it happens and okay if it doesn't happen, because I know that what's best for me is already on its way and can't miss me. I have full-time faith and the confidence to trust that I am always being guided and supported. My new definition of success is based on who I am, not what I do. I am a success because I trust in myself and the God of my own understanding, as well as my newfound ability to be open and vulnerable.

STEP 8
Embrace Your Endorphins

Joy is not in things; it is in us.

— RICHARD WAGNER

Think of someone or something that brings you joy. Whatever just popped into your mind is perfect.

For me, it's Teddy! Just thinking about my parents' dog, Teddy, fills me with such warm feelings of love and joy! He is the sweetest soul and pure, unconditional love. Teddy is a ten-year-old mini-goldendoodle with ultrasoft, fluffy hair and kind, gentle, golden eyes. He loves to hug, cuddle, and be held like a baby. My friends say he doesn't even look real; he looks more like a stuffed animal.

Thinking about how much I love Teddy, how much he loves me (and all people), and how I feel when I'm around him brings about the most pleasant, safe, loving feelings in me.

I find it impossible to be upset, fearful, or in any sort of funky mood when I am thinking about Teddy or spending time with him. If you have pets, you most likely understand what I am talking about. Just saying their names brings us joy. Think about a person or pet who creates this feeling for you. Hold a vision of him or her in your mind. Connect with these feelings of happiness and love. Breathe them in, and share them out into the world. Feel the energy in your body begin to shift and change.

Next, I invite you to think of your "happy place" or a beautiful memory. Where are you? What are you doing? Who are you with?

In my hypnotherapy sessions, my therapist, Kailah, counts me down to my "safe place," and I always find myself in Lake Como or Lisbon — two of my favorite places in the world that offer me serenity and solace. I sit or lie down, close my eyes, and open to the light within. There I see and feel myself in these magical places. In order to recall these sites later, I'm sure to be extra-present when I travel, paying close attention to my immediate surroundings, writing poetry in my mind — whether it's the vivid colors of the Cinque Terre towns; the aroma of fresh, homemade spaghetti; the taste of authentic gelato; the sound of the waves crashing against the boat in Capri; or the glint of that icy blue grotto water up close.

The screen saver on my phone is the view from my last night in Portugal, as I sat on the flower-filled terrace outside my hotel (a palace) on top of the city of Lisbon, overlooking the ocean and all the magnificent architecture, sipping on a glass of chilled Verde wine. I was enjoying the late-day sunshine from underneath the safety of an umbrella, and there was a light breeze in the air. The weather could not have been more perfect. I sat there for hours, taking it all in, knowing I would always want to refer back to that moment as one of the most exquisite pleasures of my life. I was not distracted by anything or anyone. I just got to feel like a queen for a few hours. My companions were sheer beauty, wonder, awe, and gratitude.

If you feel called, go ahead and close your eyes for a moment, and take yourself to your safe place. What do you see, feel, taste, touch, hear? Enjoy the bliss of the experience all over again if you can. Maybe you are physically in that space now.

Our challenge is to *experience* our safe place wherever we are in the world — ordinary or extraordinary — regardless of our current mood or life circumstances.

Sometimes, we can use photos or old journals, letters, or other writings as prompts to bring back the calm and comfort we experienced at a treasured time in the past. When I was in my early twenties, I went snowshoeing on Mount Rainier just outside Seattle. At the top of the mountain, I sat down in what felt like a plush snow chair and looked around in amazement and wonder. I felt so invigorated in the arms of this magnificent glacier. When I returned home, I wrote this poem. You could call it my love letter to Mount Rainier.

SNOW-CAPPED MOUNTAIN

Suddenly it appears as though the Earth has stopped,
for it is nearly motionless.
I can hear my own silent breath in the clean, crisp air.
Nature embraces me, and I can literally see the tall, thick

pine trees smile at me from under their pure, white,
snowy blankets.
They speak to me.
Now listening, I look around slowly,
in awe,
feeling the trees' mighty, yet subtle presence.
Each and every second of this calming afternoon is
savored, and I carefully photograph the images in my
peaceful mind.
Time is not an issue
and loneliness is not an option
in this simple, beautiful moment of solitude.

Just reading this again puts me back in the peaceful state
of gratitude and awe I experienced on that beautiful mountain. It's so powerful to channel the energy from these moments to help shift us back into a state of grace and calm. It's
easy, fun, and free!

Now it's your turn! What memory do you have that helps
center you and bring you back to joy? How can you jog those
memories and cultivate joy? I invite you to compose something for your happy place, person, or animal. Try not to
overthink or edit, and simply let the emotion pour from
your heart to the page. There is no right or wrong way to
write a love letter. In my experience, when we express love,
miracles occur, so be open to receiving.

You can use these simple methods to swerve out of a
powerless state and into a much more soothing place that
suits you better. The best part? You can share these feelings
with others and raise the vibration of everyone around you,
creating a ripple effect that is so needed in today's world.

What Brings Us Joy?

Our glands and brains produce endorphins that reduce our pain and increase our feelings of well-being. They release this powerful substance when we exercise (a "runner's high") and also when we connect with joyful memories and activities that make us happy. Through spiritual fitness, we can create the equivalent of a runner's high. Reflecting on what brings us joy and actively choosing to spend more time immersed in these activities enables a more blissful state of mind as our default setting.

I asked research participants, "Who or what brings you joy?" and "When you think of a moment where you felt in the flow and at peace, what were you doing?" I then urged them to reflect a bit deeper, asking them what about this particular place, activity, person, or animal made them feel at peace and in joy.

Several themes emerged as ways to experience genuine joy and feel at peace, which I'll summarize below. It's worth taking a moment to read through these common themes and make a note of any that resonate for you.

- Being present to our immediate surroundings while slowing down to notice and appreciate the beauty around us (often called mindfulness)
- Connection to self, others, something beyond ourselves, and to what matters
- Simplicity
- Ordinary moments with a loved one. One participant said having coffee every morning with her husband and dog brings her joy, for example.
- Distraction-free quiet time

- Nurturing or taking care of something and watching it grow. Gardening came up quite a few times, as did the theme of working *with* nature versus pushing, forcing, or placing *our* agenda on nature. Another participant spoke about the power of working *with* the roots, rocks, and sun while letting go of her plan for how things should go and instead being open to new possibilities. This is the joy of working together and collaborating!
- Building something from nothing
- Seeing the world through the eyes of your child. One woman talked about the simple act of watching bees doing their job (something her two-year-old son was fascinated by and made her stop and notice as well).
- Helping others develop their skills and increase their knowledge while working as a coach, mentor, or teacher
- Moments that keep us off our phones
- Anytime we aren't being self-conscious
- New experiences. Sharing these experiences amplifies the joy.
- Creating environments for ourselves that help us tap into the joy that is already within us.
- Clearing out the junk in our homes and minds.
- Being with others who have passionate and dedicated minds and embody a high degree of presence, as described by Mari Evans: "I will bring you a whole person and you will bring me a whole person and we will have us twice as much of love and everything."
- Keeping a deceased loved one's memory alive
- Challenging but doable artistic creation

- Curiosity and playfulness
- Doing something from a place of pure love and trust, not having to "think" about it

Joy occurs naturally when we open up to the goodness that is already inside ourselves. I experience joy when I trade my inner critic for empathy and just let myself *be*. My definition of joy? Complete surrender to, awareness of and appreciation for the present moment. It's also choosing to focus on *improving* rather than *proving*. Not being put in a box. Engaging in deep, meaningful conversations, preferably with people who "get" me and lovingly challenge and encourage me to be the best me, the true me.

As you can see, simple "ordinary" moments came up time and time again when people talked about what brought them joy and peace, and not one participant mentioned money, material possessions, appearance, or any of the other societal trappings we assume will make us happier.

Signs from the Universe

One of my favorite endorphin-generators is signs from the universe. I choose to believe these signs are all around us, guiding us and giving us the insight and inspiration we need in the moment, and I choose to seek them out. I've come to recognize small signs and symbols that pop up as indicators that our deceased loved ones are visiting us.

About a month after my dear friend Sam passed away, I started seeing coins in my path. I would find pennies randomly and seemingly out of place. At first, I didn't think much of it, but when I started finding coins quite frequently as I went about my day, I started paying more attention.

One day I was leaving a photo shoot at a pristine Wall Street building. I was feeling stressed and anxious about a work situation and was rushing to another appointment. As I was speed-walking through the lobby and working up a sweat in my scarf and heavy winter coat, the shiniest penny I have ever seen lay right in front of me on the immaculately kept marble floor. There wasn't even a speck of dirt on the floor, but there in front of me was a penny.

After what was by then weeks of seeing coins in my path, this no longer felt like coincidence. I slowed down, smiled, looked right at the penny, and said, "Hi, baby. I love you."

I knew it was Sam telling me, "It's okay. I've got you. Everything is going to be okay. Everything is going to work out. I am with you. You are supported. You are valuable. You are loved."

Whatever tension I was holding on to was immediately released. I relaxed. I knew it was all going to be okay.

I got used to seeing pennies, sometimes nickels and dimes, on my path, but then one day it had been about a week with no signs. I remember saying to Sam, "What's up? Where have you been? I miss you."

That same day, on the subway, I looked down, thinking I saw a penny, and it was just old gum stuck to the ground in a circular shape.

Now I was joking with Sam, like we always did in person, asking him again, "What's up? Oh, you think you're funny. Okay."

The very next day, I met my friend Melissa at a Thai restaurant in Jersey City. She was already seated and waiting for me at the table. I sat down, ordered some food, and started telling her about Sam and all the coins, and how I hadn't seen any in a while.

About a minute later, I looked over to my left and saw I was sitting next to about two hundred coins spread out all over these Buddha statues. I laughed out loud and got the chills from head to toe.

Sam and his hilarious, dramatic sense of humor! I could hear him laughing hysterically and saying, "I'll show you, Kate. I'll get your attention in a big way!" It was such a beautiful moment with my recently deceased friend. I felt so connected to him and so silly for ever doubting that he is always with me and loves and values me so very much.

Whether you have recently lost a loved one or not, finding coins is a major sign that we are highly valued. Please take this to heart, and when you notice a coin that seems out of place, take a moment to receive this important message.

Because I believe when our loved ones cross over, they want to let us know they are doing well, watching over us, and sending their love. I also believe they send small signs and symbols by placing something like a penny or feather in our path to point us in the right direction.

I continue to find comfort in these "pennies from heaven." For me, the number "1" on these pennies signifies unity and oneness. It signals to me that there is unity and oneness in the afterlife and also a unity and oneness between my loved one and me. I feel his spirit move with and through me.

I know it also means my deceased loved ones are always visiting, guiding, protecting, and loving me while showing me I am valued and never alone. The coins are a gentle reminder to slow down, enjoy the present moment, and be thankful.

The next time you see a coin cross your path, allow yourself to pause and remember:

You are valued.

You are loved.

Welcoming and accepting these signs as opportunities to feel hopeful, grateful, and loved is one of my favorite ways to boost endorphins in day-to-day life.

Seek Out Symbolism

Not so long ago, I was taking my nightly walk in my neighborhood, doing my usual laps around the same streets, committed to getting my ten thousand steps a day in while keeping my mind and spirit fit as well.

As the sky was turning to dusk, I heard loud rustling in the bushes next to me on the sidewalk. As I glanced over, I saw a skunk just inches away. Startled and scared he would spray me, I quickly ran away. *Phew!* I thought, *I'm so lucky he didn't spray me, as we both seemed to startle one another.*

As I made another lap, now back near my house, I considered going home but decided to do one more half-mile loop. It was now about 9 p.m. and dark outside. I had my music turned up in my earphones and was fully in the zone as endorphins started kicking in. As I power-walked down a dimly lit but familiar street, out of nowhere, a skunk (which I assumed was the same guy from earlier) ran right past me. He was so close he stepped on my foot! I screamed, jumped off the sidewalk — nearly out of my skin — and ran! Again, the little guy chose not to spray me, which is a miracle because my screaming must have freaked him out as well! (Sorry, neighbors!)

I had just been voice-texting a friend, telling her about my first skunk sighting, but after the second time, I said, "This is a sign. I really need to look up what it means when a skunk crosses your path, because it just happened twice in about twenty minutes!" This was unheard of.

My friend texted me the following information and then said, "Wow-wow-wow-wow!"

According to TheAstrologyWeb.com, "If a skunk crosses your path, it's a reminder for you to develop your strength and become self-dependent, for it is only through relying on your own instincts that you may turn out victorious in life."

The website TrustedPsychicMediums.com says, "The skunk meaning places the emphasis on being distinct. It symbolizes the importance of being who you are and living authentically without caring about other people's opinions. When the skunk spirit animal appears to you, it's to help you build up your self-confidence."

Never mind that so much of my work revolves around confidence building, and my first step to transcendent self-confidence is to develop self-sufficiency. It was like the skunk was winking at me, reminding me that I am on the right path and to keep going.

The world is always speaking to us through signs and symbols, whether we believe it or not. I choose to believe because I like receiving messages from divine intelligence and accepting what is important for me to know in the moment. I find that life flows better and is more enjoyable when I choose to cocreate with the universe and stay open to her magical opportunities and insights. In this way, even though I spend a lot of time on my own, I know I am never alone and am always being guided.

I Am That I Am

I believe we are all looking for the same thing in life: to love and be loved; to feel seen, heard, and understood; to know that our lives matter; to discover our purpose, live our passion, and become self-actualized.

But what many of us don't realize is just how powerful we are. We think we need more money, to look differently, be a certain age or from a certain family, wait for the "right" person to come along, rack up a million social media followers, have something or be anything other than who we are right now, in order to fulfill society's definition of success. Then there's our own definition of success that we also pressure ourselves to live up to.

Regardless of how we define success and what our goals are, I've found that two small words can dramatically improve our ability to call in the life we've been craving.

Those two words: "I am."

Whatever follows these words will eventually find you, so be very conscious and deliberate about what you attach to "I am."

For example, if you find yourself constantly saying, "I am so tired, frustrated, confused, broke, lonely, heartbroken, sad, angry," I don't need to know you to know what your life looks and feels like. I bet it's pretty tiring, frustrating, confusing, lacking, lonesome, heartbreaking, sad, and upsetting. Am I right?

That's because when you say "I am...," you're inviting in whatever you attach to it. In other words, you are giving it permission to be in your life (good or bad).

What if, instead, you said, "I am so excited, happy, free, healthy, loving, abundant, valuable, smart, kind, attractive, supported, and safe." I can only imagine how much better you would feel and how different your life would look.

This isn't about lying to yourself and saying, "I am in perfect health," when really you are sick. For example, when I am under the weather, I'm not focusing on that. Instead, I keep saying, "I am so fortunate that I get to spend the day in my cozy home resting and caring for my health."

You get the idea. So while physically I may not be 100 percent, I still feel really great! And by feeling great, I naturally attract more great things into my life. I can say this with confidence because I am witness to it day in and day out.

Another statement I hear a lot is, "I am confused."

What if you tried on, "I am seeking clarity in this moment and look forward to knowing exactly what I need to know soon."

Try it out for yourself today. Once you become more conscious of your thoughts, you will begin to see patterns and ways in which you can clean them up, thereby attracting what you actually want into your life. Remember, you are in control. Your thoughts are extremely powerful. When you blame, judge, compare, or make excuses, you are giving all your power away.

What do you want to invite into your life today?

How do you want to feel?

What or who do you want to let go of?

I'll give you another example. I was talking to a dear friend who has been trying to get pregnant for some time now. I have heard her say things like, "I'm too old to have a child. I'm so scared. I'm so frustrated, overwhelmed, disappointed."

While all these statements are valid, and it's important to be honest about how we actually feel, it's also worth trying out some new words to follow "I am."

What if the new story my friend created was, "I am having so much fun trying to get pregnant. I am loving all the quality time I get to spend with my husband. I am so healthy.

I am the perfect age for me to get pregnant. I am feeling great. I am inviting our new baby into our lives with open arms. I am so happy!"

Can you feel the higher vibration behind this language?

Clients will tell me, "Well, it's hard to say positive things about myself, my work, my partner, and so on."

Are you telling me it's easy to feel like crap all the time?

I think we can all decide to choose again and lean toward joy rather than live in scarcity and be miserable. Life is meant to be enjoyable! Let's enjoy it and be deliberate about what words we choose to attach to "I am."

Gentle reminder: I know you already know this, but it's not enough to just pay lip service to our goals. We have to also take physical action. You can hire the best physical trainer in the world who can equip you with all the motivation, knowledge, and workout routines to help you reach your optimal physical fitness level, but the trainer can't do your sit-ups and pull-ups for you. That's on you. The good news is, *you* get to experience the endorphins from putting in the work and living the results!

The Joy of the Journey

Several years ago, I embarked on a journey to the Sanctuary at Two Rivers in Cabuya, Costa Rica, for a weeklong adventure of self-discovery, transformation, and fun, along with fourteen other women ranging in age from nineteen to forty-seven. We stayed in eco-chic tree houses enclosed with screens, where we went to sleep and woke up to real-life jungle sounds of monkeys, insects, and birds — no sound machines or alarm clocks needed! The howler monkeys (who sound like shrieking, deep-voiced aliens) and the sun let us know when it was time to wake up.

We showered outside surrounded by lush jungle plants and trees. To even get a cab into town, we had to hike down an obstacle course–like path filled with large rocks and rivers (sometimes in the dark, using only flashlights to guide the way). The hike took about thirty minutes. I was soaking wet every time from the oppressive heat and humidity. Bug bites and bee stings were a common and expected occurrence.

The Costa Rican jungle was stunningly majestic, but it was also extremely uncomfortable for me. It was hot. I was wet and sweaty at all times. There were no air-conditioned rooms to retreat to. I looked and felt like a wet dog. I kept waiting for someone to care that I looked like a hot mess, but nobody did. I quickly learned it is okay to not look cute — seriously, nobody cares. It was like being eight years old again: the most important thing was to have fun, play, laugh, dance, climb mountains, get dirty, get messy, swim, snorkel, and go with the flow.

The freedom of it all made me laugh, thinking about how seriously we take our day-to-day lives, when what we should really be doing is surrendering to what is, trusting we are on the right path (even in the dark), remembering we are always supported, and sitting back, relaxing, and allowing true transformation to occur.

Stress has no place in the jungle. It gets laughed at. My absurd, self-limiting beliefs and stories I have created over the years that no longer suit me are comical. I let them all go with a deep breath and a deep, hearty laugh.

The heat made me uncomfortable but also present — I had to stop and pay attention to the fact that even my knees were sweating, and it was okay. Self-awareness is sexy. Joy is girl-next-door hot. Not needing to be anything but myself — sweaty face, bad hair day, and all — is success. It is healthy to let go. It is safe for me to be myself. I am loved.

This epic adventure wasn't about going to Costa Rica; it was about journeying inside, reconnecting with and embracing my fearless eight-year-old self, sharing my truth, and coming home to my true essence. This is my wish for everyone. You don't have to travel abroad; you just have to be willing to open up and let go.

 **JOURNALING EXERCISE**
Spiritual Jumping Jacks for Joy

I was born during a historic blizzard in Cincinnati, and I recently spent my birthday snowed in during another record-setting blizzard in New York City. (Hopefully this sentence cooled you down after sweating through the Costa Rican jungle!)

One of my favorite mantras is "Everything is perfect," so at the end of the day, I winked back at God, curled up in my favorite robe with some hot tea, and reflected on my special day (January 23). I couldn't help but think of the little girl smiling back at me in the picture on my desk.

I'm very proud of this little girl. She has been through a lot, but she never stops putting one foot in front of the other and moving forward. Who is she? Me.

When I feel the need to be self-critical, I try to think of her and remember to love and nurture her instead. She deserves the world, and I want to give it to her. My birthday wish is that you can do the same for yourself. I think we'd live in a much different world.

I invite you to take a few minutes to do a simple journaling exercise with me in the name of self-love and appreciation. I'm finding that appreciation is the antidote to judging. Find a photo of yourself as a child. If you can't find one, close your eyes and imagine that child in your mind, with his or her smile, laughter, innocence, playfulness, curiosity, and hope.

This beautiful child still lives within you and needs your care, kindness, gentleness, and unconditional love. He or she needs to feel nurtured and supported. Your younger self needs to be forgiven in a nonjudgmental way. This child needs to know that everything is going to be okay.

As an adult, I've caught myself dishing out some seriously negative self-talk and criticism. Consciously choosing to work through these negative thoughts has helped curb my indulgence in this self-destructive talk. But if someone said even *one* hurtful thing to the little girl in the photo, I would immediately go into protective mama-bear mode and fiercely roar at them.

Are you ready to give this awesome kid your attention?

This exercise will help you become more childlike, tapping into your natural creativity, playfulness, passion, and individuality.

When you feel ready, write this gorgeous soul a nurturing love letter. Tell them what you wish they had known back then. Give them the encouragement and guidance you wish someone had given you. Tell them some comforting words to get them through a challenging time.

This love note is just for you and your younger self, so no need to edit; just let your feelings flow. Really connect to this child. I find the exercise to be extremely healing, and it helps me connect back to myself, realizing I am that little girl, and I need to be kind and loving at all times.

This practice is therapeutic, as it connects you to your heart — your true self. In the past, when I was confronted with a crisis or indecision, I would seek out the advice of others, oftentimes ignoring my own inner wisdom and guidance. My mind and ego were too in the way.

Connecting with my inner child and heart space allows me to listen to my own advice, which always points me in the right direction. I make decisions for the highest good for all.

The more you do this exercise and consciously consider the welfare of your younger self, the easier it will be to honor and embrace the person you are right now.

Here's an example of a love note I wrote to my younger self:

Dear Kate,

I know you are in a lot of pain, and feel so alone. You don't know what you've done to deserve this broken heart. I'm here to tell you that the pain you are in will become your purpose in life. Your broken heart will help others heal their broken hearts. Hang in there. Be kind to yourself. You are so strong and brave. I am so incredibly proud of you. You never give up. You always manage to land on your feet because of your fierce character, and yes, that broken heart of yours will make you a deeper, richer, wiser, more compassionate woman.

When you get rejected, say, "Thank you." You are being guided to something more in alignment for you.

I have your back. You are safe. You will experience so much love and joy if you just quiet your mind and allow it to happen.

You are so incredibly loved and blessed. You are going to live the life of your dreams.

Just trust.

Just trust.

I hope you take some time to honor yourself and your inner child. He or she needs you, is waiting to connect with you, and wants to heal and grow.

Another option? Write a letter from your child self to your adult self. What would your ten-year-old self, for example, want you to know or be aware of now?

I often hear my child self say to me, "I think you should focus more on having fun. Don't take life so seriously. Enjoy it. Remember to play and make things. Go for a bike ride. Draw. Paint. Use your imagination. Bake a cake. Make your own icing. Make your own rules. Stay rebellious!"

 DIVINE WISDOM MEDITATION

This guided meditation will help you begin to put aside the ego and listen to the divine wisdom that's always available to you. I invite you to set aside at least five minutes a day (I recommend sending yourself a calendar invite and physically putting it into your schedule) to sit quietly without any noise or distractions. This helps us learn to become more practiced at listening. I find that when I give myself the time and space to listen to the divine wisdom that's always trying to make its way to me, I get more work done in less time and feel the satisfaction of ease and flow. I can't recommend this simple, but sometimes challenging, meditative exercise enough. The more we do it, the easier it becomes, and it has cumulative effects. Please let me know how it's working for you.

Get comfortable in your meditation space. Begin your meditative breathing, taking deep breaths in through your nose and out through your mouth. Feel how each breath cleanses your mind and body. Allow yourself the gift of relaxation with each letting-go breath. Continue this cycle of breathing throughout your meditation.

Begin to become more aware of your body as you breathe, noticing the rise and fall of your chest and stomach. Let any outside noises take you even deeper into your meditation.

Take a moment to scan both your physical and emotional body. Notice if there are any sensations present. It is safe to release any tension, stress, anxiety, fears, or concerns.

Relax...

Now picture yourself as the two-year-old child you once were. Go ahead and see him or her in your mind's eye. Notice what you are wearing, how your hair is styled, and the expression on your face. Are you involved in an activity? What are you doing? Who are you with, if anyone? What is the weather like? Let yourself be there now.

Ask your two-year-old self if there's someone you still need to forgive. Maybe it is you. If it's comfortable, go ahead and extend that forgiveness right now. How does this feel? If you're experiencing some resistance, continue to breathe into the discomfort. Take as much time as you need. Then when you are ready, take three breaths sending forgiveness and compassion to yourself or another person you still need to forgive. To forgive others, picture the other person as a small child.

Now imagine someone you love sending you an abundance of forgiveness and compassion.

Keep breathing.

Forgiveness and compassion go hand in hand when it comes to connecting with our divine wisdom. Repeat this meditation as often as needed to connect more deeply with your inner knowing. Smile, knowing you can share this gift with the world and make a meaningful impact in your own life and in the lives of many others. Take as long as you need to dwell in this divine wisdom and the feel-good feelings of forgiveness and compassion before slowly making your way back to full waking consciousness.

The Endorphin-Maker of Service

I've discovered that one of the best ways to experience heaven on earth is through service — putting our gifts to good use. When we're able to make a difference in the lives of others, even if it's in a small way, we feel that our existence has purpose. We have a reason to get up in the morning and keep going, even during those times when life *isn't* heaven on earth. Grand gestures are nice but aren't required. Think of a seemingly small extension of kindness that someone showed you and how much it touched your heart. Someone taking the time to write me a nice card expressing what my love and friendship mean to them feels like a million bucks but costs just a few dollars.

Every year, my aunt Judy sends out nearly two hundred (!) birthday and anniversary cards to every single one of her friends and relatives. Every single one. Every single year. Each card contains within it a crisp five-dollar bill. She has been doing this for nearly sixty years, and at eighty-one years young, she still finds a way to bless each of us with this act of generosity. It is so special to each of us because it's such a display of genuine kindness and thoughtfulness. In many ways, it means much more than an expensive gift bought without much thought or intention. Her consistency of this expression of love is unmatched, and she will always be remembered for this. What a legacy to leave!

And may I add: my aunt Judy is probably the most joyful person I know. She said she was inspired to do this because as a child her aunt Gladys sent her cards with a dollar bill inside, even though she didn't really have much money. Aunt Judy wanted to honor her aunt Gladys and show her love for her family by continuing the gesture — a reminder that kindness and generosity spread, and one simple act of love can create a huge ripple effect for generations.

My aunt Judy embodies one of my favorite quotes by author Bob Goff: "When joy is a habit, love is a reflex."

One of my favorite ways to experience heaven on earth is to give compliments. I think we live in a world where comparison, competition, fear, lack, and jealousy are the norm, sadly. I feel as though some people think if they compliment me, it somehow takes away from them. But the opposite is true, actually. On a spiritual level — we only get to keep what we give away.

I see the difference it makes in others when I take a moment to notice their pretty nails, stylish outfit, beautiful smile, radiant complexion, or inspiring speech, presentation, blog post, and so forth.

I see the act of freely giving compliments as a lost art form in our society. I remember telling one of a coach friend's basketball players that he did a great job in the game. I enthusiastically complimented his competitiveness, fight, and toughness. A friend of mine standing next to me seemed a bit taken aback, like *Gosh, don't give him a big head*, or *You sound obsessed with him*. I kindly told her afterward that I choose to compliment people and show appreciation by reminding them of their gifts. The world will beat you down enough. I'm choosing to lift others up any chance I get. The best part? It feels incredible to give! I get just as much as the recipient.

 ## DIVINE PURPOSE MEDITATION

Let's focus on finally letting go of the belief that we aren't capable or worthy of inspiring the world. Consider this a call to action designed to fill you with the overflowing energy of divine purpose. It's time to drop the act of playing small and finally step up to our divine responsibility to *be* the miracle that we are each uniquely capable of being.

> *Sit comfortably in your meditation space. Take three deep breaths in through your nose and out through your mouth. With every breath, imagine that your body is becoming more and more relaxed and open to hearing the truth.*
>
> *As you continue this cycle of breath, set an intention to learn what you need to learn in this moment without judgment.*
>
> *Just as we do in coaching to elicit deeper, more insightful responses in our clients, ask your divine self open-ended questions as opposed to closed yes-or-no inquiries.*

As you settle into a deeply relaxed and intuitive, listening state, see yourself holding the key that unlocks your divine purpose. Notice what the key looks like: see its color, texture, shape, and size. Feel it in your hands. Is it light or heavy?

Now, with this key in hand, say to yourself:

I am willing to take this inner journey and look for the answers within. I know best. Divine intelligence is always available to me.

I am willing to become more practiced at listening.

I am willing to feel fear and take the next steps anyway.

I am willing to change directions.

I am willing to feel ecstasy and know I am on the right path.

I am willing to be open to new experiences and opportunities I have never even thought of or considered before.

I am willing to be flexible as I acknowledge that my purpose can and will shift and evolve over time.

I am willing to fully express who I am.

I am willing to expand the opening of my heart.

I am willing to listen to what my divine purpose is in this lifetime.

Allow yourself to hear whatever comes up, knowing it is perfect. Continue this meditation practice to quiet the noise both in and around you and listen more deeply for additional answers to emerge. If and when you feel energy around a certain answer, that may be a sign to explore this option further. You may wish to journal about your experiences to gather more meaning or insight, or bring this topic to a coaching session for more clarity and to create an action strategy for implementation.

Multiple divine purposes may arise, which is great. Notice if there is a common theme or pattern.

Take a moment to sit in deep appreciation to honor the work you have done and will continue to do. Give yourself one of your favorite compliments.

As I mentioned earlier in this step, pay close attention to signs, symbols, and synchronicities. Embrace the fact that the universe is always communicating with you. Take a moment to dwell in this space of deep inner knowing, and when you are ready, gently return to the room.

JOURNALING EXERCISE
A Commitment to Service

I encourage you to make a commitment to service by writing a letter to your divine self or to the God of your own understanding. I find it to be a great accountability exercise to take the time to write our commitments down. It prompts us to take action rather than just talking about them or having all these grand ideas floating around in our minds. This is where the rubber meets the road and the needle is moved. This is mind decluttering coupled with an action plan, and it works!

Have fun with this exercise. Get creative. If you wrote your own wedding vows, for example, and committed yourself to another person for life in a ceremony, you know how profound an experience it can be to write a commitment letter. Be intentional with your words. Write in detail about how you will commit to service and your divine purpose. Ask your divine wisdom to lead the way. You've got this!

COACH KATE CHECK-IN

- How do you define joy?
- Who or what brings you joy?
- When you think of a moment where you felt in the flow and at peace, what were you doing?
- How can you share your joy with others?
- What can you do each day to feel more joy?

 ## STEP 8: EMBRACE YOUR ENDORPHINS
AFFIRMATION

The joy I seek is in me, and I can access it at any time. I know joy is always available to me in the present moment. I cocreate with the universe in order to tap into greater possibilities of peace and joy. I share my joy with others to double its potency. I am open to infinite possibilities of experiencing heaven on earth as much as possible. I use my divine wisdom to point me in the direction of my divine purpose.

STEP 9

Rock the
Freedom Freestyle

Abundance is not something we acquire.
It is something we tune in to.

— WAYNE DYER

The "freedom freestyle" is my term for really starting
to make spiritual fitness work for us and become a way of
life. This is about exploring what we truly want and attracting a joyful and abundant life suited to us personally. But
rather than *force* the fun, fulfilling, abundant life we desire,
we'll *allow* this abundance to unfold. I believe that mani-
festing abundance is about getting out of our own way and
allowing the universe's blessings to come to us. We ask to
be of service by putting our unique gifts to use rather than
requesting "things."

    If we trust that what we want or something better is on
the way, we can let it flow toward us easily. Part of trusting,

249

of course, means that we have to also allow disappointments and setbacks, knowing that they're bringing us closer to the abundance we seek. Our circumstances can't change until *we* change, so those disappointments and setbacks change us to get us ready for *more, better,* and/or *different.*

Abundance can mean different things to different people, and it doesn't necessarily have to relate to money. To some, abundance means time, connection, and support. To others, abundance is creativity and confidence.

I remember getting invited to a wellness retreat in Arizona that I really wanted to attend, but I didn't have any disposable income at the time. My friend Heather was also invited and really wanted to go, but said she didn't have the time, as she was strapped with the demands of being a new mother. I had more time than money; Heather had more money than time. I think of this often because our society paints a picture that money equals abundance, and while that can be true, there are many ways to feel abundant and even more ways to tap into the inner abundance that is always available to us. Ultimately, neither of us went to the retreat, but we plan to go together in the future. We trust there will be a perfect time for us.

No matter what it means to you, abundance is always present like the sun, but sometimes we don't see it through the clouds that we create with our fears, insecurities, and guilt. Maybe we think we aren't worthy of financial freedom or we don't deserve self-care.

It is our choice to accept or deny the gifts that continuously come to us. The key to attracting abundance is recognizing all the ways you're blocking it. Abundance is simply stepping out of your own way, releasing resistance, and being grateful for what you already have and open to receiving more.

How can we recognize the abundance in our lives?

When I worked full-time as a body-positive fashion model, I lost several clients all at once, which left me in a state of frustration because I felt I was losing work for ridiculous reasons. For instance, one client turned me into a computer-generated image of myself as a way to cut costs and never hired me again. Yes, my own digital mannequin took my job.

Another client decided they didn't want to work with my agency anymore. Then another decided to start shooting much smaller models. Ultimately, I lost nearly all my main clients and the majority of my income for reasons that had nothing to do with me or my performance. Initially, I dealt with it by panicking. I couldn't understand why this was happening to me, and there were months when I wondered how I was going to pay my bills.

I didn't realize my fears and insecurities were what was blocking me from receiving abundance.

So, how did I get out of my own way?

I did what I've been teaching in this book. I surrendered. I asked the universe for help. I prayed and then sat in meditation daily, asking for divine guidance and how I could serve my life's purpose.

The answer I received was that I have a much bigger purpose than modeling. That the career had taught me what I needed to learn, and it was time to move on. I was guided to read certain books and take certain courses, which led me to go to graduate school and to connect with other like-minded individuals. When I finally let go of modeling as my main source of income and opened myself up to other prospects, I came across new, exciting employment opportunities that allowed me to help others.

This experience taught me that instead of freaking out during setbacks, I should say "Thank you." Something bigger and better (or even just different) is taking shape, and abundance is coming.

How can we welcome more of it?

Here are some simple practices that helped me welcome more abundance into my life and can help you do the same. These practices draw on the skills we've worked on throughout the Full Spirit Workout so far. As you learn to put them into practice to really rock the freedom freestyle — the full spirit lifestyle — day to day, you will open yourself up to the abundance you desire and deserve.

- **Believe.** One of my personal mantras is "I trust that the universe is supporting me abundantly."
- **Be grateful for what you already have.** I've found that when I am thankful for all the ways in which I am already abundant, I easily attract more abundance into my life. Be willing to change your story. Instead of thinking, *I am not enough and don't have enough,* lead with *I am already abundant.*

  Be grateful for everything you are and have in this moment, and more of that goodness will flow your way. Decide to be certain that you are an energetic match for what you desire. You cannot have what you are not willing to *become* energetically. Begin by surrounding yourself with people who are already doing what you want to do. Attend activities with like-minded individuals. Say no to energy-draining invitations.

- **Strengthen your faith that it is your birthright to be abundant.** Recognize that you can't create the life of your dreams without first believing it is your right to do so. Then realize that you don't have to go it alone. Reach out to your support system, a higher power, or whatever you believe in. Stay open to being delighted rather than disappointed or let down. Also make a list of resources you have available to you. Even writing this down will make you feel more abundant.

- **Release fear and resistance.** Be mindful of your worldview. Do you engage with the world from a loving place or a fearful one? Ask your highest self to remove all obstacles blocking the way to abundance with this simple plea: "Please help me receive everything I need for my divine life purpose. Show me the way one step at a time. Allow me to see very clearly how I can make the world a better place and how I can be more at home within myself."

- **Still your heart and mind.** Envision what you desire in the here and now — not down the road. Believe it is already yours. Feel it in your core. Create the space for receiving abundance in all ways. Write the following phrases in your journal, or say them aloud:

I deserve to receive good as much as anyone.
It is safe for me to receive abundance now.
I open my arms to receive it.
I will be guided and given enough energy to follow
    through on that guidance.
I accept the support that is offered to me.

Opening ourselves up and allowing abundance into our lives truly frees us to live the lives we were meant to live.

What Does It Mean to "Rock It"?

We usually think of performance when we hear someone say, "You're going to rock it!" But for spiritual fitness, "rocking it" is more about getting still and protecting our emotional well-being. It is understanding that any outer limitations are just reminding us to get steady inside. We get steady and experience a stillness in spirit and mind by allowing ourselves to be guided by the sacred (service, purpose, self-actualization) rather than run by the appetite (fear, lack, control). When we are willing to accept this challenge, the universe assists us in miraculous ways.

One way I accept this challenge is to feel valuable even when I'm not achieving anything in the material world. Whether work is slow, I feel stuck in a rut, I'm lacking in creativity, or I need to press pause or reset, I've learned to stay faithful to the routine of placing one foot in front of the other. I don't have to have it all figured out today...or ever. And I don't have to go it alone. A question I ask my clients is "What support and resources are available to you?" It sounds so simple and obvious, but oftentimes we forget just how much is available to us. These are some of my core beliefs: *I live in an abundant world. There is plenty to go around. I enjoy using my privilege to help others who are less privileged claim their abundance as well.*

A question I often ask myself is *What would old Kate have done?*

To switch things up and explore untapped potential and abundance, I then do the opposite. For example, "old Kate" would have become incredibly reactive and even irate over losing clients. Now, I do the opposite by practicing nonreactivity, and if I'm feeling extra brave and bold, I even celebrate when one door closes, knowing that this is freeing up time and space in my life for something new.

I find it quite empowering to investigate new ways of being. In this way, we are abundant with options.

The Abundance of Being Ourselves

I'm discovering there are endless ways we can feel abundant. Remember, the more you recognize the abundance you already have, the more you free yourself up to claim the abundant life that is your birthright.

Lately, I've been exploring the abundance of being myself. There's also the abundance of:

- getting to know ourselves, what's important to us, and why.
- letting go of thoughts, people, and stuff that doesn't suit us any longer.
- fresh, new insights and creativity.
- stillness and silence.
- self-acceptance and forgiveness.

Isn't it great that we don't need an abundance of cash to own these priceless gifts? What are some other ways you can feel abundant?

Rejection Is Redirection

I am a great believer in the concept that you meet the people you're supposed to meet, go the places you're supposed to go, and hear the words and messages you need to hear and know.

Rejection is a part of life. We don't get accepted to the school we want, we get turned down for the job we apply for, we don't get chosen for the part, we get ditched by the partner we've set our sights on, and so on. I used to ruminate and obsess over why I didn't get a particular job I wanted, why some guy wasn't able to love me, or why some people with way less experience seemed to get my dream jobs so easily. I had a hard time accepting that "it wasn't meant to be."

While everyone has felt the sting of rejection, I believe every rejection is a protection of us. Have you ever focused your energies on someone, something, or a path that didn't turn out to work out for you? That means it wasn't for you to begin with. Have you ever struggled with letting go of someone or something you felt belonged to you and only you? Again, they or it weren't really yours. The sooner you learned and accepted those truths, the sooner you could make your way to the opportunities, people, or path that *was* for you.

Have you ever lost out on an opportunity only to have it replaced by an even better one? Can you think of a time when you looked back and thought, *Thank God that didn't work out?* What's been one of your greatest lessons or blessings contained in not getting what you thought you wanted? How can you celebrate change? What will you do? How will you allow yourself to be delighted?

There's always a blessing behind not getting what we *think* we want. I'll bet you can think back to at least a few rejections in your life that later proved to be blessings. Go ahead and jot down any that come to mind. Then use this list to serve as a reminder for when you become upset about life not going your way.

Learning to accept and even embrace rejections and disappointments is so utterly liberating, and this is a foundational skill for rocking your own full spirit freedom freestyle.

Self-Rejection

A lot of lip service is paid to the term "self-love," but I rarely hear anyone talk about self-rejection, which is so prevalent in our culture. Maybe we'd be less upset with those who have rejected, disappointed, or betrayed us if we accepted how often we reject, disappoint, and betray ourselves.

Coming to grips with our own self-rejection can be an important step toward accepting rejection from the outside world and freeing ourselves in the process. Again, this pulls in steps we've worked on earlier in the Full Spirit Workout. As you begin to really live this lifestyle, you'll be setting yourself free.

We reject, disappoint, or betray ourselves in various ways, either knowingly or unknowingly. For instance, as you know, I love eating bread, pizza, and pasta and probably could eat them for every meal. I also know this is not healthy for me, and when I consume too many carbohydrates my stomach bloats and I feel physically sick. I know this, yet sometimes I will still keep eating and eating and therefore betray myself and my health. There are times when I'm deciding what to eat for dinner, think of ordering pizza again, and hear my voice of inner wisdom say, *You know you can't eat that again tonight.* If I choose to order the pizza anyway, that is a form of self-betrayal. This isn't about beating myself up but rather consciously noticing what choices I am making and having compassion for myself. (I'm not perfect, and neither are you or anyone else. We can choose to let ourselves and others off the hook while also setting firm boundaries.)

I'm sure many of us can relate to betraying ourselves by engaging in relationships that are not healthy. Maybe we've gone back to an ex who treated us badly, or perhaps we've stayed friends with someone who isn't supportive or encouraging, or we allowed a coworker to disrespect our boundaries. Again, this isn't about judging ourselves or others but instead being aware of how often we don't treat *ourselves* the way we'd like to be treated. When we recognize this, we can do something about it and make better choices. I'm also noticing that it isn't someone's mistreatment of me that causes so much pain but rather my judgment of the person mistreating me.

I see self-rejection often disguised as self-love. Another word for self-rejection is the *ego*, which is all about judgment and small-mindedness. Our ego is the voice that rejects us, insisting we have to be different from who we really are, whether it's what we look like or how we perform. The ego is never satisfied and thrives on our self-hatred. I would be so hurt and offended if someone else said half the stuff my voice of self-rejection, or ego, has said to me.

A self-inquiry exercise I like to do with my clients involves asking simple questions about each belief that causes us stress. Ask yourself:

1. Is this belief accurate?
2. Am I certain that it is accurate and verifiable?
3. How do I feel when I believe this?
4. What would my life be like without this belief?

Then choose a reframe, or a statement expressing a different or even polar opposite belief. For instance, "He confuses me" could become "I confuse him" or "I confuse myself."

This reminds me of a relationship I had with a man who told me up front that he didn't want to be in a serious relationship. I said okay, even though I wanted something more. But then the whole time we were dating, I couldn't understand why he didn't want a serious relationship with me when we got on so well and he always expressed how much he liked me. "You're so confusing," I would say. But that wasn't true. The truth is that I confused myself by choosing to date someone who did not share my relationship goals, and I confused him by saying I wanted to be in a committed relationship yet stayed in an unsatisfying situation.

Another example I hear frequently is "My boss doesn't value me."

Is this belief accurate? Maybe.

Are you certain that it is accurate and verifiable? Probably not. Of course, you could ask her, but she may or may not tell you the truth.

How do you feel when you believe this? I know I'd feel hurt and unsure why she didn't value me.

What would your life be like without this belief? Your life would be yours; you'd be free, less weighed down, and more empowered.

A reframe to this is "Maybe I don't value her" or "I don't like the part of me that cares if she values me or not because that's out of my control."

This is an exercise we can turn to again and again. Anytime a thought pops up that causes us discomfort, we can shift the energy by first asking ourselves, *Is this belief accurate?*

Two truths about the brain: it is lazy, and it doesn't like gaps. This explains why our minds create so many stories, many of which are not true. When the brain has incomplete data on a person or situation, it rushes to fill in the gaps, and because it is lazy it doesn't always paint an accurate picture. That's why it's so important to press the pause button and ask ourselves these reflective questions, so we can live in truth and feel at peace, not at war, with our thoughts. I always find that I feel much lighter without the clutter of false stories floating around in my head. Talk about a headache! This reframing exercise is like pain medicine for the mind.

Resistance Training

One of my favorite workouts to do at the gym is TRX, which stands for total-body resistance exercises. It's an ultimate challenge for your entire body, and the result is a strong core. TRX is a two-strap suspension system that tones your body and burns fat by using two simple resources: gravity and your body weight.

A full spirit resistance workout uses emotional gravity like fear, stress, anxiety, judgment — anything that weighs us down — to build a strong spiritual core and burn off self-doubt and insecurities by sweating out toxic thoughts and then refueling with radical self-acceptance.

This kind of resistance training is about looking at how we've tended to resist what's good for us and resist letting go of our ideas about what we must have. When we try to control outcomes, we actually block blessings and miracles. As we've learned, we can begin to disengage from this strong-hold that resistance has on us by choosing to loosen our grip and give ourselves permission to trust in the present moment. It's not about fighting against — resisting — what we don't want; it's about letting in what we fear and then replacing or transforming it with a more loving thought, feeling, or approach to the situation.

Full spirit resistance training is done with an open heart, regardless of outside circumstances. Building strong attitudinal muscles is accomplished in the moments we get still on the inside. In this stillness, we are able to lay judgment aside. As I mentioned, I've found that rejection itself isn't what's so painful; it's our judgment of it and what we think it means about us when we don't get the money, promotion, relationship, and so forth.

When working with clients, I often find that some cling to what isn't working and the pain it causes, because at least that pain is familiar. The consistent effort it takes to create new thought patterns and behaviors can be more uncomfortable than the pain. I recognize the resistance others have to facing their own darkness because I was once in their shoes, too.

In his book *Without Buddha I Could Not Be a Christian*, theology professor Paul Knitter says,

> If we can truly be mindful of what is going on in us or around us — that's how we can find or feel "the Spirit" in it. Then our response to the situation will be originating from the Spirit rather than from our knee-jerk feelings of fear or anger or envy. And whether the response is to endure bravely or to act creatively, it will be done with *understanding* and *compassion* — which means it will be life-giving or life-creating.

There's such a big difference between what we want and what we *really* want. For example, I want to buy a ton of stuff online. But what I *really* want is to save money and make smart, responsible financial investments, saving for my dream home. I want to eat the entire pizza, but what I really want is optimal health. I want to tell that person that he's a complete jerk. But what I really want is to feel at peace, and I know that spiritually speaking, whatever we do to another (in this case, attack/blame/judge), we are also doing to ourselves.

Beating ourselves up or blaming others doesn't move us forward. Compassion and commitment to being the person we say we want to be moves us closer to becoming the men and women we are capable of being. It takes practice like anything else. It's like going to the gym and exercising our physical muscles. We all know that we have to do that to combat gravity. If you don't work at keeping your muscles up, they're going down!

The same is true for our attitudinal muscles. Every time we choose what we really want over what we "want," we build strong emotional muscles — the kind of muscles that are big enough to absorb any setback or heartache. And that's sexier than a six-pack, if you ask me!

 **JOURNALING EXERCISE**
Allowing Abundance

1. Take a moment to think about and write down what rejections you have still not let go.
2. Now consider what you likely would never have experienced had that "rejection" not taken place.
3. Next, reflect and write about the possibilities your life still has, even without having received what you believed you *had* to have.

4. What are you learning about yourself through or thanks to rejection?
5. What changes can you celebrate?
6. Journal about how thrilling it will feel to claim the new gifts that are making their way to you now.
7. In what ways can you allow yourself to be surprised, delighted, and abundant?

 INFINITE POSSIBILITIES MEDITATION

Take a moment to get comfortable in your meditation space. Allow your eyes to gently close as you move your focus to your breath. Start by taking a couple of deep, cleansing breaths in through your nose and out through your mouth.

In your stillness, melt into the quiet and listen. Open your mind in presence. Center and ground your spirit. Now bring this openness and centeredness down to your heart. Feel it expanding. Allow your breath to fill you with infinite possibilities. Hear the guidance and inspiration that are making their way to you now. Feel the wave of relief from knowing you don't have to make your way through the world all on your own. Feel how supported you are physically, mentally, emotionally, and spiritually. Take a moment to take in this support.

The support and the love you feel here is your gentleness, your calm, your stillness, your sacredness, your authenticity, your inno- cence, your vulnerability, your strength, your full spirit.

Open yourself up to the infinite possibility within you. The truth of who you are is an infinite possibility. Try not to reject this inner wisdom that wants to deeply connect with you and show you a more complete and purposeful way to live.

Convince yourself of this truth: you are an infinite possibility. The infinite possibility you desire is you. This is the power of our spirit. What a world it would be if we could tap into this sacred space more often — where we become one with the divine and its abundance.

Become radiant with compassion as you extend infinite possibilities from your heart down to your hands. Give your hands permission to carry out the infinite possibilities in your heart, and take the inspired next steps to bring your possibility into existence for all to experience.

Now extend this compassion to everyone you encounter, friends and strangers alike. Share your infinite possibilities with them, reminding them of their own power of infinite possibilities, and watch as the vibration of the world is raised... together.

I invite you to continue to slow down so you may remember who you are. There is time to remember now. In the stillness you become awake and alive, free and fearless. Allow your spirit to come out and stay out of hiding to breathe life into the world so desperately in need of your love, power, truth, and limitless possibilities. Be captivated by this present moment, and allow it to remind you that the infinite possibilities you seek are within you. They are you. Take as long as you need before gently opening your eyes and coming back to the room.

Full-Time Faith

Have you ever noticed how much you can hear when you get quiet? I'm not talking about noticing the birds chirping or the sound of the air conditioner or the neighbors next door, I'm referring to our inner wisdom — the divine downloads that are always available to us but often get muted by the noise of our overscheduled lives and the chaos of current events.

When I get still and allow myself the space to just *be*, without any distractions or sounds, I find myself with an abundance of brilliant guidance. For instance, while stressed and spinning out in my apartment one day over an issue I do not even remember, I heard the voice of God say, quite loudly, "It is no longer okay to just trust part of the time. You have to have full-time faith!" Boom! It was like someone threw freezing-cold water on my face. I woke up!

This is how allowing abundance and rocking the freedom freestyle occur — through developing full-time faith. Just like it isn't enough to work out every now and then, it isn't enough to trust every now and then. To see real results, we have to be consistent, even when it doesn't appear that anything is happening for us. That's when we must learn to trust that the wheels are turning behind the scenes in our favor. And to live our full spirit lifestyle every day and return to these exercises and practices again and again to keep our skills sharp and our spirits free.

Life keeps teaching until we get it. Despair is when we think tomorrow is going to be like today. That's a lie. Life is always in motion. Choose to cocreate and work out with the ultimate personal trainer — the universe.

Believe in your greatness and that the universe wants you to succeed. Be willing to trust that life can and will be way better than anything you could have ever imagined...if you allow it and don't resist it. Remember, resistance keeps us firmly planted in our comfort zone.

Welcoming Our Abundance by Turning It into Service

I was sitting on my front porch, having my morning cup of coffee while talking on the phone with a friend. I saw the FedEx truck pulling down my driveway, and I laughed, thinking, *How embarrassing — it's 10 a.m., and I'm still in my pink pajamas and slippers, with messy, unbrushed hair and no makeup.* When I saw the driver was an African American man, I quickly became embarrassed for another reason.

It had been just two days since a Caucasian woman walking her dog in Central Park called the cops, screaming that an African American man was threatening her life. The truth is, she was breaking clearly marked park rules by having her dog off its leash, and the man, Christian Cooper, a birdwatcher, nicely asked her to leash her dog.

And it had been just two days since George Floyd, an unarmed African American man, died while in police custody. A bystander captured a now-viral video of Floyd pleading for his life, saying, "I can't breathe. They're going to kill me." It shows Floyd handcuffed and pinned facedown on the pavement, with a Caucasian police officer's knee on the back of his neck in broad daylight. The explosive footage has ignited outrage and a call for justice throughout Floyd's community and the entire country. Protesters took to the streets, demanding the officers involved be charged with murder, something Floyd's family was peacefully requesting as well.

The unjust and inhumane incident has rightfully reignited deep-seated anger, rage, and unimaginable pain across a racially divided United States.

So, as the friendly, smiling FedEx man approached me, I cheerfully said, "Hi!" and flashed him a toothy grin. He handed me my package (a dress from Bergdorf Goodman), and I smiled, saying, "Thank you!" But what I really wanted to say to him was "I'm so sorry."

I wanted to hug this man and apologize on behalf of all white Americans. I wanted to tell him I'm sorry that despite the fact that we both live in the same free country, I have freedoms and privileges he doesn't and may never have. Unlike him, I will never be racially profiled or have to worry about being a victim of police brutality, at least directly. It is highly unlikely that someone in any park or anywhere will ever call the cops on me and say, "A blond white girl is threatening my life." If someone did, it would most likely be met with roaring laughter — not guns and violence, and certainly not death.

There's so much I want to say about this topic and so much pain in my heart to express, and yet it's challenging for me to do so because I feel too privileged to even share my thoughts. I know life isn't fair, but these injustices are unacceptable, and our society somehow allows them to keep happening again and again. Innocent lives are being taken. This isn't an African American problem or a police problem; this is a white American problem. We have blood on our hands through silence, ignorance, denial, and inaction. It's on us to demand justice. That doesn't happen by any of us pretending our voices — especially as privileged as they are — don't matter. They do. But our hearts matter even more, and it starts with atonement.

The word originally meant "at-one-ment" or being "at one" or in harmony with someone. I think it's way past time we all rise up to be ambassadors of love and oneness in our communities. I personally stand committed to using my privilege in service of justice and equality.

It is my wish that you, too, will find it in your heart to take action, acknowledge our country's history, be willing to apologize or forgive, and stay committed to educating and healing yourself and others.

We need you.

There are numerous ways to stay informed and take solidarity action that can help dismantle racism. A link to some anti-racist teachers, leaders, organizations, and resources you can learn from and support is provided in the notes section.

In an article for Medium.com, my friend Gerard McGeary, an African American man, said it will take a "sustained attention span, compassion, and moral clarity of purpose" to address the centuries-rooted systems that haunt the African American community. "And make no mistake about it," he said. "Sustained moral clarity of purpose is what is required because racism is not a bug but one of the foundational features of the system."

Sustained moral clarity of purpose. These five words resonate so deeply with me because we can all vote, protest, speak, write, teach, educate ourselves and others, sign petitions, donate money, demand policy reform, and help get laws changed. We can be kind, compassionate human beings. All these things are important, imperative, and the minimum requirements to help bring about justice and equality for all.

But real change and "a sustained moral clarity of purpose" ultimately begin and end with our core belief systems. We have to learn and unlearn, challenge some of our beliefs, release others, and replace many. We can do all the work in the outside world, but if we still harbor hatred and judgment in our hearts and prejudices and unconscious biases in our bones, the change we will see, if any, will be fleeting and superficial at best.

The real work is and always will be being brave enough to navigate the raw, messy, uncomfortable, deep inner journey into the parts of ourselves that need to be confronted, the parts of us that scare us and force us to change. This is about holding ourselves (and others) accountable for the work we are doing (or not doing). This means having difficult conversations while also taking unprecedented action. This is exercising our inner power so we can more effectively exercise our political power.

This is a consistent lifetime practice. This is like being a mom — there are no days off. You don't get to wake up one day and say, "I don't feel like being a parent today or anymore because it is too hard, too frustrating, too exhausting, and makes me look at my own limitations and feel bad about myself."

Part of this journey can be welcoming the abundance that we have in order to turn it outward into service and action. In my case, recognizing my abundance of privilege can help me step out of a place of feeling powerless (or even voiceless) and into a place of action. This is not just empowering; it is a way to start being a part of the change I want to see in the world. What abundance do you have or can you welcome that you can turn into service?

Many people talk about "fixing the system." I believe the system is working exactly how it was designed, unfortunately. And systems are created by people who share a particular mindset. Therefore, it is *our minds* that need to be fixed. We can change our minds through radical self-reflection, awareness, and resilience, along with a willingness to change our hearts. The ego (mind) is out for itself, but our heart (love) and spirit (truth, authenticity, power) don't have to fight for justice and equality; they already embody it. When we show up for ourselves in this way, we automatically show up for others and this cause.

In this way, the Full Spirit Workout is not just about our own personal fitness. Many lives depend on us strengthening these vital muscles and getting fit on a deeper level. While I don't pretend to know the cure for racism, I do know that spiritual fitness is part of the solution. When you understand that every human being is an innocent child of the universe or the God of your understanding — and you consistently train your attitudinal muscles and practice getting still on the inside — you treat yourself, and therefore everyone else you meet, with more love and respect. It sounds simple because it is. The challenge, however, is prioritizing this act of love and respect on a daily basis.

 ## COACH KATE CHECK-IN

- What does it mean to you to be of service?
- What does being of service look and feel like?
- Who do you have to be in order to put your unique gifts to use in service of a higher purpose?
- Why is serving your life's purpose important to you? Why now?
- How will you show up in this way? What will you do, and by when?

STEP 9: ROCK THE FREEDOM FREESTYLE
AFFIRMATION

Abundance is always available to me. I am ready to release all the ways I knowingly or unknowingly block abundance. I step out of my own way and, more importantly, God's way. I am grateful for what I already have while staying open to receiving more. I ask God to use me, so that His will can be done and I can best serve my life's purpose, rocking my own personal freedom freestyle.

STEP 10
Cool Down
with Inner Calm

Within you there is a stillness and sanctuary
to which you can retreat at any time and be yourself.

— HERMANN HESSE

Congratulations! You have worked so hard and come
so far. It's time to get off the treadmill and cool down with
newfound inner calm. Regardless of where you feel you are
on your spiritual fitness journey, I invite you to set a goal
called "radical self-acceptance." This is about embracing
who and where you are in this moment, while liberating
yourself from the grip of your shame and insecurities about
not feeling good enough. Radical self-acceptance invites
you into a space of deep awakening, compassionate healing,
and transcendence.

This step contains a series of cool-down exercises to help
you practice radical self-acceptance and let the benefits of

your Full Spirit Workout begin to sink in. The great thing about these exercises is that you can return to them again and again. Each time, you may learn something different about yourself. You will see how much you've grown stronger in some areas and where you can still improve. Try to see this as an open invitation to limitless possibilities for yourself and your life. And grab a workout buddy if that feels more fun for you!

"To-Be" Lists

When was the last time you asked yourself, *How am I doing? What can I do for myself? What do I need to feel better?*

We're all familiar with "to-do" lists and the stress and shame that can come with trying to do all we think we should be doing, while rushing around trying to feel accomplished in our busyness. We've mastered the art of exhausting ourselves in an effort to feel good enough and worthy of a break, happy hour, or vacation — at least I have.

Let's try something different: let's create "to-be" lists instead. Everything we desire in life is because of how we think it will make us feel once we have it. Think about how you want to feel in your life. It could be anything from confident to kind, authentic to alive.

Making a "to-be" list involves asking yourself what qualities make you feel your absolute best — not the fantasy version of you, but the real you. The fantasy version of me, for example, is adventurous and loves to try extreme sports, climb huge mountains, and go camping. But the real me craves quiet time at home by myself to rest, recharge, reflect, read, and write. This is your list, so think about what makes you, not others, feel really happy.

Here is an example of one of my "to-be" lists:

Confident
Courageous
Authentic
Vulnerable
Kind

It has everything to do with how it makes me *feel*, and the act of writing and later rereading it actually helps me embody these feelings. For example, if I am feeling angry, I can refer to my list, lean into the qualities I want to embody, and then act the way I want to feel (confident, courageous, authentic, vulnerable, and kind). I end up experiencing just that, and my anger vanishes.

Another way to come up with your "to-be" list is to ask yourself, *What qualities do I need to embody to attract what I desire and deserve in life?* If we want to attract a loving partner who treats us with respect and is romantic, thoughtful, and funny, then our "to-be" list might include:

Loving
Respectful
Romantic
Thoughtful
Funny

The key is to treat ourselves how we would like to be treated. Loving, accepting, honest, forgiving, nonjudgmental, open, compassionate, peaceful, focused, warm, and friendly are some more feelings that come to mind for me.

To give you some encouragement, here are five proven benefits to creating and sticking to a "to-be" list:

1. It helps us slow down, center ourselves, and consider the day ahead.

2. It enables us to set boundaries — to say no to things that will take us farther from the qualities on our list. For example, imagine this scenario: I feel like I should go to that work event, but I don't really want to. I'm tired, don't have any more energy to be "on," and I desperately need to clean my house and rest. In the past, I may have gone to the event and even had fun, but I would feel depleted, and the feeling of abandoning myself and my needs is not self-care. Today, I am committed to practicing self-care, even if it means disappointing others.

3. It enables us to create our own reality and choose how we will be, regardless of what our day brings us. So, if I have chosen to be optimistic, I will remain optimistic even when I don't book the job or my love interest does not call me back like he promised.

4. Taking a more intentional approach to life is empowering. It gives us the opportunity to take our time back and therefore be more centered, creative, and in the flow. We get more done by exerting less effort and feel better doing so.

5. Our "to-be" lists make us more mindful and self-aware and give us space for quiet consideration to reflect. Our peace of mind and pleasant mood are a top priority, making everything else we do in our lives (even those "boring" to-do lists) more peaceful and pleasant as a result.

Different days will require us to add different qualities to our lists depending on our schedules and how we are feeling spiritually, emotionally, mentally, and physically. Feel free to make a "to-be" list every day, being open to whatever arises within you, and change it up based on your schedule or what will suit you best that particular day. Here's how to do it.

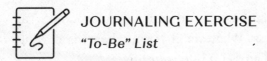

JOURNALING EXERCISE
"To-Be" List

1. List five things on your "to-be" list today — five ways you would like to feel. Here are some prompts to help you come up with your list:

    - What qualities make you feel your absolute best?
    - What words, concepts, or feelings really excite you right now?
    - What qualities do you need to embody to attract what you need and deserve in life?

2. List five to ten experiences that will make you feel this way.
3. List three things you can do today to generate these feelings.
4. List the people who can support you in feeling this way.

After you've done this initial "to-be" list, I invite you to get into the habit of writing your "to-be" list on a piece of paper or in your phone so you can take it with you and refer to it throughout your day.

Remember, this is a gentle cool-down exercise, so please

do not take on any shame or judgment if you don't stick to your list, forget about it, or need to skip a day. With practice, it will become like second nature, and you will be building a strong spiritual muscle to guide you.

Just *Be* It!

Love. Money. A relationship. A dream job. Acceptance. Validation. Forgiveness. Whatever it is your heart is craving, there is one way to attract it into your life.

Are you ready?!

The answer is to *be it*. Yes, we can *become* what we want.

If you want love in your life, *be love*, which is actually everything that we truly are! Take yourself out on a date, make yourself a delicious home-cooked meal, buy yourself chocolate or fresh flowers, write yourself a love letter, and accept, honor, and validate yourself. In other words, romance yourself. Treat yourself to a massage, Reiki session, or trip to your favorite park or museum. Volunteer, tune in to what your heart is trying to communicate, make a cup of green tea, buy yourself that rose-scented facial cream. Whatever makes you feel loved by others, do for yourself, and watch those icky feelings of neediness, desperation, and fear dissolve from your life and clear space for more love.

Tip: some of the most powerful things you can do to love and honor yourself don't cost one penny, such as these:

- Forgiving yourself. You did the best you could at the time. Say to yourself, *I forgive you.*
- Accepting yourself — "flaws" and all. Look in the mirror and say, "You look gorgeous today."

- Being your own standard of beauty. You decide what's beautiful.
- Validating yourself. You are good enough.
- Being proud of yourself. Great job today!
- Listening to yourself. You already know the answer. Trust what you hear.
- Letting yourself rest and relax. Practice stillness, and allow yourself time to recharge your batteries.
- Seeing yourself clearly for who you truly are. Look in the mirror and say, "I love you." The old way of beating yourself up is no longer acceptable. It's a new day. Choose love.

There have been times in my life when I wanted to hear and feel these things so badly from another person. We can't control anything other than our own thoughts and behavior, so if you're desperately craving love, attention, affection, and forgiveness, give them to yourself first. It's also the quickest and easiest way to attract these things into your life from others. It's a simple concept but takes discipline and commitment.

I used to think, *When I get that job/money/relationship/ house/ring/apology, and so on, I'll be happy*. That mentality translates into *I will never be happy*. Yikes!

The trick to having everything you want flow into your life is to be happy now! That is one of my favorite lessons from the late, great Dr. Wayne Dyer. Let that sink it for a second. *Be happy now.*

Dyer would say, "Act as if…" you already have and are everything your heart desires. That's the surefire shortcut to attract abundance of any kind into your life. Be a magnet for miracles, not a repellent to them.

Having an abundant life is all about being in alignment with your thoughts, the energy you put out into the universe, and your actions. Commit to dwelling in a high-vibe, loving, blissful state, and watch the uplifting people and situations you attract. Your daily life will feel more energizing and fulfilling. It may not be easy to dwell in this higher vibrational state at first, but try to stay committed to wanting to feel your best and living the life of your dreams. It will be well worth the effort, and you will get better and better at returning to your "happy place" quickly in times of stress.

You Don't Have to Choose between Pleasure and Wellness

How often have you enjoyed a delicious meal with family, a festive drink with friends, or a decadent dessert with yourself and felt immediate shame for overindulging?

Our society's obsession with perfection is very real. Whether it's "Keep off those holiday pounds!" or "Burn off the belly bloat!" we're bombarded with messages telling us we're not enough. But it doesn't have to be that way.

Lately, I've been embracing a more radical approach to eating, and with it, I feel less and less guilt around enjoying myself at the table or elsewhere. How, you ask? Instead of agonizing over any additional pounds, I affectionately call this fluctuation my "prosperity pounds."

How do you indulge in a balanced way?

While consciously choosing to increase my intake of vitamin P (for pleasure, of course), my pants can become a little bit tighter. And rather than beating myself up for indulging while traveling (like having pizza in Italy when you've been eating low-carb) or catching up with old friends (over incredible grass-fed steaks, say, when you usually avoid red meat), I reframe my slightly curvier figure as a sign of success, abundance, luxury, and well-being.

This isn't about "letting myself go," and I have no desire to be overweight. This is simply an act of love for myself. I'm committed to maintaining a healthy weight while enjoying each moment without the guilt.

Some days that commitment looks like a slow walk in nature instead of a high-intensity sweat fest at the gym. I may not burn as many calories or feel quite as fit, but my body appreciates the rest. Not to mention, my mind and soul feel nourished.

When I'm traveling, I tend to indulge more, eager to experience the culture. I balance that indulgence with protein shakes and more fresh fruits and veggies when I return home.

Nutritional psychologist Marc David says the level of enjoyment we experience in eating our food has very real biochemical consequences that directly affect our metabolism and digestion. "*What* you eat is only half the equation of good nutrition. *How* you eat is the other half," says David, founder of the Institute for the Psychology of Eating and author of *The Slow Down Diet: Eating for Pleasure, Energy, and Weight Loss.*

David notes that feeling guilty for eating our favorite foods takes away from the pleasure. We all know it's not healthy to eat ice cream every day, but he believes conscious doses of pleasure put us in a state to honor our desires while nourishing our bodies in a thoughtful way.

I can choose to feel terrible about myself for eating pasta at almost every meal in Italy. Or I can lean into gratitude for the experience of working and traveling in such a magical country. There is so much freedom in enjoying exactly where we are — both geographically in the world and physically in our bodies.

I'm not suggesting you make choices that feel unhealthy. I'm just proposing we each consider that food and life are meant to be savored and enjoyed, and we don't have to choose between pleasure and wellness.

But how do you really start enjoying your food?

There is a wealth of evidence that focusing on food's sensual pleasure actually can help you find a healthful balance. And to get the most pleasure from food, I recommend slowing down while you eat rather than shoveling it in. Remove distractions like the phone and television, so you can eat mindfully.

Be sure to use all your senses to fully experience your food. Appreciate colors, textures, aromas, and presentation. Notice every flavor you are tasting while chewing thoroughly. Studies show that when people eat more slowly, they tend to take in fewer calories and feel just as satisfied. You'll also digest your food better and absorb more nutrients.

Instead of trying to avoid foods I enjoy, I find it more effective to stop labeling certain foods (and myself) as "bad." I'm relabeling "forbidden foods" as "fun foods" instead. Since making this mindset shift, I've noticed that I crave my fun foods much less, and when I do partake, I enjoy them so much more.

For me, eating a balance of nutrient-rich health foods coupled with some fun foods is the ultimate healthy diet.

And healthy pleasure is something we can all agree on for dinner. Cheers!

Change the Channel

In 2001, in the days that followed 9/11, I was glued to my television, watching hours upon hours of horrific imagery from ground zero. I would flip between channels and will always remember seeing legendary TV news supergiants Tom Brokaw, Peter Jennings, and Dan Rather break down in tears during their live coverage, which is something I'd never seen before. I was living clear across the country from New York City in Los Angeles, but I feared a terrorist attack would hit us next. I sat in my condo terrified and grieving the loss of so many innocent American lives, while sobbing day in, day out, and yet, I couldn't turn away from the news.

Fortunately, I had just hired my first life coach, a lovely woman named Sonia Jeantet. I called her to schedule a session because I was reeling. Like every other American, she, too, was struggling to navigate the shock and horror of what just happened. Sonia offered me a piece of advice that I've kept close to my heart all these years. She said to me kindly, "You need to change the channel."

Yes, I literally needed to change the channel and switch from the news to a cartoon or comedic movie, but I also needed to change the channel in my mind from extreme fear to acceptance, love, peace, and calm. I knew that was going to be a much harder task, so I started with just changing the channel on my TV. I did notice that I felt much more at ease watching something light and fluffy after so much input that was so intense and heavy. Sonia also suggested I go to the movies to "change the channel." I went and saw a

Vivica A. Fox romantic comedy, and it made me laugh out loud. Other moviegoers were also laughing along with me in the theater, so it amplified the feel-good feelings throughout my body. I began to understand more deeply how laughter is not just fun; it changes the channel and can actually improve our health and well-being.

Many modeling sets are in dark, windowless rooms. Crew members are often grumpy and look at us with blank stares — no smiles — while we are required to look way happier than we actually feel, jumping around in swimsuits and ill-fitting clothing to "get the shot."

One trick I always used was to imagine I was standing on a gorgeous beach, looking out at the ocean. I would picture my best friend skipping toward me with a gigantic grin on her face and a margarita in her hand. I would get such a genuine smile on my face, hearing, "Hey, girl, hey!" in my mind and actually laugh out loud on set to get an authentically energetic, pleasant-looking shot. While modeling, I always took myself somewhere else in my mind to "change the channel" and simulate the feeling. I would say out loud on set, "Ha, ha, ha!" and actually laugh. The entire crew would follow suit. It raised the vibe and made for genuine, gorgeous photos, which, in turn, sold more clothing.

Side note: saying, "Ha, ha, ha!" is a wonderful way to get children and adults alike to smile genuinely and jubilantly in photos. Try it!

Studies show that "it is possible to laugh without experiencing a funny event — and simulated laughter can be just as beneficial as the real thing."

I had to get creative on all those modeling sets to find

not just my light but also my "happy place," and you can, too. I find that simulated laughter always turns into spontaneous laughter, and like anything, the more you do it, the more it becomes second nature. If you're anything like me, you'll find yourself laughing a lot more and will understand how much it enhances your personality, relationships, and life. Laughter will always be my favorite and most effective way to "change the channel." It's highly contagious, and it can be hilarious to watch it spread!

Like any effective coach, Jeantet offered me a tool I can use again and again to pull myself out of an emotional rabbit hole or even just a situation that lacks good energy. It's inevitable that we will get caught up in fear, anger, or low vibes from time to time, but changing the channel in our minds is an empowering practice we can choose to exercise in any moment. This feels much better than taking our negative emotions out on others or arguing with someone in our heads all day, robbing ourselves of the peace we could feel if we just chose to change the channel instead. Besides, who wants to watch the same (horror) show over and over again? Try mixing it up! You are always the lead character, but you can choose different emotions, who you choose to spend your time with, where you go, and what you do. Have fun with it! Get creative with the choreography. Direct yourself into actions that will better suit you and lead you toward the happy ending you wish (and deserve) to experience.

When we practice forgiveness, compassion, appreciation, and exuberance in these moments, we shift out of negativity quickly, reinforcing and strengthening the muscles we've built and toned in other full spirit exercises. With practice, we can begin to change the channel on our energy so that we learn how to evoke feelings of tranquility and glee at will.

Apply Love in Action

The ancient Greeks used several words for love to help them distinguish between different types of love. In a *Psychology Today* article, psychiatrist Neel Burton discusses seven types of love that he says are loosely based on classical texts, like those of Plato and Aristotle, plus J. A. Lee's 1973 book, *Colours of Love*. The seven types are *eros, philia, storge, agape, ludus, pragma,* and *philautia.*

Burton describes *agape* love as universal love. It is also considered to be the most divine love, love at the highest level, or God's perfect, unconditional love.

Burton said,

> Unlike storge, it does not depend on filiation or familiarity. Also called charity by Christian thinkers, agape can be said to encompass the modern concept of altruism, defined as unselfish concern for the welfare of others. Recent studies link altruism with a number of benefits. In the short term, altruism leaves us with a euphoric feeling — the so-called "helper's high." In the long term, it is associated with better mental and physical health, as well as longevity. At a social level, altruism serves as a signal of cooperative intentions, and also of resource availability and so of mating or partnering potential. It also opens up a debt account, encouraging beneficiaries to reciprocate with gifts and favors that may be of much greater value to us than those with which we feel able to part. More generally,

altruism, or agape, helps to build and maintain the psychological, social, and, indeed, environmental fabric that shields, sustains, and enriches us. Given the increasing anger and division in our society, and the state of our planet, we could all do with quite a bit more agape!

Stanford University professor Anne Firth Murray, who teaches the course Love as a Force for Social Justice, spoke about a neuroscientist who visited her class and described his concept of love as "perfect communication" or "perfect connection."

Murray says she is often asked, "What does love have to do with justice?" She says philosopher and political activist Cornel West summed it up best when he said, "Justice is what love looks like in public." In her online course, Murray said, "I see love very much like a coin, with one side being 'compassion' and the other 'loving kindness.' 'Compassion' is the desire to prevent pain, while 'loving kindness' is the desire to promote happiness."

The course teaches that agape widens our circles of human connection and concern and that love applied in action is a force for social justice. As students in the course, we were asked to observe an instance of someone using love as a force for social justice every week, then write about it and put it up on the class blog. If we did not notice an instance, we were to practice love as a force for social justice ourselves and write about it.

We're discovering that love can be learned, observed, and practiced. Just like other skills can be practiced and improved upon, so can the act of loving, and its effects are powerful! I think sometimes we take for granted how much a simple act of kindness that we consider to be no big deal can impact another. For example, I could see that a woman I met just once on a TV set, who I follow on Instagram, was visibly upset over a news event that hit a little too close to home for her. I sent her a direct voice message letting her know I see her, support her, and stand with her in solidarity. I said, "Please call me anytime. I care."

She took me up on my offer and was able to release so much anger and pain, as well as gratitude, to me over the phone while I sat quietly and listened. I've had friends do this for me, and there are few greater human experiences than feeling truly seen, heard, and acknowledged. You know that feeling where you know in your bones that you matter because the person you're talking to isn't distracted or thinking only about themselves but is truly present for and invested in *you* instead? That's agape love in action.

Has someone has ever helped you pack and move? Agape in action! With so much social justice work to be done, it's easy to slip into the hopeless "I feel so small" game, where we think our "little" actions don't really add up to much or move the needle. But I've seen the enormous impact that little acts of kindness can have on both an individual and collective level.

I always remind myself that the abolitionists and the suffragettes were the minority. The majority of people did not want to swim against the tide or even end slavery or give women the right to vote. Up against such odds, I'm sure the activists felt tired, overwhelmed, and like their efforts weren't making a difference at times, but they kept going, and they kept using love as a force for social justice. And we all know their love in action made history!

Can you think of a time when you created positive change in the life of another? Murray said, "The changes of heart that truly transform the world will always be occurring at an individual level."

Strengthening our kindness, empathy, and love for the purposes of social change, says psychology professor Barbara Fredrickson, can:

> help to pull us out of our self-absorption. They can counter an excessive self-focus and build habits of greater other-focus, so that when we see others we see more of them — we see their humanity and we don't just see them as a means to the end of what we want to accomplish that day. Being able to see and appreciate others in their full humanity is something that we get lulled out of by self-absorption or by our increasing reliance on technology.

 LOVING-KINDNESS MEDITATION

I learned about loving-kindness meditation from Christine Carter, PhD, a senior fellow at the Greater Good Science Center in Berkeley, California. Scientist, writer, and meditation teacher Jon Kabat-Zinn, PhD, calls this practice a "transfiguring of the heart." Think of it as "open-hearted, nonreactive, nonjudgmental presence," which allows us to expand our heart's field while also inviting others into our warm embrace. Before we can expand the field of loving-kindness,

Kabat-Zinn reminds us to work on ourselves first. "Think of it as tuning your instrument before you can play it for the world."

> *With that in mind, start by sitting comfortably in a meditation space with your eyes closed. Take a couple of nice, deep, cleansing breaths. Now bring your breath down to your heart. Feel your heart breathing in and out. Good.*
>
> *As you tune in to the loving-kindness within you, notice how you feel in your body. Continue to breathe in and out while inviting in feelings of peace and calm.*
>
> *To begin, bring to mind something you desire for your life. To help guide you, here are the phrases that I've chosen to use in my own practice. You're invited to create your own phrases that resonate most with you and express your wishes of loving-kindness toward yourself and others:*
>
> *May I be filled with loving-kindness.*
> *May I be safe and protected.*
> *May I feel at peace.*
> *May I be happy and healthy.*
>
> 1. *Start by directing the phrases to yourself: May I be filled with loving-kindness. May I be safe and protected. May I feel at peace. May I be happy and healthy.*
>
> 2. *Next, direct the phrases to someone dear to you who you love: May you be filled with loving-kindness. May you be safe and protected. May you feel at peace. May you be happy and healthy.*
>
> 3. *Now visualize someone you feel neutral about — someone you neither like nor dislike: May you be filled with loving-kindness. May you be safe*

and protected. May you feel at peace. May you be
happy and healthy.

4. *Now bring to mind someone you don't like or who*
   you are having a difficult experience with. You
   may find it challenging but also extremely empow-
   ering: May you be filled with loving-kindness. May
   you be safe and protected. May you feel at peace.
   May you be happy and healthy.

5. *Finally, direct the phrases to everyone universally:*
   May all sentient beings everywhere be filled with
   loving-kindness. May you be safe and protected.
   May you feel at peace. May you be happy and
   healthy.

6. *If you can, try sitting for a while and basking in*
   the energy of loving-kindness that may have been
   generated here.

In a world where we are all craving connection and a
deeper sense of community, loving-kindness meditation
has proven results: "One study showed that a single seven
minute loving-kindness meditation made people feel more
connected to and positive about both loved ones and total
strangers, and more accepting of themselves. Imagine what
a regular practice could do!" said Carter.

In an article for Mindful.org, Kabat-Zinn, founder of
mindfulness-based stress reduction (MBSR), said, "No doubt
the world benefits and is purified from even one individual's
offering of such intentions. The relationship within the lat-
tice structure of reality and the web of all life slightly shifted
through our openness and through our willingness to let

go of any rancor and ill will we might have been harboring, however justified we may think it is."

The Holistic Practice
That Snapped Me Out of a Funk

When I think back on my life before I began my own Full Spirit Workout, I picture a hamster on its wheel, feverishly chasing some illusive thing and getting frustrated, exhausted, and depressed when that thing remains out of reach.

I used to think if I just ran harder, faster, and longer, I could have, be, and do anything I wanted. Living and working in an overstimulating city like New York only made matters worse, and I felt as though I were in a constant state of fight-or-flight.

My nervous system was overwhelmed by the hectic pace I had established for myself. My adrenals were shot, my cortisol levels were off the charts, I felt hot and sweaty even in the winter, and fatigue followed me around like a lost puppy.

I wasn't happy or at peace in my body. I was surviving rather than thriving.

It was only when I learned to slow down and go within that I began to cultivate the inner calm that allows any human to thrive.

One way to cool down and relax after all the hard work we've been doing delving into our counterproductive habits, limiting beliefs, and self-fulfilling fears is to draw on the ancient Japanese healing method of Reiki. Reiki is based on the idea that an unseen "life force energy" flows through us; perhaps this is what we call spirit. If this energy starts to run low, we are more likely to get sick or feel stressed, and if it's abundant, we are more capable of health and happiness. Reiki supports deep relaxation and healing by removing internal blocks and balancing the body's energy centers.

Reiki practitioners are trained to act as conduits for the universal energy to flow through. They break up stagnant energy by using their hands to gently touch different areas of the body, releasing blocks and promoting relaxation in the process. I've found that it helps reconnect us with our hearts, realigning us with our higher selves.

Reiki is about creating a sacred, safe, compassionate, nonjudgmental environment where we don't have to hide from our emotions — where we can embrace whatever comes up and release it. I tell my clients to imagine energy that no longer serves them shooting out of their feet or head in a bright golden light — into Mother Earth or the cosmos to be transformed.

I recommend that anyone who's curious schedule a session with a certified Reiki practitioner. But whether you do so or not, you can draw on the principles of Reiki yourself to cool down after your Full Spirit Workout and give yourself space to recover and assimilate the benefits of all your hard work. You can repeat the following Reiki affirmation to start your post-workout day of rest. You might just like it so much you start every day this way!

Just for today, I will not worry.
Just for today, I will not be angry.
Just for today, I will be grateful.
Just for today, I will do my work honestly.
Just for today, I will be kind to every living thing.

REIKI HEALING MEDITATION

To further draw on the healing power of Reiki tradition as part of our cooldown, let's tap into this beautiful, pure, loving life force energy and do a Reiki healing treatment on ourselves.

To begin, take deep breaths in and out. Feel the energy within your body flowing freely as you tap into your inner wisdom and power. Envision a positive shift occurring, and notice any energy you are willing to release. When you're ready, deeply exhale any unwanted energy.

Good. You're doing a great job.

This practice is a combination of a body scan, light touch, and energy sweeping designed to calm, ground, and realign your body, mind, and spirit.

To begin, gently rub the palms of your hands together to activate the energy within. Close your eyes and take a few rounds of nice, deep, letting-go breaths. Imagine the crown of your head opening and a stream of healing white light flowing from the top of your head, into your heart, and out through your arms and hands, legs and feet. Imagine this healing white light filling you up where you need healing most. Place your hands gently on that area — it may be your heart, it may be your face or the top of your head or your abdomen. Take a moment to scan your body and see where you could place this pure, loving life-force energy.

Good.

As you feel the flow of energy, continue to breathe,

and if your mind begins to drift, come back to your breath. Envision yourself as a vessel for healing. Then set an intention or prayer to receive healing of the highest good.

Continue to scan your body with your eyes gently closed, bringing awareness to any sensations or areas that may be holding on to tension or blocking the flow of energy. Allow yourself to feel any emotions that arise. Notice them, but try not to judge them. Let them flow out of your body with the cleansing, healing white light.

If you'd like to give yourself a full Reiki self-treatment, gently place your hands on or directly above the crown of your head for a minute or two. No pressure is needed. Touch very lightly, then move down to the face, throat, back of the head, upper chest, lower ribs, navel, and lower abdomen.

Go at your own pace and feel the calm, cleansing peace and healing wash over your entire body and mind. Return to this practice as often as you need to.

 COACH KATE CHECK-IN

- What insights are emerging for you as you complete your first Full Spirit Workout?
- Who can you call on for support to help you stay accountable?
- Why is it important for you to stay spiritually fit?
- How can your life be used for the purposes of love?
- How can you heal the separation between yourself and the God of your own understanding or love?

STEP 10: COOL DOWN WITH INNER CALM AFFIRMATION

I am committed to maintaining my spiritual fitness — living the fun and fulfilling life I'm meant to live and inspiring the world along the way. I can return to these practices at any time. I stand in gratitude for myself and my full spirit while allowing the following words to be heard and felt by my heart:

Thank you for showing me love.

Thank you for caring for me, guiding me, supporting me, comforting me.

Thank you for allowing me to feel deeply, care, learn, heal, and grow.

Thank you for never leaving me alone.

Thank you for the continued health, harmony, and blessings in my life.

I rest comfortably in my own confidence and calmness.

I dwell in gratitude for all the wellness I have created for myself.

Acknowledgments

This book is possible because of my powerful angels, Sam and Raf. You put this idea in my heart and guided me from start to finish. You are my why, and the reason I keep going even when it's hard.

A very special thank you to my beautiful and brilliant literary agent, Wendy Sherman. My wish is that every person has someone who believes in them as much as you believe in me. Forever grateful. Thank you to my lovely editor, Georgia Hughes, and the entire team at New World Library for helping me bring my words and my full spirit to the world.

To the gorgeous souls who have supported me on this journey in such a meaningful way: Alana Gentry, Alberti Popaj, Allison Hendrix, Bonnie Beck, Courtney Carver, Josh Smith, Julie Reisler, Justin Clynes, Kailah Cone, Kathe Crawford, Kira Hug, Laila Weir, Melanie Votaw, Natasha Orslene, Richelle Fredson, and Vanessa Tennyson.

Thank you to my family: Mom, Dad, John, Natalie, Melia, Ross, Teddy, and Winnie.

And most of all, thanks to you, the reader, for taking the time to "work out" with me. Your commitment to spiritual fitness will help heal the world, and that inspires me in countless ways. I am honored to be on this journey of self-discovery with you. I love you.

Notes

Step 1: Stretch Your Comfort Zone

p. 13   *employees have said in surveys*: Craig Dowden, "Why You Want to Be
Stretched Outside Your Comfort Zone," *Psychology Today*, August
2016, https://www.psychologytoday.com/us/blog/the-leaders
-code/201608/why-you-want-be-stretched-outside-your-comfort
-zone.

p. 14   *"Nobody ever died of discomfort*: T. Harv Eker, *Secrets of the Millionaire
Mind: Mastering the Inner Game of Wealth* (New York: Harper Business, 2005), 172.

p. 17   *The idea of a "comfort zone"*: Robert M. Yerkes and John D. Dodson,
"The Relation of Strength or Stimulus to Rapidity of Habit-
Formation," *Journal of Comparative Neurology and Psychology* 18
(November 1908): 459–82, http://psychclassics.yorku.ca
/Yerkes/Law/.

Step 2: Lift Yourself Up

p. 43   *"The beginning of freedom is"*: Eckhart Tolle, *Practicing the Power of
Now: Essential Teachings, Meditations, and Exercises from* The Power
of Now (Novato, CA: New World Library, 1999), 18.

p. 53   *"There is no diet or doctor"*: Marianne Williamson, *A Woman's Worth*
(New York: Ballantine, 1993), 27.

Step 3: Feel the Burn

p. 59   *what psychological science says about the good life*: Laurie Santos, The
Science of Well-Being, Coursera, https://www.coursera.org/learn
/the-science-of-well-being.

p. 60   *Researchers Dan Gilbert and Tim Wilson argue*: Dan Gilbert and Tim Wilson, "Miswanting: Some Problems in the Forecasting of Future Affective States," in *Thinking and Feeling: The Role of Affect in Social Cognition* (New York: Cambridge University Press, 2000), 178–97.

p. 61   *"our minds don't think"*: Victoria Husted Medvec, Scott Madey, and Thomas Gilovich, "When Less Is More: Counterfactual Thinking and Satisfaction among Olympic Medalists," *Journal of Personality and Social Psychology* 69, no. 4 (October 1995): 603–10.

p. 61   *So if our goal is to make*: Sonja Lyubomirsky, *The How of Happiness: A New Approach to Getting the Life You Want* (New York: Penguin, 2007), 44.

p. 61   *What about true love?*: Richard E. Lucas et al., "Reexamining Adaptation and the Set Point Model of Happiness: Reactions to Changes in Marital Status," *Journal of Personality and Social Psychology* 84, no. 3 (March 2003): 527–39.

p. 61   *"psychological immune system"*: Daniel T. Gilbert et al., "Immune Neglect: A Source of Durability Bias in Affective Forecasting," *Journal of Personality and Social Psychology* 75, no. 3 (September 1998): 617–38.

p. 61   *that awful diagnosis or event*: Elizabeth W. Dunn, Timothy D. Wilson, and Daniel T. Gilbert, "Location, Location, Location: The Misprediction of Satisfaction in Housing Lotteries," *Personality and Social Psychology Bulletin* 29, no. 11 (November 2003): 1421–32.

p. 62   *Want to know how to double*: Erin Vogel et al., "Social Comparison, Social Media, and Self-Esteem," *Psychology of Popular Media Culture* 3, no. 4 (October 2014): 206–22.

p. 63   *In a 2004 TED Talk*: Martin Seligman, "The New Era of Positive Psychology," TED Talk, February 2004, https://www.ted.com/talks/martin_seligman_the_new_era_of_positive_psychology?language=en#t-9791.

Step 4: Strengthen Your Core Confidence

p. 94   *"Indigenous cultures call this gift"*: Gail Larsen, "Original Medicine — Your Expression to the World," Transformational Speaking, April 25, 2018, https://realspeaking.com/original-medicine.

p. 100 *our emotions are essential*: Kathleen Taylor and Catherine Marienau, *Facilitating Learning with the Adult Brain in Mind* (San Francisco: Jossey-Bass, 2016), 4–7.

p. 105 *college students who based their self-worth*: Jennifer Crocker, PhD, "Self-Esteem That's Based on External Sources Has Mental Health Consequences, Study Says," *Monitor on Psychology* 33, no. 11 (December 2002): 16, https://www.apa.org/monitor /dec02/selfesteem.

p. 109 *At its root,* confidence *means*: "Confidence," Online Etymology Dictionary, accessed January 6, 2020, https://www.etymonline .com/word/confidence#etymonline_v_18184.

Step 5: Build Your Emotional Muscles

p. 121 *"There's more to life than basketball"*: Phil Jackson, *Sacred Hoops: Spiritual Lessons of a Hardwood Warrior* (New York: Hachette, 2012), 124.

p. 135 *"In my defenselessness my safety lies"*: Foundation for Inner Peace, *A Course in Miracles: Workbook for Students* (Novato, CA: Foundation for Inner Peace, 2007), 284.

p. 139 *antidepressant use has skyrocketed*: Yoichiro Takayanagi et al., "Antidepressant Use and Lifetime History of Mental Disorders in a Community Sample: Results from the Baltimore Epidemiologic Catchment Area Study," *Journal of Clinical Psychiatry* 76, no. 1 (January 2015): 40–44, https://www.psychiatrist.com/JCP /article/Pages/antidepressant-lifetime-history-mental-disorders -community.aspx.

p. 144 *"Thoughts become things...choose the good ones"*: Mike Dooley, TUT (The Universe Talks), accessed April 2020, https://www.tut.com.

Step 6: Boost Your Mental Metabolism

p. 164 *"I am a lover of what is"*: Byron Katie, *I Need Your Love — Is That True? How to Stop Seeking Love, Approval, and Appreciation and Start Finding Them Instead* (New York: Crown, 2005), 190.

p. 173 *"Wrong remedy, but right instinct"*: Johanne Picard-Scott, "The Drummer's Lair: How to Retreat, Recharge, and React with Power in Today's World," Harlem Chi Community Acupuncture, September 27, 2020, https://harlemchi.com/author/johanne/.

p. 179 *I learned this technique*: Martin Seligman et al., Foundations of Positive Psychology Specialization, Coursera, https://www .coursera.org/specializations/positivepsychology.

p. 180 *To begin, identify a situation:* Martin Seligman et al., Foundations of Positive Psychology Specialization, Coursera, https://www.coursera.org/specializations/positivepsychology.

Step 7: Step Up Your Spiritual Stamina

p. 199 *"Emotional bypassing is quite helpful":* Chris Tecce, PhD, author's interview, May 2020.

Step 8: Embrace Your Endorphins

p. 228 *"I will bring you a whole person":* Mari Evans, from her poem "Celebration" (1993), The Poetree House, https://poetree-house.tumblr.com/post/15726767590/celebration.

p. 233 *"If a skunk crosses your path":* "Skunk Meaning and Symbolism," The Astrology Web, accessed May 2020, https://www.theastrologyweb.com/spirit-animals/skunk-meaning-symbolism.

p. 233 *"The skunk meaning places the emphasis":* Imelda Green, "The Skunk Spirit Animal," Trusted Psychic Mediums, accessed May 2020, https://trustedpsychicmediums.com/spirit-animals/skunk-spirit-animal/.

p. 244 *"When joy is a habit, love is a reflex":* Bob Goff, *Everybody, Always: Becoming Love in a World Full of Setbacks and Difficult People* (Nashville: Thomas Nelson, 2018), 21.

Step 9: Rock the Freedom Freestyle

p. 261 *"If we can truly be mindful of what is going on":* Paul Knitter, *Without Buddha I Could Not Be a Christian* (London: Oneworld Publications, 2013), 162.

p. 268 *"sustained attention span, compassion, and moral clarity of purpose":* Gerard McGeary, "Do Not Look to Me for Hope," Medium.com, June 4, 2020, https://medium.com/@GerardMcGeary/do-not-look-to-me-for-hope-795e56cd5e6d.

p. 269 *We can change our minds through radical self-reflection:* See Sarah Sophie Flicker and Alyssa Klein, "Anti-racism Resources," May 2020, https://docs.google.com/document/u/1/d/1BRlF2_zhNe86SGgHa6-VlBO-QgirITwCTugSfKie5Fs/mobilebasic?fbclid=IwAR2woG6N3uUBlWbo312Xt6vCc4TdD1uzbTt57iYbkINSEyh9NHhECWZsBkg.

Step 10: Cool Down with Inner Calm

p. 281   "What *you eat is only half the equation*": Marc David, *The Slow Down Diet: Eating for Pleasure, Energy, and Weight Loss* (Rochester, VT: Healing Arts Press, 2015), 5.

p. 284   *"it is possible to laugh without experiencing"*: Lawrence Robinson, Melinda Smith, and Jeanne Segal, "Laughter Is the Best Medicine," Helpguide, November 2019, https://www.helpguide.org /articles/mental-health/laughter-is-the-best-medicine.htm.

p. 286   *"Unlike storge, it does not depend on filiation"*: Neel Burton, "These Are the 7 Types of Love," *Psychology Today,* April 27, 2020, https://www.psychologytoday.com/us/blog/hide-and-seek/201606 /these-are-the-7-types-love.

p. 287   *Stanford University professor Anne Firth Murray*: Anne Firth Murray, Love as a Force for Social Justice, Coursera, https://www .coursera.org/learn/love-social-justice.

p. 289   *"help to pull us out of our self-absorption"*: Barbara Fredrickson, quoted in Michael Edwards, "Can Love Change the World?" *Greater Good* magazine, August 19, 2013, https://greatergood .berkeley.edu/article/item/can_love_change_the_world.

p. 289   *I learned about loving-kindness meditation*: Christine Carter, "Greater Happiness in 5 Minutes a Day: How to Teach Kids Loving-Kindness Meditation," *Greater Good* magazine, September 10, 2012, https://greatergood.berkeley.edu/article/item/better _than_sex_and_appropriate_for_kids.

p. 289   *Jon Kabat-Zinn, PhD, calls this practice*: Jon Kabat-Zinn, "This Loving-Kindness Meditation Is a Radical Act of Love," *Mindful,* November 8, 2018, https://www.mindful.org/this-loving -kindness-meditation-is-a-radical-act-of-love/.

p. 291   *"No doubt the world benefits"*: Kabat-Zinn, "This Loving-Kindness Meditation."

About the Author

Kate Eckman is a broadcast journalist and TV personality who brings her expertise in communications, performance, and mindfulness to her practice as a success coach for business leaders and professional athletes. She earned a BA in communications from Penn State University, where she was an Academic All-American swimmer, and received her master's degree in broadcast journalism from Northwestern University's Medill School of Journalism. She graduated at the highest level from Columbia University's executive and organizational coaching program and is a certified International Coaching Federation coach (ACC) and a licensed NBI consultant. Passionate about mindfulness practices for both brain and body health, she is also a meditation teacher and course creator for Insight Timer, the world's number one–ranked free meditation app. Visit her online at www.kateeckman.tv.

NEW WORLD LIBRARY is dedicated to publishing books and other media that inspire and challenge us to improve the quality of our lives and the world.

We are a socially and environmentally aware company. We recognize that we have an ethical responsibility to our readers, our authors, our staff members, and our planet.

We serve our readers by creating the finest publications possible on personal growth, creativity, spirituality, wellness, and other areas of emerging importance. We serve our authors by working with them to produce and promote quality books that reach a wide audience. We serve New World Library employees with generous benefits, significant profit sharing, and constant encouragement to pursue their most expansive dreams.

Whenever possible, we print our books with soy-based ink on 100 percent postconsumer-waste recycled paper. We power our offices with solar energy and contribute to nonprofit organizations working to make the world a better place for us all.

Our products are available wherever books are sold. Visit our website to download our catalog, subscribe to our e-newsletter, read our blog, and link to authors' websites, videos, and podcasts.

customerservice@newworldlibrary.com
Phone: 415-884-2100 or 800-972-6657
Orders: Ext. 110 • Catalog requests: Ext. 110
Fax: 415-884-2199

www.newworldlibrary.com